TACKLING SOCIAL EXCLUSION

The concept of social exclusion has been a central focus of government policy for the past ten years and is now at the core of much practitioner activity.

Thoroughly updated, this much needed new edition shows how social workers can combat the social exclusion experienced by service users and at the same time promote social inclusion. It clearly and accessibly demonstrates how concepts and theories of social exclusion can be used to improve practice. *Tackling Social Exclusion* covers:

- social work perspectives and approaches promoting social inclusion;
- contemporary issues such as preventive work with young children and families, anti-social behaviour and tensions relating to ethnicity, immigration and faith;
- the role of the voluntary sector and how service agencies can change their organisation to promote inclusion;
- the skills needed when working with specific groups including children and families, young people, vulnerable adults and communities, as well as new material on social exclusion in more rural areas.

Each chapter is grounded in up-to-date practice examples and explores, through activities, case studies and exercises, how the perspective of social exclusion is changing social work today.

John Pierson was formerly a senior lecturer in Social Work and Applied Social Studies at Staffordshire University. He now works as a consultant and visiting lecturer at the Creative Communities Unit at Staffordshire University. He is co-editor and author of the *Dictionary of Social Work, Rebuilding Community: Policy and Practice in Urban Regeneration* (2001), and *Going Local: Working in Communities and Neighbourhoods* (2007).

TACKLING SOCIAL EXCLUSION

2ND EDITION

John Pierson

Routledge
Taylor & Francis Group

LONDON AND NEW YORK

First published 2010
by Routledge
2 Park Square, Milton Park, Abingdon, Oxon, OX14 4RN

Simultaneously published in the USA and Canada
by Routledge
270 Madison Avenue, New York, NY 10016

Routledge is an imprint of the Taylor & Francis Group, an informa business

© 2010 John Pierson

Typeset in Sabon and Futura by
Bookcraft Ltd, Stroud, Gloucestershire
Printed and bound in Great Britain by
TJ International Ltd, Padstow, Cornwall

British Library Cataloging in Publication Data
A catalogue record for this book is available from the British Library

Library of Congress Cataloguing in Publication Data
Pierson, John, 1944–
Tackling social exclusion / John Pierson. – 2nd ed.
p. cm.
Includes bibliographical references.
1. Social service. 2. Marginality, Social. 3. Poor. I. Title.

HV40.P535 2009
361--dc22   2009015968

ISBN10: 0-415-47833-2 (hbk)
ISBN10: 0-415-47834-0 (pbk)
ISBN10: 0-203-86925-7 (ebk)

ISBN13: 978-0-415-47833-5 (hbk)
ISBN13: 978-0-415-47834-2 (pbk)
ISBN13: 978-0-203-86925-3 (ebk)

For Peter Llewellyn Frank Sharp and in memory of
Joyce Yvonne Sharp 1928–2007

In gratitude for the support, guidance and love

CONTENTS

FIGURES

ACKNOWLEDGEMENTS

I am grateful for the help and advice that I received from many quarters while writing this volume. As so often in the past I have benefited from regular conversations with two close friends and colleagues, Terry Philpot, former editor of *Community Care* and now author and freelance journalist, and Martin Thomas, former head of the Institute of Social Work and Applied Social Studies at Staffordshire University. Grace McInnes and Khanam Virjee from Taylor & Francis have been supportive, facilitative and patient by turns. The volume is more readable for their efforts and advice. I also pay tribute to the three anonymous reviewers who commented helpfully on the proposal for this second edition.

Social exclusion is a very large theme to capture within a single volume. Without the help of advice from the field it would have been difficult to keep pace with developments. Among these I would like to thank: Bob MacLaren, formerly of Wrexham Social Services, Paul Boylan, consultant with 4 Children, Neil Jameson of the Citizens' Organising Foundation, Keith Puttick, principal lecturer in law at Staffordshire University, Conrad Parke of Regeneration West Midlands, and Sally Sharp and Eric Beak of Malpas Young Person's Centre.

Finally, I would like to thank Marilyn Brookstone and her colleagues of Cheshire County Libraries based at the Bishop Heber High School who systematically and cheerfully met my every request for scores of books and other documents.

INTRODUCTION

For ten years and more the concept of social exclusion has remained central to government social policy. It will continue so for the simple reason that profound inequality and disadvantage still shapes our society. Tackling social exclusion sets a fundamental agenda for the major public services – health, social services, education, neighbourhood regeneration, housing and the police. Within the concept, for all its many shades of meanings, lies a pathway to social justice, to fairness, to equality, to the guarantee of inalienable rights.

As we shall see there is much debate, even conflict, about *how* to tackle it. Since 1997 social exclusion has been widely used as a way of describing a cluster of factors that cut the links between individuals, families and indeed whole communities, and the society in which they live. As a concept it points to many different forms of disadvantage and has stimulated just as many innovative practices to counteract it.

There are also criticisms of the concept that need to be made, not least that it can shift the spotlight away from the fact that poverty pure and simple is the central feature that shapes society and toward a focus on the behaviour of the excluded. For social work this presents a special challenge, since in its approximate 140 years of history the profession has laboured long and hard to join its theories of personal responsibility and individual behaviour to wider understandings of how society functions. In this sense, investigations of social exclusion and the development of a practice based on those investigations present something of a chance to lay down new directions that social work should take for the twenty-first century.

This volume intends to contribute to that project. It is a second and completely revised edition of a book first published some seven years ago. At that point in the early 2000s many of the programmes launched under the Labour government to tackle exclusion had been launched but had not yet had time to show whether they were working. We now have some of that evidence – child poverty is reduced (but not halved as the government had hoped by 2010), teenage pregnancies are down (but rates remain too high for comfort), children's services have been unified (but there is some evidence that as a society we are struggling to maintain high levels of children's wellbeing), older people are living longer and are better off (but are still vulnerable to poor levels of hospital care and their social links to neighbourhoods an afterthought).

This edition has been written with greater knowledge of what works and does not work. It has also been written in the context of significant changes in services – not least the explicit division in many authorities between adult and children's services and the development of outcomes specifying for the first time universal conceptions of well-being that all services whether working with adults, children or young people should work toward. There have been significant pressures on policy and practice as well. The war in Iraq has come and gone to be replaced by renewed war in Afghanistan, funding streams for particular programmes mentioned in the first volume, such as Sure Start local programmes and neighbourhood management pathfinders, have come to an end, and a serious global depression at time of writing has played havoc with governmental budgets. At the same time government has redirected some of its efforts more toward changing behaviour of excluded individuals through programmes such as Think Family, multi-systemic therapies and adults facing chronic exclusion making even more complex the huge range of programmes that have been brought to bear on exclusion.

Thus there is much to do. As I wrote in the Introduction to the first edition, when social work explicitly focuses on social exclusion it also takes on new ways of looking at social problems and of new approaches to these problems. As long as it is subject to reflection and critical analysis the concept of social exclusion can change the way social workers think about society and in particular the consequences for practice, for it highlights the nature of inequality, whether of income, social supports, access to services, or health and wellbeing. It re-orders practice priorities toward universal outcomes, preventive work, building social networks and maximising income. To accomplish this, social work – in its many forms – is asked to work in close partnership with a range of other professions and voluntary groups.

The first edition addressed a wide audience and this second edition does no less. As used here social work is again viewed as a big tent which includes social workers with local authority or voluntary agencies, social-care workers of every description, advice workers, youth workers, youth justice workers, probation officers, social care managers, community support workers, children centre staff, youth workers, lead professionals, education social workers, home-care workers and social workers with primary care and hospital trusts. It is also aimed at a range of community practitioners and community engagement officers whether in community arts or public health. In an age of specialisation, we too easily forget that these roles all involve social work skills, even if the professional designation varies.

Ten years into the new century it is clear that combating exclusion roles and tasks are evolving continuously. Local authority social workers and social workers with large voluntary organisations have been handed a multiplicity of new responsibilities. Extra care housing teams, integrated care teams, floating support teams, youth offending teams, disability service teams, teams looking after care leavers or smoothing the pathway for older people as they resettle in the community after a stay in hospital are just part of the evolving landscape. Then too there is the growing number of staff working with local organisations – housing associations, community centres, cultural resource centres and advice centres. All deal with aspects of social exclusion and all draw on social work components – assessing need, collaborating in partnerships, giving advice, building networks, marshalling resources. They too are among the intended readers of this volume.

But the conviction behind the first edition of this book lies at the heart of this one as well: the core of social work practice prepares it well for these new challenges. While social work shares certain elements of professional organisation with medicine, law or teaching Bill Jordan has noted that it is different in this one important respect: it exerts its influence on individuals, families and communities through informal negotiation (Jordan and Jordan 2000). Social workers are thus distinguished from other professionals by their willingness and capacity to move away from their formal roles and by meeting people in their own, natural settings. This provides informality and the means for negotiating solutions to problems rather than imposing them. Jordan (1987) has also argued that a unique quality of social work is found in the close attention it pays to individuals' own understanding of their situation and to the informal processes by which client or user and social worker broker a solution. This unique way of working provides social work with many opportunities for tackling exclusion and promoting inclusion of their service users.

THE STRUCTURE OF THE BOOK

The book as a whole is designed to provide an introduction to the different dimensions of social exclusion that social workers will encounter. The first three chapters lay foundations. Chapter 1 introduces the concept of social exclusion itself, how it is defined and measured and the arguments between different perspectives over what it really signifies. Chapter 2 brings social work into the picture by discussing those values, approaches and skills that are relevant to tackling exclusion. The aim here is to ground practitioners in those perspectives that help make sense of the tasks ahead. Chapter 3 lays out the five building blocks for practice: maximising income, strengthening networks, developing partnership for holistic practice, increasing the participation of users and residents and finally the importance of small areas or neighbourhoods.

Chapters 4, 5 and 6 each focus on a broad group of users – families with young children, young people and excluded adults. Recognising that many social workers practise within broad specialisms, these chapters aim to establish links between the every day work that social workers are already familiar with and the kinds of roles and tasks required to tackle the exclusion of users.

The next three chapters look at further elements of practice with the focus on different kinds of communities. Chapter 7 looks at neighbourhood-based work and lays out approaches to engagement in excluded neighbourhoods. Chapter 8 considers the particular impact of social exclusion in rural areas and shire counties where it often remains hidden but no less potent. Chapter 9 examines the powerful role that racism continues to play in enforcing exclusion upon a range of ethnic groups, looking in particular at the concepts of institutional racism and community cohesion. Chapter 10 concludes by discussing the learning organisation and the importance of evaluating initiatives.

Throughout the aim is to inform and stimulate thought and reflection. The case studies and even more, the activities prompt the reader to look more closely at practice, to judge what might be useful, to think anew and build anew.

CHAPTER 1

WHAT SOCIAL EXCLUSION MEANS

OBJECTIVES

By the end of this chapter you should:

- Understand the concept of social exclusion and the different ways it is defined.

- Know which groups in society are excluded and why.

- Reflect on how social work practice can reduce the social exclusion of service users, their families and neighbourhoods.

This chapter begins with an overview of the concept of social exclusion and the different meanings that people find in it. For all its widespread use any discussion of social exclusion provokes sharp debate and these controversial aspects are considered next. The chapter then explores in more detail some of the components of social exclusion using case studies to draw these out as clearly as possible for the reader. The aim here is to provide practitioners and managers in the field with a workable understanding of what social exclusion is. The final section of the chapter explains why tackling social exclusion, and promoting social inclusion, are key social work tasks for the twenty-first century.

INTRODUCING THE CONCEPT OF SOCIAL EXCLUSION

Any discussion of social exclusion inevitably raises contentious issues and strong feelings, principally because people with quite different points of view find different meanings in the concept. At stake are deeply held views about society and the causes of social problems. Some of the differing viewpoints that emerge in such discussions can take the following form:

- As a concept social exclusion is overly vague but government likes it because it downplays the destructive influence of poverty in people's lives and allows government to reconcile a bland notion of social justice with a market economy.
- Social exclusion is caused by people excluding themselves from mainstream society through their own actions and delinquent moral values.
- Work is the most effective way of overcoming social exclusion because it provides social connections and higher levels of income than benefits. Welfare policy therefore should contain forceful encouragement and even compulsion for all on benefits – including disabled people and lone mothers – to take on paid employment.
- Focusing on poverty means only looking at income as the basis for quality of life; social exclusion by contrast focuses more on social relations and the extent to which people are able to participate in social affairs and attain sufficient power to influence decisions that affect them.

Are such assertions right? In fact every one of the above points has those who agree and disagree with it. For example, on the third point, advocates and representatives of disability organisations would strongly contest what they regard as the pressure from government on disabled people *themselves* to find work when in fact they face job discrimination on an institutional scale. Those who argue for the second point, that social exclusion is a consequence of individual habits and personality, maintain that exclusion is the individual's responsibility. But others would argue that many of the forces of exclusion lie outside the individual's capacity to act. Although we can not resolve these questions one way or another for now, as practitioners accumulate experience they will begin to develop their own understanding of its causes, of what the experience of exclusion is like, what defines it and the ways in which they may be able to counter it.

ACTIVITY 1.1: DEVELOPING AN UNDERSTANDING OF SOCIAL EXCLUSION

In your practice you will encounter the term social exclusion frequently and with different shades of meaning. To help give you a better idea of what social exclusion means for people read the following three case studies and make a note of those aspects of their lives that you think contribute to their exclusion.

CASE STUDY 1: AN ASYLUM SEEKER

Mrs. K. N. is originally from Poland. She settled in Britain some five years ago and is now the mother of two young children; her husband and father of the children is from Nigeria and is seeking asylum in Britain. The family is currently living in a west midlands city and has been refused assistance from the local social services department who said it was not responsible for paying for accommodation for the family nor for subsistence for the family as their last settled address was in a city in the northeast of England. The family were told they would have to apply for assistance from that city.

CASE STUDY 2: PAULINE

Pauline is the mother of a son David who is 12 and has a mild learning disability. She also cares for a grandson, aged 11 and a granddaughter aged 4, who are the children of Pauline's daughter Marcia who lives near by. Pauline has long been known to social services with a succession of social workers having concerns about the cleanliness of her house. The files are replete with comments about how the cycle of problems is inter-generational. Social workers repeatedly try to negotiate written agreements that are rarely adhered to. Pauline says, as she has on occasions in the past, that she does not want social work involvement.

CASE STUDY 3: A DISADVANTAGED NEIGHBOURHOOD

A large disadvantaged housing estate lies on the edge of Leeds with clearly demarcated geographical and transport boundaries that separate it from the city. The estate was built in the 1930s to replace extensive slums in the area. A large part of the population of the estate live below the poverty line. Over two-thirds of households in the area live in council accommodation; about one-third of households with dependent children are headed by a single adult. A dispersal order – that is a measure that empowers local police to disperse groups of young people in order to prevent anti-social behaviour – has been granted to cover most of the estate. Now when residents see groups of young people gathering they ring the police who respond quickly to break the groups up.

Before reading any further, think about what social exclusion means for those in the case studies above. In the first, the family's precarious position in relation to public authorities stems from the father's claim to asylum which overrides the entitlement to financial support of other family members. Although asylum seekers are sometimes mixed with refugees in popular imagery, the tabloid press portray them not as 'invited' as refugees who are recognised under international convention. Their reason for seeking asylum in the UK may stem from civil war, cultural practices that oppress women, or flight from severe economic hardship. These are new and different circumstances – at least in the public and the media mind – from those of, say, refugees under the Geneva Convention of 1951 who are fleeing well-founded fears of persecution for reasons of race, religion or nationality. In general the children of asylum seekers are not subject to the Children Act 1989 although local authorities do have responsibility for unaccompanied children.

The circumstances of asylum seekers graphically illustrate the various forces that shape exclusion: barriers to the jobs market, thin or non-existent support networks of their own, extreme difficulties in obtaining the safety-net benefits of the welfare state, children facing poverty and marginalisation in the school system. Although it is difficult to assert that one group of people is 'more excluded' than another, asylum seekers' experience demonstrates exclusion's raw power more than most.

The second case study highlights a very different kind of an excluded individual – a person who seems to want to reject helpful services, one of those called in government parlance 'the hard to reach'. Government social exclusion policies have increasingly focused on those who are beset by a multitude of problems from which they and their children cannot seem to get free. Initiatives such as 'Think Family' and the offer of 'multi-systemic therapy' are aimed at connecting with those who seem resistant thus far to services.

The third case study gives a different perspective entirely: how a whole estate or neighbourhood can suffer exclusion. Derelict or over-crowded housing, abandoned public spaces, the disappearance of local shops, poor services, postcode stigma, lack of trust between neighbours all combine to exclude the residents living there. This case study also involves young people who, locals are afraid, have a tendency to engage in anti-social behaviour. Since 1997 government has focused particularly on young people as providing a ready pool of the potentially excluded such as young offenders, young teenage mothers, truants and those excluded from school, children in care and young rough sleepers. Local and central government have invested heavily to curtail the disorder and crime that disaffected youth cause in local communities. Cracking down on forms of anti-social behaviour, raising the school leaving age and compelling all young people to remain in education, employment or training, and placing responsibility on their parents for ensuring discipline – all are advocated in the name of fighting social exclusion.

ORIGINS OF THE CONCEPT SOCIAL EXCLUSION

Despite the many meanings that social exclusion has acquired in recent years in Britain, the concept itself arose in a specific context in France in the 1970s. There it was used to describe the condition of certain groups on the margins of society who were cut off both from regular sources of employment and the income safety nets of the welfare state. *Les exclus* lacked the substantial rights of *les citoyens*, either in practice because they were victims of discrimination – such as disabled people – or because they were not citizens of the state, such as asylum seekers. Nor did they have access to or connections with those powerful institutions that might have helped them gain voice such as the trade unions or residents' associations. It is important to remember that the concept of social exclusion arose in France and not in Britain or the United States, both of which have substantially different political cultures in which privatisation and the expansion of the free market in delivering public services play a far more prominent role. In France in particular there has long been an emphasis on citizenship and social cohesion reflecting a strong nation and a stronger commitment to providing a social safety net for those outside the labour market.

From France the term gained wide currency in the social policy of the European Union particularly in the Maastricht Treaty of 1996. When the Labour Party came to power in the UK in 1997 it swiftly adopted the concept for its own. From the start the Labour administration saw how its range of social goals could be presented in terms of reducing social exclusion. As a first important step very soon after its election it set up the Social Exclusion Unit in the Cabinet Office to ensure that all departments co-ordinated their efforts in tackling exclusion. This in turn was replaced in 2004 by the Social Exclusion Task Force, still within the Cabinet Office, as government recognised that it had to restructure its inclusion policies to focus on chronically excluded adults and multi-problem families.

In the transition from continental Europe to the UK, social exclusion became more flexible as a policy vehicle, amalgamating with earlier strands of welfare policy in the UK, particularly whether individuals are defined as eligible for services and benefits through means tested and targeted resources. Yet the importance of what was new should not be underestimated. Using social exclusion as the focal point for policy marked a profound break with government philosophy of the two decades from the mid 1970s to the mid 1990s. During this period Britain not only saw a large rise in the proportion of its people living in poverty, particularly children, but had the fastest rate of rising inequality *in the world* with the exception of New Zealand. Even so ministers in that period from time to time suggested there was no such thing as poverty in Britain. From 1997 on the British government at least recognised that poverty and exclusion undermined social and individual wellbeing to an unacceptable degree and announced its intention to do something about it.

Tackling poverty and exclusion and promoting inclusion for all people and groups in mainstream society gained wide appeal across the political spectrum. For the left it suggested a greater push toward equality with a focus on tackling deprivation and the lack of rights, while for the right it suggested shaping a more cohesive, unified society uniting behind a strong national regime. As we shall see both of these tendencies were and are to be found inside the Labour party.

Equally the Conservative Party has come to recognise that it cannot ignore the concepts of relative poverty and social exclusion. Its recent policy statements have underscored the underlying consensus between both political parties that work is the route out of poverty for *all* major groups claiming benefits – whether lone parents on income support, adults on incapacity benefit or young adults on job seeker's allowance. Thus the Conservative Party has prescribed tough conditions on people with disability who are to be required to work or actively seek work for a minimum of 20 hours a week (or 5 hours 'depending on capability') after completing a work capability assessment. (Although to its credit party policy does say that those who cannot work at all should be treated with complete respect.)

Conservative policies also require lone parents to work a minimum of 20 hours a week when their youngest child reaches five years and to work full time (30 hours a week) when their child reaches 11 years. Even more than the Labour Party, the Conservative Party places great faith in 'state determined but not state delivered' services and is calling for a large-scale system of contracting out back to work services into the private and non-profit sector (Conservative Party 2008; Centre for Social Justice 2007).

SOCIAL EXCLUSION: CONTROVERSY AND DEBATE

As used in the UK the concept of social exclusion is sufficiently broad to allow different understandings of society and social problems to exist side by side. Practitioners will find that social exclusion is interpreted differently and that these different interpretations frequently relate to different political points of view. For instance there are those using the term who prefer to focus more on the threat that the socially excluded themselves present to social cohesion and mainstream society. But there is also the view that social exclusion should primarily concern the poverty and disadvantage that people suffer in the midst of an otherwise wealthy society; those who hold this perspective tend to think that only by making the UK more equal in wealth through redistribution and personal resources will the scourge of exclusion finally be overcome.

The three strands of social exclusion

In an influential text Ruth Levitas uncovered three different interpretations or 'discourses' within discussions on social exclusion (Levitas 2005).

1   RED: the redistributionist discourse which has as its prime concern those living in poverty and the social forces that make this happen. RED includes within these concerns the extreme extent of inequality in Britain. Those holding this view argue that only through the redistribution of wealth across society as a whole, through taxation, benefits and services, will poverty and inequality be eradicated in Britain. It is especially critical of the idea that individual attitudes, for example toward work, or that moral and cultural attributes are in any way responsible for exclusion of groups or individuals.

2   MUD: the moral underclass discourse which concentrates on individual delinquency and lapses in attitudes and morality. Proponents extend this argument to whole neighbourhoods or social groups. For example they will view low-income neighbourhoods as falling prey to criminalised behaviour or as lacking a work ethic. MUD is also a gendered discourse; it highlights what it regards as moral weakness in which gender plays an important role. It pinpoints, for example, the behaviour of absentee fathers who evade child-support responsibilities, young male offenders, and young teenage women who have children outside a stable relationship. Proponents argue that the excluded in effect exclude themselves by

engaging in certain behaviours such as drug addiction, crime and having children out of wedlock. This position is found frequently among those who argue that there is an 'underclass' in society that has become detached from mainstream social institutions, adopts anti-social behaviour and has values that seem to justify this behaviour.

3   SID: a social integrationist discourse whose primary focus is on paid work and entrance into the labour market as a way of achieving a cohesive society. Levitas argues that this discourse remains uppermost in the policy and practice of the Labour government since it came to power in 1997. Although it shares some of the features of the redistributionist discourse insofar as it uses tax and benefits policy to support people in need while they train or search for work, it tends to equate social exclusion with exclusion from the labour market (Levitas 2005).

ACTIVITY 1.2: THE DIFFERENT MEANINGS OF SOCIAL EXCLUSION

Below are three texts each of which reflect one of the three discourses associated with social exclusion discussed by Levitas above. Try to identify which one exemplifies RED, MUD and SID as discussed above.

1   'It turns out that the clichés about role models are true. Children grow up making sense of the world around them in terms of their own experience. Little boys don't naturally grow up to be responsible fathers and husbands. They don't naturally grow up knowing how to get up every morning at the same time and go to work. ... And most emphatically of all, little boys do not reach adolescence naturally wanting to refrain from sex, just as little girls don't become adolescents naturally wanting to refrain from having babies. That's why single-parenthood is a problem for communities, and that's why illegitimacy is the most worrisome aspect of single-parenthood' (Murray 1996: 31).

2   'Well I think there's a growing body of evidence now that says actually that probably in many cases, the worst response that we can make to someone who's developing a problem – maybe it's a mental health problem, maybe it's something else – is to exclude them from the world of work is not always the right thing to do. So we have been piloting, again in some parts of the country, putting some of our employment advisors into GPs' surgeries so that the GP can consult and discuss and so can the patient' (Hutton 2006).

3   'Britain remains a highly divided country with grotesque extremes of income and wealth. Until the cause of these disparities are addressed, the work of the Social Exclusion Unit could seem at best to be marginal, at worst a political smokescreen. ... Social inclusion is no more than an organised attempt by the state to incorporate people at the margins into this flexible and global labour market, characterised by insecurity, low wages and poor conditions, a task made politically more urgent by the growing numbers of those currently excluded' (Craig 2000: 6).

When thinking about social exclusion it is important to have all three strands in mind, although of course you will rarely encounter them in pure form as above. But in reflecting on the policies and practices you are having to carry out knowing which strand is uppermost provides a key signal for what formally you are being asked to achieve. There is real tension among the three discourses over what forces shape human behaviour. To what degree is behaviour shaped by *either* social, economic and political structures, such as low income, prejudice and economic decline, *or* by individual character, personal attributes and moral codes? This central question has existed since the earliest days of social work in the late nineteenth century and, as befits such a complicated issue, there is evidence on both sides. The concept of social exclusion can point to both kinds of influences and so it remains vital that practitioners think long and deeply on what is at stake here since social work is often required to make finely balanced judgements on user behaviour precisely on this issue.

A broad definition of social exclusion

Reflecting the broad nature of social exclusion a number of definitions have been advanced by various authorities including government.

The Centre for the Analysis of Social Exclusion defines social exclusion in this way: An individual is socially excluded if (a) he or she is geographically resident in a society, (b) he or she cannot participate in the normal activities of citizens in that society, and (c) he or she would like to so participate, but is prevented from doing so by factors beyond his or her control (Burchardt, *et al.* 1999).

This definition is broad brush emphasizing that the person is excluded if resident in a neighbourhood, community or country but is kept from participating in society through circumstances not of their own making. It is significant because unlike many other definitions – individuals cannot exclude themselves.

With fundamental arguments over human behaviour at stake it is not surprising that reaching a single, reliable definition of social exclusion in practice is difficult. On balance the viewpoint offered in this volume places a greater weight on poverty, poor housing, and the impact of disadvantaged neighbourhoods as shapers of human behaviour than on individual motivation, moral capacity and characteristics of personality. Social exclusion, in the view of this author, drastically reduces the range of choices that individuals and families have at their disposal. What appears from the point of view of mainstream society as reasonable and responsible actions for individuals and families to take are often simply not available to the excluded. This is because the access, the resources, the means, the knowledge and the support are not there. In short, broad social and economic factors – social class, access to political power, knowledge of professional systems, discrimination based on race or physical ability – shape the capabilities of all individuals, augmenting some, and drastically curtailing others.

Reflecting the contradictory nature of the way in which social exclusion is used in policy and practice we adopt the following definition:

> Social exclusion is a process over time that deprives individuals and families, groups and neighbourhoods of the resources required for participation in the social, economic and political activity of society as a whole. This process is primarily a consequence of poverty and low income, but other factors such as discrimination, low educational attainment and depleted environments also underpin it. Through this process people are cut off for a significant period in their lives from institutions and services, social networks and developmental opportunities that the great majority of a society enjoys.

Of course practitioners do not have the luxury of endless debates over definitions and perspectives. They are, however, charged by their agency at local level and by central government to undertake certain responsibilities either by law or by professional commitment and many of these hinge on tackling exclusion and promoting inclusion of service users. The National Occupational Standards for Social Work for example refer frequently to advocacy, to respecting individual rights, to promoting independence and adopts for its own the International Federation of Social Workers (2009) statement on the key purpose of social work as:

> a profession which promotes social change, problem solving in human relationships and the empowerment and liberation of people to enhance wellbeing. ... Social work intervenes at the points where people interact with their environments. Principles of human rights and social justice are fundamental to social work.

Social workers are as well fitted as any of the helping professions to undertake this work. They have long been familiar with the effects of social exclusion on individuals and families for a century or more – family breakdown, mental and physical ill-health, educational under-achievement, unemployment and loss of self-esteem – and are in a better position than others to negotiate the complex boundaries between individual and social dynamics required to achieve a greater measure of that social justice.

In coming to grips with exclusion, advancing knowledge has enabled us to ascertain its extent in particular geographical areas and with particular groups of service users. For example, researchers from the New Policy Institute (Palmer *et al.* 2008) have developed indicators that show the extent of exclusion suffered by various groups in society. Their careful research into social exclusion has shown that these are the most reliable and effective signposts for social exclusion taking place. As an example the indicators for the extent of socially excluded children in Britain are the number of:

- children living in workless households
- low-birth-weight babies under 2.5 kg
- infant deaths per 1000 of population

- 16 year olds failing to get five or more GCSEs at A to C
- permanent exclusions from school
- births to girls conceiving under 16
- children cautioned for or guilty of an indictable offence.

In using such indicators it is important not to confuse 'causation' with 'correlation'. Indicators do not identify the 'causes' of social exclusion nor do they provide evidence for arguing individuals or families are responsible for their own exclusion. But they are quantifiable signposts – ways of estimating the degree of exclusion within a particular area and for the country as a whole year after year – that shed light on the real world consequences of exclusion (Palmer *et al.* 2008).

As our definition above suggests whole neighbourhoods and communities can also face exclusion. The indicators of exclusion at this level include, among others, the extent of overcrowded housing, the extent to which people feel unsafe, a high percentage of residents without a bank or building society account and high levels of burglaries among others (Palmer *et al.* 2008: 96–110). For neighbourhoods, as for families, social exclusion has devastating effects. Certain long-term trends gather pace: vital services as well as commercial and financial outlets withdraw, vulnerable groups such as lone parents find themselves housed together in particular areas and the incidence of social disturbances rise. Social workers are less familiar now with the skills for tackling the social problems of whole neighbourhoods than they used to be when 'community work' was routinely on the training curriculum. But as we shall see in Chapter 7 there is a strand within social work of working in neighbourhoods and communities dating back to the nineteenth century, that when combined with a contemporary skill set can mean that social workers can address this area based dimension of exclusion also.

THE COMPONENTS OF SOCIAL EXCLUSION

We have thus far discussed the tension within the concept of social exclusion, have begun to think about what being socially excluded actually means for people and neighbourhoods, and formulated a working definition of social exclusion as a process that extends over time. This section follows up these first thoughts by examining its different components in greater depth.

Of the important forces that drive the process of social exclusion five stand out:

- poverty and low income
- lack of access to the jobs market
- thin or non-existent social supports and networks
- the effect of the local area or neighbourhood
- exclusion from services.

These five components intertwine and reinforce one another which means that tackling social exclusion and promoting its opposite, social inclusion, requires a multi-pronged approach to practice that address each of these domains: maximising options for income, strengthening social networks, tackling the quality of life in neighbourhoods and making services more accessible. Let us examine each more closely.

Poverty and low income

The most potent element in the process of social exclusion is poverty and low income. Any social work practice that aims to reduce exclusion cannot avoid this central fact. Many commentators, both in government and out, now refer to 'poverty and social exclusion' to ensure that this is understood. Indeed a family with a reasonable income, or a local neighbourhood with reasonable median income, will usually have ready resources to overcome barriers and exclusions that they may encounter.

Definitions of poverty have themselves become more diverse and flexible and have begun to incorporate elements that parallel aspects of social exclusion. Increasingly it is acknowledged that any definition of poverty, as with social exclusion, is based at least in part on value judgements, for example whether government should or should not play a vigorous role in reducing poverty or whether obtaining work is the main way out of poverty.

Conventionally poverty has been defined in one of two ways – as either absolute or relative.

Absolute poverty is defined by a fixed standard below which individuals and families experience complete destitution and so cannot meet even minimum needs for food and shelter. Many aid agencies and the World Bank and the United Nations Development Programme use this standard for measuring poverty in the developing world which they have fixed at two (US) dollars a day. Below that level of income families face severe malnutrition and dangerous levels of ill-health. This notion of poverty is thus broadly fixed at the level of income necessary for basic subsistence. Above that level families can survive if only barely. Below that level they may starve. No other criteria are used.

Absolute standards of poverty have the virtue of allowing us to calculate poverty across different countries. Thus the United Nations Development Programme was able to estimate in the mid 1990s that within the developing world 30 per cent of all children under five are malnourished (UN 1995). But such absolute standards can also have an exploitative function: the old workhouse system in Britain often relied on an absolute notion of poverty to decide whether or not a person was truly poor. Only if they were on the verge of starvation would a person or family agree to come into the local workhouse where the regime was hard and often tyrannical. When John Moore, then secretary for social security in the Conservative government, said in 1989 that there was no such thing as a poverty line he was hewing to a primary definition of poverty and concluded that in Britain there was no poverty, only inequality (Moore 1989).

Relative poverty on the other hand refers to the lack of resources needed to obtain the kinds of diet, participate in the activities and have the living conditions and amenities that are widely approved and generally obtained by most people in a particular society. A person who suffers this form of poverty has resources so seriously inferior to those commanded by the average individual or household that they are, in effect, excluded from ordinary living patterns and social activities.

The work of Peter Townsend (1979) in particular helped us to understand that the basic standards of living that most people enjoy are implicitly defined within each society. These standards have not only to do with income but also consumer purchases, levels of health and wellbeing, and access to goods and services. Those investigating relative poverty look at the ways in which individual and family life is affected by the experience of deprivation. The notion of relative poverty focuses on the degree to which people are prevented from sharing the living standards, opportunities and norms of wellbeing that society as a whole has created for itself. In this sense the concept of relative poverty is closely allied to social exclusion.

Both concepts imply that as society becomes more sophisticated and living standards rise so do the necessities that an individual or family requires to participate in the benefits of that society. Information and communication technology (ICT) presents a good example. In a relatively short time access to a computer and the ability to use it has moved from the margin of economic and social activity to its core. Add in its networking and educative functions and it becomes a central tool that impacts widely on the lives of individuals. Families with no access to or knowledge of ICT have yet another dimension in which they are poor – 'information poverty' and 'computer illiteracy' – which 20 years ago was not even recognised as a source of concern.

DEFINITIONS OF POVERTY

Absolute poverty
- 'a condition characterised by severe deprivation of basic human needs, including food, safe drinking water, sanitation facilities, health, shelter, education and information. It depends not only on income but also on access to services' (UN 1995: 57).

Relative poverty
- 'persons, families and groups of persons whose resources (material, cultural and social) are so limited as to exclude them from the minimum acceptable way of life of the Member State in which they live' (EEC 1985)

People are said to be living in relative poverty if their income and resources are so inadequate as to preclude them from having a standard of living considered acceptable in the society in which they live. Because of their poverty they may experience multiple disadvantages through unemployment, low income, poor housing, inadequate healthcare and barriers to lifelong learning, culture, sport and recreation. The standard for determining low income is generally accepted at 60 per cent or less of the average household income in any given year. In 2005/06 nearly 13 million people or a fifth of the UK population were living below this income threshold; only five other countries of the EU had higher rates of relative poverty (Palmer *et al.* 2008).

The notion of relative poverty raises a key question: what does society deem as the standard for deciding who is poor? What are 'the necessities of life'? Determining the norms of society is a crucial part of coming to understand what it is that people are being excluded from when they are poor.

One of the most influential studies that has attempted to define what are the necessities was 'Breadline Britain' which through several rigorous public surveys established what the British people considered to be necessities as they have changed since the 1980s. The surveys showed that the public hold wider-ranging ideas about the necessities of life than expert opinion might have thought. In those surveys people of all ages and walks of life move well beyond the basic necessities to acknowledge that social customs, obligation and activities form a platform for needs (Howarth *et al.* 2001: 14).

There is a striking consensus over many items deemed 'necessities', that is those things that all adults should be able to afford and which they should not have to do without. For example, in the most recent of these surveys, 95 per cent thought beds and bedding were necessary (although interestingly 4 per cent thought they were unnecessary) while 94 per cent thought heating to warm the living areas of the home was necessary. Other items deemed necessary by the vast majority (with percentages in brackets) were things like two meals a day (91), a refrigerator (89), fresh fruit and vegetables daily (86), money to keep the home in a decent state of decoration (82) and a washing machine (76) (Howarth *et al.* 2001).

The same consensus however does not always exist over what is *not* necessary. There is disagreement, especially over a range of items that are new, technological or labour-saving.

These two main definitions of poverty – relative and absolute – reveal different ways of looking at human needs. Absolute definitions provide a universal threshold by which to measure poverty while relative definitions are concerned not just to look at what is required for subsistence but at a range of social and psychological resources needed to fulfil the promise of the autonomous, capable adult participating in their social milieu.

ACTIVITY 1.3: THINKING ABOUT POVERTY

Before reading any further look at the list of items below which have been taken from the most recent Breadline Britain survey, mentioned above. They have been scrambled to give you the chance of testing your opinion on what constitutes necessities against the results of the public survey. Which of the following would you define as 'necessities', that is 'items which you think all adults should be able to afford and which they should not have to do without' (list the items in order of importance):

two pairs of all-weather shoes, television, holiday away from home once a year, dictionary, car, carpets in living room, microwave oven, daily newspaper, regular saving of £10 per month, an evening out once a fortnight, visits to friends and family, visits to the children's school, a leisure activity, having a telephone, small amounts of money to spend on self weekly, dressing gown, coach or train fare to visit friends and family every three months.*

---

* The public's view was (figures in brackets are percentages): two pairs of all weather shoes (71), television (56), holiday away from home once a year not with relatives (55), dictionary (53), car (38), carpets in living room (67), microwave (23), daily newspaper (30), regular saving of £10 per month (66), an evening out once a fortnight (37), visits to friends and family (84), visits to the children's school (81), hobby or leisure activity (78), having a telephone (71), small amounts of money to spend on self (Gordon et al. (2000: 13).

Access to the jobs market and paid employment

While unemployment has long been viewed as a principal factor in causing poverty, our awareness of its many effects has become more sophisticated since the 1990s. In particular, our understanding of what exclusion from the labour market means for individuals and families across their life cycle has expanded considerably. Those with low levels of skills face the toughest barriers to entering or re-entering the job market. This mismatch has arisen in part because of the increased requirement for 'soft skills' – skills that relate to motivation, teamwork and problem-solving reflecting the move toward services and retail, team-production processes, together with emphasis on quality of service (Giloth 1998: 5). The emerging service economy itself does not provide orderly advancement (as did the earlier manufacturing economy) because of the gulf between high-wage, high-skill jobs at one end and low-wage, low-skill work at the other. Some economists now argue that skills in the technical sense are less critical to employability than attitude, and that the notion of 'soft skills' is simply a way of denoting the willingness to learn and to accept the disciplinary requirements of most workplaces.

One strand of government policy applies both enticement and pressure on specific groups of people to prepare for and seek work more actively. The various Welfare-to-Work programmes are for groups with an insecure or disadvantaged relationship to the labour market such as 18–24 year olds, the long-term adult unemployed, people with disabilities and lone parents. The programmes aim at 'enhancing employability' of such groups through training, job search and general 'work readiness'. The thinking behind such programmes is that through work those who lived previously on benefits are able to lift themselves out of poverty and also enjoy the connections and further opportunities that employment provides. Recent initiatives have taken this line of thinking even further with claimants on new benefits such as Employment and Support Allowance having to undergo renewed medical assessment and enter work readiness programmes (see Chapter 6) and lone parents with children over seven having to secure training places and employment as they are transferred from income support to jobseeker's allowance (see Chapter 4).

This emphasis in government policy on the jobs market and finding work presents practitioners with another potential conflict over values. How much encouragement or pressure should be applied to people of working age to find a job? This is a particularly acute question for those adults that social workers often serve – disabled people, people with mental health problems or lone parents. Each group has a range of requirements to be met and barriers to overcome before they can readily find work. Many social workers may feel uncomfortable in being part of a wider policy goal of pressuring people into work. They may well share the redistributionist perspective which accepts that many individuals not able to work because they are raising children or are disabled should be supported through adequate levels of benefits.

The effects of discipline of the labour market and being 'work ready' are not always clear cut for particular individuals. On the one hand employment does in general provide levels of income higher than most state benefits. Work can also provide a sense of purpose and social interaction and networks that are difficult to find anywhere else. It also can facilitate contact with relatively powerful institutions such as trade unions or professional associations. As a result groups that social workers work with want greater access to the jobs market. Young adults leaving care need training schemes, adults with a learning disability look for supported employment as do young offenders leaving custody.

On the other hand jobs, particularly in the service sector such as restaurants or call centres, pay low wages, are often casualised (that is, are part time and temporary) and stressful and do not bring either the higher income or the valued sense of inclusion in a work place where a person is trusted and respected (Sennett 2007). Recent research examining lone parent employment for example has pointed to the existence of a 'low pay – no pay' cycle. Evans and colleagues show that although lone parents are moving into paid work at a rate similar to that of other non-employed people, they are twice as likely to leave that work, with low pay one of the main factors associated with exit (Evans *et al.* 2004).

While official long-term unemployment decreased by half between 1997 and 2004 it has since been rising again – very substantially in 2008–9. Only two-fifths of those who want paid work but do not have it are officially unemployed while a further fifth are long-term sick or disabled (Palmer *et al.* 2008: 67). So we have to be cautious therefore in assuming that 'labour market activity' produces an easy answer to helping individuals out of social exclusion.

Social supports and social networks

A third component of social exclusion is the weakness in social networks experienced by groups, families or individuals. 'Network poverty' deprives users of social supports and informal help that we all need to participate in community life and to enjoy the standards of living shared by the majority of people. Social workers have informally recognised this to be the case for some while. For example, since the implementation of the Children Act 1989 they have preferred to place children with relatives and as near to home as possible rather than in a children's home or with distant foster parents, thus preserving the child's natural networks. But in general focus on networks has been intermittent and often of low priority. For instance in social care for older people social workers have reduced their engagement with 'non-care' activities such as developing luncheon clubs, providing specialist transport services and befriending activities which has undermined the network-enhancing role of social care practice. This is despite the clear evidence that networks and neighbourhood involvement are instrumental in underpinning older people's wellbeing (Wenger 1997; McLeod 2008; see Chapter 7).

Mastering what social networks are and how they thrive is therefore an essential element in tackling the social exclusion of users. Fortunately our understanding both of the importance of social networks and how they function has developed considerably in the last 20 years. There are various ways of describing and measuring the characteristics of networks. One helpful distinction is to think of networks for 'getting by' and those 'for getting ahead'; they are very different and perform very different functions.

Networks for getting by

These are the close, supportive networks embedded in everyday relationships of friends, neighbourhood and family. When we think of the social supports offered by extended families and friends or by close-knit communities, these are networks for 'getting by'. Through these last minute gaps in childcare are filled, a sick person is looked after, a small loan or cash to make ends meet are provided and family celebrations or rites of passage are extended by their participation.

As social workers we are vitally interested in how these networks are viewed by the people with whom we are working. They may be seen as affirmative, nurturing or accepting or as antagonistic and inaccessible. At their very worst they can be sources of heavy responsibility, aggression and scapegoating. Understanding how such networks function helps us to understand better the distinctive characteristics of socially excluded and isolated individuals and families (Briggs 1997).

Networks for getting ahead

These networks provide crucial information for individuals and families on jobs, education, training and on a range of options for advancing individual interests. In many ways they are the opposite of networks for getting by but can achieve important goals in their own right. Mark Granovetter has summed up this kind of network in the phrase the 'strength of weak ties' (Granovetter 1973). The 'weak ties' he refers to are the networks found outside the immediate neighbourhood and family and friends; they are occasional and episodic in nature and are more tenuous than a close personal relationship. They may be based on 'someone who knows someone' about a job possibility or on the links obtained through a skills agency half a city away which a person visits only occasionally (Briggs 1997). Such networks are often referred to as 'bridging social capital' – the kind of network that provides access to institutions and employment markets that personal relationships simply cannot offer.

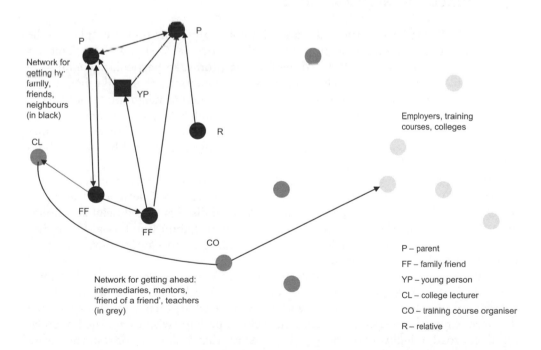

FIGURE 1.1   Networks for getting by and getting ahead

'Weak ties' can in fact be very powerful by providing information and opportunities for self-development. This is particularly so in relation to the jobs market which has become complex and difficult to navigate for all young people but particularly so for those from low income urban neighbourhoods or adults who have been out of the labour market for a lengthy period. Job descriptions are more fluid and firms, focusing on 'core competencies', have hived off entry-level jobs to other organisations that once were routes to secure positions. Increasingly the networks to which low-skilled workers and prospective employers belong fail to intersect. As a result it is increasingly clear that excluded individuals, whether through low income or discrimination, no matter how highly motivated, cannot on their own reconstruct and negotiate a city's map of job connections. Finding a job is no longer an individual transaction where a person simply acquires skills and then joins a job queue, where they are individually assessed without other intermediaries being taken into consideration.

Creating new networks of either kind or bolstering existing ones offers a fertile field for practice, as we shall see in the next chapter. Network mapping, capitalising on existing strengths within networks for getting by, creating new networks around existing points of service such as family centres and schools, or by using mentors and volunteers, are all approaches which social workers should be developing to achieve practical ends in their work – whether to provide more informal social care, support people in finding work or helping young parents become more effective in managing their children's behaviour. Networks are particularly important when working with individuals that employment gatekeepers view stereotypically as ill-equipped for the jobs market, such as young males without qualifications – black and white – or long-term unemployed.

Importance of neighbourhood

Since the 1990s we have learned an immense amount about the power of 'place' – the impact of neighbourhood on the lives of those that live there. We know that conditions of poverty and exclusion interact and reinforce each other in particular geographical locations to create a qualitatively different set of conditions that make it virtually impossible for individuals or families to escape these negative 'neighbourhood' effects. This dynamic between poor schooling, vulnerable families and low income is found throughout the UK, often on social housing estates on the edges of towns and cities but also in low-income areas of mixed tenancy and owner-occupied housing in both urban and rural neighbourhoods.

Yet people's attachment to their neighbourhood, to their 'place' can be deep and enduring. It tends to be strongest in areas with effective social networks and where people perceive their area as 'safe'. While residents in disadvantaged neighbourhoods *in general* have lower levels of attachment to their neighbourhood as a whole they nevertheless express strong attachments to their social networks as a resource in coping with social problems (Livingston *et al.* 2008).

When we refer to 'neighbourhoods' we are not trying to evoke a cosy well-defined area where the residents all know and support each other in frequent face-to-face transactions. Far from it. In working with poor and excluded neighbourhoods we use that term simply to refer to a recognisable vicinity, perhaps with established boundaries like a road or highway or the edge of an estate, that a majority of residents themselves would acknowledge.

The built environment of a neighbourhood or local area – such as the quality of the housing, the existence or not of leisure facilities and the road system – is of course important to the quality of life, but we have come to understand from the range of research since the 1990s that the social fabric is even more important to understanding exclusion in a locality. By social fabric we mean the social connections between people, the strength of local organisations and associations and the extent and vibrancy of local activity whether commercial or civic. These are assets stored in effect in human relationships of the area, and are often collectively referred to as 'social capital'. Such assets may be stronger, weaker or even non-existent but knowing something of these relationships for a given area should be fundamental to practice.

In working with low income neighbourhoods, increasing the levels of participation by local residents – whether in local organisations and institutions, decision-making affecting the locality or in public services themselves – becomes an important goal. There are three reasons why. First, raising levels of participation ensures that the expressed needs of local residents are heard directly and are not shaped subtly by the interests of service providers or local officials. Second, local people can build skills and confidence that make them more effective in articulating their needs and demands and that of their neighbourhood. Third, as local residents learn to participate more effectively, their experience helps develop skills for further successful collaborations in solving local problems (Ferguson and Stoutland 1999: 51).

That is the theory at least. But there are practical barriers to participation by local residents, especially in low-income neighbourhoods, to take into consideration. The sheer amount of time required, the lack of pay or expenses for that time, the complicated professional and managerial language that service providers often deploy and burnout by those who regularly step forward to volunteer to sit on management boards or oversee yet another survey or attend yet another meeting are all obstacles to be surmounted by local people.

DISTRESSED HOUSING ESTATES

In her research on distressed social housing estates, Anne Power has shown the intensifying effects of exclusion in particular areas. In *Dangerous Disorder*, which she wrote with Rebecca Tunstall in 1997, the authors report on their findings from 13 areas where there had been serious disorder.

There was a vacuum within the estates which tough boys sought to fill – too little work, too little cash, too few adult male workers and fathers, too many buildings, too many young boys outside any system. There was too little for these boys to do and too many useless places for them to attack. The vast majority of estates in difficulty had some empty property, abandoned land and unsupervised areas, inviting vandalism, fires, gangs, hideaways and other forms of trouble. Empty property was a signal that their community was worthless to the outside. But empty property gave boys room for destruction. The damage caused further abandonment with the consequent weakening of controls.

(Power and Tunstall 1997: 46)

Exclusion from services

Closely allied to the importance of locality in the social exclusion of individuals, families and groups is the lack of access to basic services. By 'services' we mean the whole range of private and public, in-home and out-of-home services which individuals, families and groups continually draw on for a variety of purposes. In-home services include everything from electricity to care for those who need it; out-of-home services include transport, post office, banking, doctor and hospital facilities or those such as day care for children and day centres for older people. In poor or disadvantaged neighbourhoods there are often barriers to obtaining such services beyond the means of any one individual or family to surmount. All such services do have a relationship to the locality. They may be remote in their style or even conspicuous by their absence while others will have ready points for local contact but in one way or another through their quality they have a wide impact on the degree of inclusion or exclusion that people experience.

Take the example of what the withdrawal of financial services can mean for neighbourhoods and those that live there already experiencing other forms of exclusion. The number of adults without a bank account fell from nearly 3 million in 2002 to 2 million in 2005 yet many households remain vulnerable to financial exclusion. High levels of financial exclusion have been found in particular groups such as housing association tenants, care leavers, lone parents, disabled people, members of ethnic minorities, migrants and asylum seekers. They are vulnerable to higher-interest credit and loan sharks, they are badly covered by lack of insurance, they have no bank account into which income can be paid and often pay a higher cost for their utilities.

ACTIVITY 1.4: FINANCIAL EXCLUSION AND PREDATORY LENDING

Choose a social housing estate where you or your team work and find out which financial services are and are not provided. Don't forget to consider services such as extending credit to families or individuals, counters for cashing benefit cheques and services to small shops or businesses. It is important to examine the informal services that people might come into contact with such as credit unions or loan sharks.

Focusing on exclusion from services requires looking hard at how social work services are currently delivered and finding ways for increasing access to them. To take one example: the proportion of older people receiving home care has fallen by over a quarter between 1998 and 2007 (New Policy Institute 2009). The reasons for this are complex and have to do with local authority home-care resources focused on those deemed most in need, higher charges for home care and the availability of free health care in hospital. This means that services such as home care, respite care to relieve regular family carers occasionally, meals services and day-care centres are all contributing less and less to maintaining older people at home. The example raises a number of important questions. Why is this happening? Is this the consequence of political decisions and local authorities deciding to fund other services? Can people now not afford such services? Are there other barriers that we do not know about in place that prevent their being used?

ACTIVITY 1.5: REFLECTING ON WHAT SOCIAL WORK CAN CONTRIBUTE TO TACKLING SOCIAL EXCLUSION

Before going on to the next chapter read the list below of social problems that the government's Social Exclusion Task Force (2004) associates with social exclusion.

- lack of opportunities for work
- lack of opportunities to acquire education and work-related skills
- childhood deprivation
- families disrupted through high levels of conflict, separation or divorce
- barriers to older people living active lives
- inequalities in health
- poor housing
- poor neighbourhoods
- fear of crime
- groups disadvantaged through poverty or discrimination.

Think of your current set of job or student placement responsibilities and decide which of the social problems listed above you and your team could tackle. You might want to categorise those problems according to whether you and your team's job specifications would have scope for tackling those problems on your own or in collaboration with others. If you are a social work or social care student pick out those skills and competencies that you think could be applied to reducing the exclusion of various service user groups.

KEY POINTS

❑   Social exclusion is a process that deprives individuals, families, groups and neighbourhoods from obtaining the resources for participation in social, economic and political activity that the great majority of society enjoys. These resources are not just material but have to do with the quality of social interaction. Social exclusion undermines or destroys channels of access for support and opportunity.

❑   The five main components driving the process forward are

    ○   poverty and low income

    ○   barriers to the jobs market

    ○   lack of support networks

    ○   the effects of living in extremely poor or distressed neighbourhoods

    ○   lack of access to good-quality services.

❑   Social exclusion presents a number of interlinked problems for social workers to deal with, in the form of individuals with depression and poor mental health, families under stress, children living in poverty, and older people cut off from activities and social engagement. Perhaps the biggest challenge for social workers in tackling social exclusion is to develop approaches that deal with these problems on a neighbourhood or community level.

KEY READING

Guy Palmer, Terrence MacInnes and Peter Kenway, *Monitoring Poverty and Social Exclusion* (New Policy Institute and the Joseph Rowntree Foundation, 2008). The authors measure the extent of social exclusion in Britain based on a range of important indicators. The information is provided in clear graphs that are easy to interpret; produced annually.

John Hills and Kitty Steward (eds), *A More Equal Society?: New Labour, Poverty, Inequality and Exclusion* (Policy Press, 2005). Combines hard data with a reflective exploration of exclusion across a number of aspects of British society in the twenty-first century.

Gerald Smale, Graham Tuson and Daphne Statham, *Social Work and Social Problems: Working Towards Social Inclusion and Social Change* (Macmillan, 2000). The late, far-seeing Gerry Smale and colleagues describe how in practice social workers can move from providing short-term aid to families to long-term development work and social change.

CHAPTER 2

PERSPECTIVES AND APPROACHES TO PRACTICE

OBJECTIVES

By the end of the chapter you should:

- Know the key professional values that underpin a practice committed to reducing exclusion.

- Be able to examine your own values and attitudes toward poverty, deprivation and exclusion.

- Be familiar with those social work approaches which provide the greatest scope for tackling exclusion.

- Understand the specific skills for tackling exclusion.

This chapter is designed to help practitioners prepare for a practice dedicated to reducing social exclusion. It aims to do this by discussing the values, approaches and skills which are useful for guiding practice development and at the same time examining your own values and attitudes which are crucial to motivation.

Tackling social exclusion requires collaborative approaches focusing on the key forces of exclusion: low income, health inequalities, low educational attainment, constricted opportunities for women and race discrimination. This raises particular challenges for social work practitioners not least because much of this collaborative work is often deemed 'preventive', that requires the practitioner to look beyond risk oriented, day-to-day decisions in relation to individuals and families on their caseload. Specific trends in social care, which focus on financial assessment and criteria for eligibility, and an emphasis on child protection have only reinforced social work's reliance on crisis oriented work with individuals and families leaving less time for addressing social and economic dimensions of users' lives (Audit Commission 2000; Barr *et al*. 2001).

SOCIAL WORK VALUES AND ATTITUDES TOWARDS POVERTY AND INEQUALITY

Social work is a distinctive profession because of the emphasis it places on social justice. Its values represent the profound aspirations of professional commitment, 'held aloft as the ultimate and, perhaps, never wholly attainable ends of policy and practice' (Clark 2000:31). While values can be thought of as attributes of persons, professions and organisations they are less precise than we might presume. As Clark puts it they are 'the ongoing accomplishments of knowledgeable and reflective human intelligences immersed in a social world' (ibid.: 31).

Social work values emerged from a wide range of beliefs, theories, religious affiliations and moral and political understandings. Although social work educators and professional associations refer to values as if they were well established, conflicting strands make it difficult to find a unified set of values for the whole profession. The picture is even more complicated because beliefs and values are closely intertwined; indeed, values have been regarded as well-entrenched core attachments and sentiments which result in deep beliefs (Lipset 1996). Since beliefs are deep-seated, often life long and integrated with identity this interconnection between values and beliefs means that values may be resistant to change and even immune to evidence concerning practice outcomes.

One of the most profound and difficult questions the profession faces concerns the nature of poverty and why some people are poor and some are not. Social work has worked with people in poverty since the origins of the profession in the second half of the nineteenth century. Yet to this day its values and beliefs about poverty are contradictory and at times overlook the significance of this. One constant thread in social work practice was and is the 'pathologising' of poor people, that is viewing users' poverty as the result of that person's perverse choices, for example spending too much on alcohol and tobacco (or drugs), being apathetic towards work and failing to recognise family responsibilities. This deep-seated belief often prompted the social worker to examine personal expenditure and to offer guidance on users' moral conduct and led to two of the earliest (and still potent if often disguised) assessment categories: the 'deserving' and the 'undeserving' poor (Jones *et al*. 2005). There are some similarities between this approach and that of the 'moral underclass' perspective discussed in the previous chapter.

The dominant casework tradition in social work is built on this framework. It tried to secure good personal habits such as thrift, sobriety and hard work through developing a personal relationship between user and the social worker and to achieve individual and family change with techniques such as counselling combined with compulsory interventions sanctioned by law (Pearson 1989). Social work's professional values were constructed around the notion of the user as an individual and the centrality of the worker's relationship with that individual. A Catholic priest, Father Biestek (1961), codified these in a number of principles:

- individualisation and the uniqueness of each individual
- purposeful expression of feelings
- controlled emotional involvement
- acceptance
- non-judgemental attitude
- client self-determination
- confidentiality.

Although criticised for putting too much emphasis on the individual relationship between client and practitioner and not enough on the social environments of users (Pearson 1989; Jones *et al*. 2005), the principles of casework continue to influence how social workers view their work and in particular the remedies for tackling exclusion.

WHAT ARE VALUES?

The evidence for the existence of a distinctive and coherent set of normative professional social work values is extremely tenuous; and the actual range and content of social workers' personal and professional values can be conjectured from the professional literature but is not evidenced by any significant body of empirical social research. The identification of social work values can therefore be no more than approximate, provisional and inherently controversial. In broad terms, the values of social work are clearly rooted in Christian ethics blended with modern Western secular liberal individualism. They share their origins with the dominant Western tradition of morality.

(Clark 2000: 360).

How effective they are in grounding practitioners to combat social exclusion and disadvantage is an open question which readers should keep in mind.

Clark finds four broad principles present in social work values:

1   The worth and uniqueness of every person: all persons have equal value regardless of age, gender, ethnicity, physical or intellectual ability, income or social contribution. Respect for individuals is active and needs to be positively demonstrated rather than just assumed.
2   Entitlement to justice: every person is entitled to equal treatment on agreed principles of justice that recognise protection of liberties, human needs and fair distribution of resources.
3   Claim to freedom: every person and social group is entitled to their own beliefs and pursuits unless it restricts the freedom of others.
4   Community is essential: human life can only be realised interdependently in communities and much of social work aims to restore or improve specific communities.

(Clark 2000)

USERS ARE SMARTER THAN YOU THINK

Some users have long understood social workers' undying interest in depth psychology and complicated family relationships as the platform from which they launch their work. Clients could sometimes work this to their advantage. 'Tailgunner' Parkinson, a probation officer known for his capacity to pierce social work's pretensions, captured this four decades ago in a short article entitled simply 'I give them money'. He wrote, 'Clients tried to talk about the gas bill, workers tried to talk about the client's mother. Perceptive clients got the gas bill paid by talking about mother' (Parkinson 1970, cited in Dowling 1999).

One strand of social work values developed around the notion of the uniqueness of each individual, self-determination and the empathy that practitioners should bring to their work. Other fundamental values emerged to embrace more explicitly political commitments. Radical social work in the 1970s sought to change economic and social structures while somewhat later anti-oppressive practice from the 1980s on has sought to reverse all forms of discrimination (Langan and Lee 1989). The notion of empowerment provided yet another set of commitments, enabling people without power to have more control over their lives and greater voice within institutions and extending a person's ability to take effective decisions (Braye and Preston-Shoot 1995: 48).

Beliefs about poverty

Professional values are only as effective as the practitioner makes them. For that reason *personal* values are extremely important too. Both professional and individual values may combine either to distance from or push practitioners toward anti-poverty work. Personal beliefs about poverty are based in part on your own upbringing and experiences but also on how familiar you are with what it is like to be poor, your understanding of society and social structure and what motivates individuals in conditions of scarcity. In the realm of values and beliefs it is easy to lose the complexity as to why a person, family or an entire neighbourhood is poor. Yet beliefs and values have a large influence on the way we understand explanations of poverty. For example, if you believe that people are themselves largely free to make choices for what happens to them in life you quite likely will also think that people are poor because of personal failures for which they bear responsibility. Conversely if you believe in equal opportunity for everyone you may focus on the barriers that limit opportunity as a cause of poverty. From the dominant casework perspective poverty is too often seen as the inevitable backdrop to service provision, the responsibility of other agencies. This is despite evidence showing that users' poverty remains the single factor most widely associated with social work contact.

ACTIVITY 2.1:   UNDERSTANDING THE REALITY OF POVERTY

Here is a thought experiment. Imagine that you bank on-line and that you have responded to an email from the bank asking for you to confirm your identity because there has been some suspicious withdrawals. The email asks for your user name and password – and, because you are very busy and preparing for a case conference in a couple of hours time, you supply the information requested without reflection. An hour later your bank phones you to say that your account has been cleaned out and your debit card invalidated.

- What would your first reaction be?
- What would you actually do?
- Would you be able to concentrate on the conference as it went ahead?
- What would happen to the networking and relationship building with other professionals that you were planning on?

Now assume you are a lone parent with two small children, living on jobseeker's allowance paid into your bank account. You have just been informed that there is some official concern about your benefit that requires investigation and in the meantime benefit payments have been suspended and you will be informed when they are to start again. Do you see similarities with the scenario above?

ACTIVITY 2.2:   YOUR BELIEFS ABOUT POVERTY

To begin to clarify your views on individual responsibility and poverty consider the following short scenarios.

1   Ms Neema is white British, 24 years old and the mother of two young children. Her husband is an asylum seeker and as a family they have been refused assistance from the local social services who say they are not responsible for providing or paying for temporary accommodation and basic subsistence because their last settled address was in that of a neighbouring authority. The council say that it is that authority that should provide assistance. (Note: the main aim of the Asylum Act 1999 was to exclude those seeking asylum from drawing benefits and instead introduced vouchers for essential purchases. It also established zones where new arrivals were to be dispersed and increased the capacity for detention and deportation for failed applicants.)

2   Mr Kaur is 70 years old, a Sikh and originally from the Punjab. He has been living in Birmingham for some thirty-five years. He has diabetes and smokes; as a result of the diabetes he is partially blind and has restricted mobility from leg ulcers. He says he has worked hard all his life but now feels he is a burden on his wife who has to attend to his many care needs. The couple have two working sons who live in other parts of the city. The

Kaurs live on a state pension and have several outstanding debts for their utilities – gas, electricity and water. The gas company has written to them recently about their unpaid bill of some £560 and are threatening court action.

What do you consider to be the main reasons for each family's low income? To what degree do you think the following are responsible for the family's predicament:

- personal or individual choices and actions
- cultural and moral attitudes within the family or neighbourhood in which they live
- pressures associated with social and economic status such as the impact of social class or the jobs market on their lives?

ACTIVITY 2.3: VALUE REQUIREMENTS IN THE NATIONAL OCCUPATIONAL STANDARDS

According to the National Occupational Standards social workers *must* hold the following values:

a   Have respect for:
- individuals, families, carers, groups and communities regardless of their age, ethnicity, culture, level of understanding and need
- the expertise and knowledge individuals, families, carers, groups and communities have about their own situation.
b   Empower individuals, families, carers, groups and communities in decisions affecting them.
c   Be honest about:
- the power invested in them, including legal powers
- their role and resources available to meet need.
d   Respect confidentiality, and inform individuals, families, carers, groups and communities about when information needs to be shared with others.
e   Be able to:
- challenge discriminatory images and practices affecting individuals, families, carers, groups and communities
- put individuals, families, carers, groups and communities first.

(TOPSS 2002: 4)

Which of these do you think are most applicable to tackling social exclusion? Do you think certain of these values could inhibit approaches to tackling exclusion?

Poverty is too often seen as the inevitable backdrop to service provision, the responsibility of other workers and agencies. Even where local authority social service departments have direct control of important resources, whether grants for children in need, direct payments to disabled people, or payments to care leavers and foster carers, they use these powers variably and not as part of an anti-poverty strategy. This limited engagement in anti-poverty initiatives means that local authority social service departments have little accumulated experience in tackling poverty as the central pillar of social exclusion (Dowling 1999; McLeod and Bywaters 2000).

This attitude is reinforced by social work organisations themselves in which the hierarchy of skill locates the experienced social worker at the top undertaking 'complex' work particularly in child protection while leaving bread and butter issues to family support workers. Nor is anti-poverty work seen as part of the restructured role of community care manager and purchaser of care. Welfare rights work, on the other hand, if done at all, is carried out frequently by under-trained staff or assistants. Many social work training programmes do not stress the importance of obtaining full and accurate benefits for users while students show less commitment and less dedication to acquiring expertise and skills than in virtually every other area of the work.

USEFUL PERSPECTIVES

No single social work theory maps out a pathway for combating social exclusion. The importance of poverty, social networks, neighbourhood environments, partnerships and participation has long been recognised in social science and social work theory as separate subjects for investigation but they have not been conceptualised as forming a single process as components of exclusion.

Some groundwork, however, has been laid and the aim of this section is to familiarise practitioners and educators with those perspectives that help clarify social exclusion and get to grips with it.

Anti-oppressive practice

Anti-oppressive practice merges the separate struggles that social work undertook against discrimination into a single coherent approach. Feminism, anti-racism and disability campaigns have all contributed to this approach as has gay and lesbian thinking. It locates the sources of oppression and disadvantage in social structure and focuses on how powerful groups retain dominance by exploiting existing political institutions, language and everyday 'common sense' which goes unchallenged because it seems universal.

Oppression arises from the extreme imbalance of power. Confronting such pervasive power is the key element that binds the experiences of the oppressed together. Certain groups are dominant in society, such as white or able-bodied people, those with wealth, and men. As a result these groups are able to construct institutions, from the family to parliament, that promote and expand their own interests while preserving their political and social power. The point is that this process of domination will appear natural and an aspect of what is to be expected rather than as something that has been socially constructed. For example, the difficulties that we 'naturally' associate with being disabled – lack of employment opportunity, barriers to mobility – actually arise not from the physical impairment a person has but from the elaborate social attitudes that able-bodied people have constructed around those impairments and which disadvantage and oppress people who have impairments.

ANTI-OPPRESSIVE PRACTICE

Anti-oppressive practice is based on a belief that social work should make a difference, so that those who have been oppressed may regain control of their lives and re-establish their right to be full and active members of society. To achieve this aim, practitioners have to be political, reflective, reflexive and commited to promoting change.

Dalrymple and Burke 2006: 48

A social work practice that is anti-oppressive begins with this awareness that barriers to full human development are socially and politically created. Part of any social work assessment therefore should uncover these ideological constructs and stereotypes, and the barriers that restrict service users' freedom to act should be challenged through workers' alliance with users. Social workers strive then to improve the material level of resources for oppressed groups, work to amplify their power, and challenge dominant groups' oppression of the marginalised. Braye and Preston-Shoot (1995) argue that in working with people who are oppressed, it is not sufficient to increase their say in decisions; the sources of their oppression must also be challenged. For the individual practitioner engaging in anti-oppressive practice Dalrymple and Burke link three levels: augmenting the practitioner's own sense of power, acknowledging the connection between personal problems and existing power structures, and undertaking social and political action (Dalrymple and Burke 2006).

While anti-oppressive practice clearly has much to offer in contesting exclusion it has certain limitations. First, it often pays little direct attention to poverty, or to the power of social class and the means for maximising a family's income. Jordan has written that the principles of anti-oppressive practice 'fail to capture the essential element in most service users' oppression – exclusion and marginalisation stemming from poverty'. By focusing on 'oppression' in relations between men and women, white and black, able and disabled, young and old, social work fails to address the fact that it is itself deeply implicated in the oppression of users. This is because it fails to tackle the fundamental source of social injustice for users – their poverty (Jordan and Jordan 2000: 49–50).

Second, anti-oppressive practice is suspicious of notions of neighbourhood and community because it regards them as masking difference and allowing already dominant interests to speak for a whole community. Yet 'the neighbourhood' is a critical arena of practice where the engagement of local people in initiatives to tackle social exclusion can be implemented (Barnes 2007). Third, anti-oppressive practice places a premium on language as the medium through which oppressive ideologies are cemented in place and requires close examination of language to reveal the extent of oppression. One of its main emphases lies in the arena of challenging others' use of language – whether that of users, other agencies, professions or community groups. As necessary as this is it nevertheless directs attention away from the brute constraints that poverty places on individual families and sees language constructions as foundational to oppression rather than income levels and social class.

An ecological approach

The ecological framework provides a holistic way of looking at the connections between family, neighbourhood and society and how each level is affected by the others (Bronfenbrenner 1979). It offers a powerful guide to showing how you can map out the interconnections through which social exclusion occurs.

Bronfenbrenner looked at an individual's environment as a set of structures nesting within structures through which it is possible to picture how institutional decisions, social attitudes and market operations promote or curtail the opportunities and well-being of individuals (Figure 2.1). Individuals develop within the:

- micro-system of home and family
- meso-system of school, neighbourhood and other local institutions such as churches, clubs and associations
- exo-system through which more distant but powerful institutions and practices bear on the individual's life. For a child such institutions may be the parent's

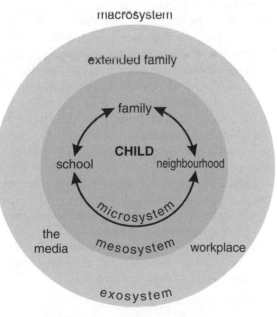

FIGURE 2.1   Bronfenbrenner's ecological system of human development

workplace (and its level of pay and working conditions), the conduct of local agencies such as youth clubs or something as everyday as the local public transport system. For a young adult it may be how information regarding job opportunities or skills training is transmitted. For a person with disability it may be the attitudes of local employers or the supported employment opportunities or more skills training.

Finally there is the macro-system – a large field embracing the cultural, political, economic, legal and religious context of society. It includes social attitudes and values which, although not always articulated in daily life, nevertheless have a huge impact on individuals. For example our images and opinions on gender, older people, HIV, crime and punishment emerge often from the macro-system (Barnes 2007).

The ecological approach has several elements that are useful in attacking social exclusion.

1   It is holistic. It understands that human development is a product of interaction of forces with a powerful role played by the wider social context or macro-system so that it prompts social workers to be concerned with the way social environments impact on different individuals and groups.
2   It stresses that the individual's perception of these interactions and the social pressures with which they have to contend are best understood and explained by that person.
3   It underscores the importance of social supports, social networks and the institutions within communities as fundamental to individual development.

The ecological approach compels the practitioner to consider a range of factors across the community and family level. As you read through the chapters and in particular consider the case studies it will be helpful to keep these levels in mind: for example, for creating a basic map of the forces and structures that socially excluded people have to contend with (see for example Chapter 3). The ecological approach highlights a range of responses that might otherwise have been overlooked: the importance of income and concrete resources such as child care and employment opportunities, and better co-ordinated services around health, education and housing. It also highlights the changes that can only be achieved by community building where the capacities of local people and neighbourhood organisations are developed (see Barnes 2007). However the way in which a person's ecology is portrayed in four concentric circles can be misleading. This seems to suggest that each of the different levels are self-contained and that there is a practice competence related to each but not one that extends across all four. In fact the ecological model, like all models, is a construction and does not capture the dynamic of a person's life course through time. It is also a systems-based model which tends to emphasise the virtues of equilibrium and smooth running with change following only in the event of system-breakdown. It is important to recognise that all the factors the ecological model highlights are intertwined and dynamic so that practitioners' competences need to engage at all levels.

Community social work

Community social work flourished in the 1980s as a kind of bridge between the radical social work of the 1970s and the more market oriented, privatised policy and practice environments of the 1990s. Radical social work often sought directly to change social and economic structures (at least locally) by raising the consciousness of users and bringing welfare claimants and trade unionists together in a wide agency for local change. The premise of community social work is that people in difficulty most often receive help from other individuals from within their locality and social network. In this understanding of the assets of networks, community social work sees social services as peripheral to many people's lives. For example, the care of vulnerable adults is largely undertaken in the community by family, relatives or friends and not by public services. Child care is offered by family, friends and neighbours. The anti-social activities of young people are controlled informally at local level without the intervention of the criminal justice system.

Community social work recognises this capacity within localities and works to bolster those networks or to bring new networks to life where they are insufficient to provide help. Rather than focus only on an individual client and their immediate family it recognises that social problems arise in part through a malfunctioning social network (Hadley *et al.* 1987; Darvill and Smale 1990).

The work of the principal proponents of community social work, especially that of the late Gerald Smale (1988), still offers solid grounding for a practice dedicated to reducing social exclusion. Its main concerns are acutely relevant: the emphasis on social problems, interest in networks, the need to 'go local', formation of partnerships and the requirement for practitioners to be 'bridge builders' between service systems and different interest groups (especially those without resources).

In framing its practice community social work avoids the alternative of intervention in the 'community' or with the 'individual'. Community social work teams see both as legitimate, each requiring planning and resources, and engage in a whole spectrum of activities. The spectrum of work includes:

- Direct intervention – work carried out with individuals, families and their immediate networks to tackle problems that directly affect them.
- Indirect intervention – work with wider community groups and other professionals and agencies to tackle problems which affect a range of people including the individuals involved in the direct work.
- Change agent activity – this seeks to change the ways that people relate to each other that are responsible for social problems whether at individual, family, or neighbourhood levels. Change agent activity has to do with reallocating resources, such as staff time and money, in different ways to tackle social problems. This includes making such resources available to neighbourhood residents and organisations and joining with other agencies in holistic solutions.
- Service delivery activity providing services that help maintain people in their own homes, to reduce risks to vulnerable people, and to provide relief for overloaded parents and carers. This includes making resources available to community organisations for this purpose (Smale *et al.* 2000).

PRACTICE IS PREVENTIVE

Practice that tackles social exclusion is 'preventive' practice; that is, a practice that aims to direct resources and intervention towards addressing early signs of social difficulties or social problems before they accelerate and intensify into emergencies that require vastly greater resources in terms of time, energy and money. The notion of 'preventive work' is not wholly satisfactory, first because it raises the question preventing what? Second, it suggests that it is a kind of optional extra as if social work is not really social work until it is reacting to harm or imminent crisis. Gerald Smale *et al.* (2000) prefer the phrase 'development work' instead of preventive work and distinguish it from 'curative' or crisis work through which social work offers aid in a reactive way in times of emergency.

Safeguarding children provides a good example of how the emphasis on risk ebbs and flows in relation to preventive work. From the mid 1990s there was official concern from the Department of Health that too many resources were being drawn into safeguarding children and that social workers with children and families could use resources more effectively if they got out from under the shadow of reactive protective work (Department of Health 1995). The development of outcome oriented work and the creation of separate children's services following the publication of Every Child Matters in 2003 seemed to further underscore the importance of prevention and early intervention in children's lives (see Chapter 4). The Scottish Executive in its enquiry into social work in the twenty-first century also firmly committed itself to a preventive strategy (Scottish Executive 2006). Then in 2008, following the death of Baby P, that policy went into reverse with the numbers of children being looked after by the local authority escalating sharply. Some argued that social work discourse around risk and child protection had all but disappeared and that this was a needed correction.

A balance between risk oriented intervention and preventive work nevertheless has to be struck. The aim is both to overcome the effects of social disadvantage for families and to reduce crime and other anti-social behaviour in the interests of their local community and wider society.

One widely endorsed model for understanding the relationship between curative and preventive practice is Pauline Hardiker's, which she developed for work with children and young people (Hardiker 2004).

Practice designed to tackle social exclusion in Hardiker's model (see Figure 2.2) in general flows up along the diagonal aiming to embrace larger numbers of people through its range of collaborative interventions. But this is not exclusively the case, and those practitioners who clearly work around risk or engage in casework should also be able to see how their practice fits in tackling social exclusion. Social exclusion has consequences of self-esteem, mental health problems, violence and the acute consequences of exclusion that affects behaviour requires counselling and therapeutic skills. Many of the initiatives discussed later in this volume are aware that social deprivation causes immense individual stress and has personal consequences.

DEFINING PREVENTION AND EARLY INTERVENTION

Williams and colleagues (Williams *et al.* 2005) differentiate between the two as follows:

> *Prevention* refers to strategies or programmes that prevent or delay the onset of health and behaviour problems, while *early intervention* refers to strategies and programmes that reduce the harms and health consequences of behaviours that have been initiated (Williams *et al.* 2005: 93).

Little and Mount (1999) made a similar distinction in relation to services for children in need:

> *prevention*: an activity to stop a social or psychological problem happening in the first place;
>
> *early intervention*: activity aimed at stopping those at highest risk of developing social or psychological problems, or those who show the first signs of difficulty from displaying unnecessarily long or serious symptoms (Little and Mount 1999: 48–9).

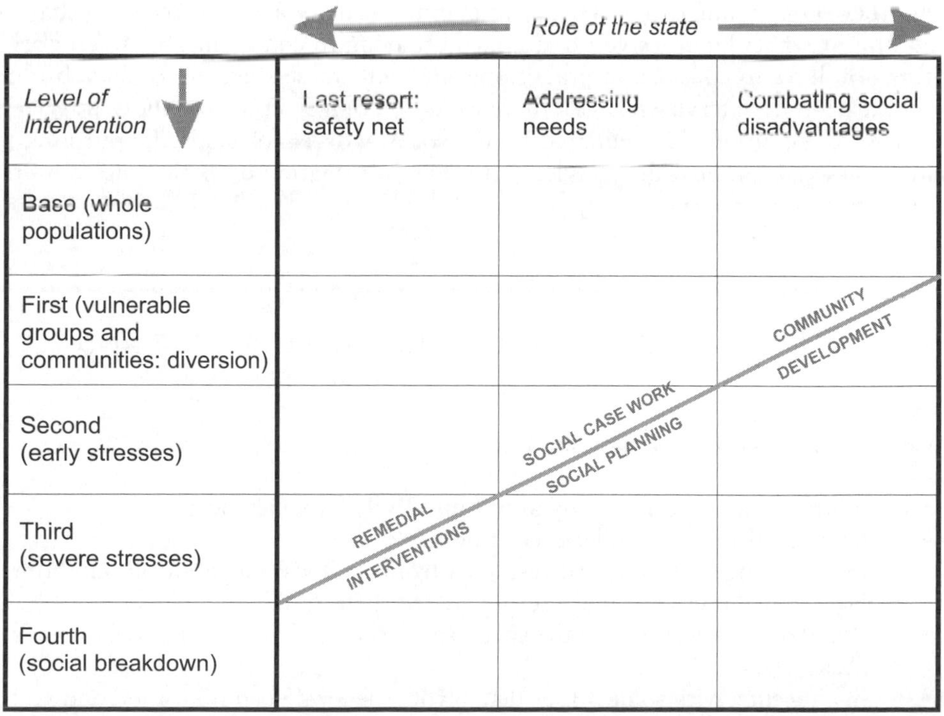
Role of the state
Level of Intervention
Last resort: safety net
Addressing needs
Combating social disadvantages
Base (whole populations)
First (vulnerable groups and communities: diversion)
Second (early stresses)
Third (severe stresses)
Fourth (social breakdown)
COMMUNITY DEVELOPMENT
SOCIAL CASE WORK
SOCIAL PLANNING
REMEDIAL INTERVENTIONS

FIGURE 2.2 Hardiker's model: locating preventive practice

SOCIAL WORK SKILLS FOR TACKLING EXCLUSION

Trevithick argues that 'skill' in social work is difficult to define because it overlaps with other key terms with which it is used interchangeably, such as 'intervention' and 'competence'. Hence trying to isolate 'skills' from other techniques and approaches can be at best a provisional task. Trevithick defines skill broadly, encompassing knowledge, expertise, judgement and experience that is difficult to separate from a given situation, course of action or intervention (Trevithick 2005: 64). For her, skill involves reaching sound judgements on how to work best in a particular environment. Among her list of 50 skills many have to do with interviewing; among these she includes planning and preparing for interview, creating rapport, knowing the different types of questions – open, closed and circular – and when to use them, clarifying and summarising, providing advice and information and offering encouragement and validation. But she includes many others such as modelling and teaching others social skills training, counselling skills, containing anxiety and mediation skills (*ibid.*).

In the following section we consider those key skills that are particularly pertinent in combating social exclusion.

Communication skills

Communicating with people is the bedrock of social work practice aiming to reduce social exclusion. All the building blocks discussed in the next chapter rely in one form or another on communication. How you communicate, what objectives you have in mind and in what situations you find yourself having to communicate are all critical factors you have to consider. In practitioner manuals these skills are often subsumed under the heading 'interviewing' as if there were a set of techniques to follow. Interviews in general are conversations initiated by the social worker for a specific purpose, for example assessment, providing advice, gathering information or explaining to users a particular statute or agency policy.

ACTIVITY 2.4:   COMMUNICATING – WHAT, WHERE AND TO WHOM

Consider the following situations. You are:

- talking to a 15-year-old boy about his family circumstances
- having a drink with colleagues after work
- in a meeting with some 30 residents from the local neighbourhood about how to make services more responsive to their needs
- asked to write a report on the social care needs and priorities in your team's area
- in a meeting with some 30 residents from the local neighbourhood and you have been asked at the last minute to chair the meeting

- given ten minutes at a multi-agency forum to convince those present to undertake a particular project.

All the above are tasks in communication. Arrange them in the order of the difficulty that each would present for you, starting with the most difficult. Why are they difficult? What makes the easy ones easy? What do you need to do to improve your communication skills in the difficult situations?

Listening

Social workers have to be good listeners, and be able to absorb and respond to what users and their families are saying. Often listening is part of a therapeutic endeavour, reflecting back to the user what the practitioner has heard so that the person can respond and react to their own statements. However in working to reduce social exclusion with service users the emphasis in communication shifts in a different direction. The mission is to build capacity and extend capability in work that is often locally based and preventive or 'developmental' in Smale's terms. A key objective of this work entails gathering experiences and information on exclusion in the area from the experts: those who are excluded. You listen to users' and local residents' accounts in order to hear histories, make links between what may appear to be only individual problems, gather information on networks, become aware of neighbourhood issues, find out where users' strengths and resources are and where those of the neighbourhoods are.

This might best be described as listening to stories, or 'gathering stories' in Cedersund's phrase (Cedersund 1999), where the focus of listening becomes the experiences, obstructions and hardships that a person or family has encountered. The value of stories is that they have many sides to them and may be told and heard in different ways depending on the life experiences of those telling them and those listening. Stories, as Parton and O'Byrne argue, are also a way of creating beliefs in that they impose a coherence on a person's life experience and have a unique power for 'setting forth truth claims' (Parton and O'Byrne 2000: 49).

Getting people to tell 'their' story acts as a way of bringing elements of their life to awareness – yours, theirs and others. One of the elements of a story that you are looking for is local knowledge. We may think of local knowledge as *partisan knowledge*, because the person who holds it has a passionate interest in a particular outcome (Scott 1998). As you become more familiar with the range of stories and their local knowledge the problems that people feel strongly about will emerge. This is the keystone of what we will refer to in Chapter 7 as 'relational organising', which borrows much of social work's emphasis on relationship building, and the patience and empathy that that requires, but applies it to extending the capability of individuals and their neighbourhood.

Listening to stories means departing from the question and answer format of the standard interview. In stories knowledge, according to Parton and O'Byrne is 'ready-made to be listened to, needs no proof and [is] capable of creating an obedience that makes reframing or reinterpretation difficult later' (2000: 49). But while stories, in particular 'family stories', may be used to maintain traditional authority – men over women, parents over children – they have other functions.

Parton and O'Byrne examine the effect of 'externalising conversations' which seeks to re-politicise experience. Externalising conversations facilitates the 'naming' and 're-naming' of the dominant forces in people's lives, inviting them to identify the influences of oppressive 'truths' and the practices associated with them. 'In being assisted to evaluate these influences, people are encouraged to establish alternative stories or "preferred identity claims and alternative preferred practices of self and relationship"' (Parton and O'Byrne 2000: 84).

Practitioners addressing the experience of social exclusion should be interested in 'externalising' conversations. To begin this process they may ask questions about the social fabric of people's lives, what they have done and achieved, what they hope to achieve, the history of their family. For example, they could ask: 'how did you come to be living here?' 'What was it like living through a period of racial harassment?' 'I noticed a couple of neighbours calling in for advice – they seem to respect you a great deal. Do you think that's the case?' 'You obviously had to fight for your child's dignity – that must have taken a lot of courage at times.' The aim of such comments is to identify what you sense the person feels most passionate about and to encourage them to talk about it. Unlocking what people care most about is an effective first step in encouraging them to articulate problems and push ahead for answers.

The practitioner's task is to see how social exclusion as a process is experienced by service users. When talking to specific groups of users and citizens, the emotions, stresses, decisions and behaviours that people engage in become an important part of the equation. For example: it is one thing to observe and deal with the barriers that exclude refugee children from mainstream society; it is another to hear directly about the trauma and loss of their separation, perhaps from family, certainly from their home country. This capacity to hear first hand the experiences of deprivation and hardship has always characterised social work from its beginnings although it has not always known how to respond effectively.

Excluded individuals will not necessarily see themselves as 'victim' or 'oppressed'. But their stories often do describe the hidden injuries of disadvantage. Overt divisions between social classes used to be obvious and observable; disadvantage, poverty and lack of opportunity were directly linked to a person's position within the class structure and could be described and understood as such. Now, as Richard Sennett has explained, the hidden injuries of disadvantage have produced a 'crisis in self-respect' because social difference appears as a question of character and personal responsibility when it is not (Sennett 2007). This personalised sense of defeat in a winner–loser culture is another aspect of what practice has to deal with.

Focusing on strengths not weaknesses

Historically, social work has tended to base its practice on a person's or family's deficits and weaknesses. The complexities of personal, cultural, physical and environmental adversities have been reduced to narrow compartments of diagnostic or assessment schemes and responded to accordingly. Instead of asking what is wrong with this individual, this family or this neighbourhood we can ask 'What strengths do users have that have helped them cope so far? What are their aspirations, talents and abilities?

What social, emotional and physical resources are needed to support their growth and wellbeing?'

Saleeby (1992) has outlined three assumptions of this strengths perspective:

• Every person has an inherent capacity for regeneration and transformation.
• This power is a potent form of knowledge that can guide personal and social change. Accepting and honouring the personal experiences of others creates the basis for knowledge exchange. A dialogue between equals replaces hierarchical knowledge structures so no individual or group can wield power through a monopoly on knowledge.
• When people's capacities are respected and supported they are more likely to act on their strengths.

Negotiating skills

Negotiation is a process of communication between parties that takes place over a period of time during which the parties involved are trying to reach an agreement that both sides find acceptable. They may have interests in common and be able to reach an agreement that meets at least some of these interests. They may have no common ground to speak of, in which case the negotiation will fail. In this communication each party brings information to try and educate the other, lays out what it wants to see in a final resolution and brings pressure to bear to have those interests realised (Shell 1999). The parties may be individuals, organisations or nations (in which case it is called diplomacy). In their classic work, *Getting to Yes,* Fisher and Ury write 'Whether a negotiation concerns a contract, a family quarrel, or a peace settlement among nations, people routinely engage in positional bargaining. Each side takes a position, argues for it, and makes concessions to reach a compromise' (Fisher and Ury 1982: 3).

Social workers are distinguished from other helping professionals such as doctors, teachers or nurses, precisely by their willingness to engage in informal negotiation through which they balance interests of various parties and stakeholders and facilitate the emergence of a consensus. In this way they work with ordinary people in their natural settings, using the informality of their methods as a means of negotiating solutions to problems rather than imposing them (Jordan 1987; Parton and O'Byrne 2000: 33). Much of this negotiating involves dealing with conflicting interests among family members or with conflict between individuals and various agencies, or in securing agreement from users to pursue a jointly negotiated plan, whether through task-centred work or a written agreement.

In tackling social exclusion the informal negotiating role of social workers expands into new arenas and becomes more formal. As social worker you may now be involved in negotiating:

• With other agencies – in constructing a partnership in which resources are pooled and sacrifices of 'turf' inevitable.
• In acting as advocate or representative on behalf of a user or a neighbourhood group.
• In support of users or local residents who are entering into their own negotiations

and for whom you are providing back-up support as they deal with project funders, various public authorities, elected councillors or technical experts.
- In community development work with political or corporate authority on behalf of neighbourhood organisations.

Approaches to negotiation

Fisher and Ury (1982) present a set of techniques to structure virtually any negotiation:

Separate the people from the problem. Treat your negotiating partner with respect even if you reject their position totally: nothing will be gained by rejecting, criticising or otherwise insulting the person who holds a position that you cannot accept. If you do that you close off avenues for future agreements. Equally it is to be expected that people will get angry, depressed, fearful, frustrated or offended in the process of negotiation. They confuse their perceptions with reality or fail to interpret what you say in the way you intend. Whatever else you are doing at any point in negotiation you should ask yourself 'Am I paying enough attention to the people problem?' (Fisher and Ury 1982: 19). This does not mean trying to please the other party by making offers that will elicit a pleasant response. Negotiation is not about maintaining pleasant responses but neither is it about character assassination or demonisation of the other party.

Focus on interests and not positions. A negotiating position is often concrete and explicit but behind every negotiating position lie the deeper, perhaps unexpressed, intangible interests of the different parties. For example, agency representatives negotiating a collaborative service agreement for hospital after-care may fight stubbornly for a certain task to be included, when in fact they care less about the task itself than insuring a continuing role in the joint work going forward. Figuring out what these interests of the other parties are is often just as important as knowing what your interests are. To do this Fisher and Ury suggest the simple technique of putting yourself in the other party's shoes. Examine each position its representatives take and ask why they reach that particular position as well as why they have not taken certain other decisions.

Invent options for mutual gain. In many areas of public life much can be achieved by understanding the self-interest of others and focusing action around shared interests. As Stokes and Knight put it, 'When people are acting together in common self interest, significant power can be exerted. When people are kept apart and their self interest is managed by others, powerlessness results' (Stokes and Knight 1997: 14).

Techniques such as brainstorming, seeking preferences and weighting them according to importance, inventing multiple agreements with different strengths, and dovetailing or reconciling deeper interests all assist in this endeavour.

Establish objective criteria. These are used to define or measure negotiated outcomes in a way that is separate from the subjective or personal feelings of the various parties. Broadly, such criteria either have to do with fair standards for judging outcomes or fair procedures for resolving conflicts. Fair standards, for example, may be rules for evaluation, targets for distributing resources, or specified outcomes for a project as a whole or for the individual parties to the process. Developing such criteria is a task to be undertaken early on in the negotiating process so it is helpful to prepare in advance, working through alternative standards beforehand so as to gauge their impact on your case (Fisher and Ury 1982: 88).

ACTIVITY 2.5: WHAT KIND OF NEGOTIATOR ARE YOU?

Richard Shell (1999) identifies five types of negotiating personality which, in descending order of aggressiveness, are: competitors, problem-solvers, compromisers, accommodators and conflict avoiders. He poses this simple thought experiment to see which style you are most inclined to:

Imagine you are one of ten people, all of whom are strangers, sitting around a big table in a conference room. Someone suddenly comes into the room and makes this offer: 'I will give a prize of £1000 to each of the first two people who can persuade the person sitting opposite to get up, come around the table and stand behind his or her chair.' What would you do and what tactics would you use? What style would suit this situation? How aggressive could the 'competitors' become? (Competitors might hastily offer their anticipated £1000 to the person opposite them to come around in order to ensure they were absolutely first.)

Advocacy skills

Advocacy seeks to represent and secure the interests of relatively powerless users when dealing with powerful service organisations, the media or in coping with repressive public attitudes. Advocacy takes several forms:

- self-advocacy in which people with similar experiences of social exclusion, for example discrimination arising from a physical or learning impairment, form an organisation to alert the public, pressure service officials and politicians and mobilise for increased resources;
- citizen advocacy;
- practitioner advocacy on behalf of users or local resident groups.

You may be involved in facilitating the first two forms through information, advice or resources, but it is the last that you will be carrying out yourself. Neil Bateman (2005) has laid down six principles for effective advocacy:

1   Always act in your client's best interests. This principle is easily overlooked when facing multiple and competing pressures from managers in your own organisation or other agencies. It means constantly reminding yourself of the person on whose behalf who you are acting.
2   Always act in accordance with your client's wishes and instructions. This is fundamental: the advocate's actions have to be driven by the client's wishes and instructions. Developing what Bateman calls an 'instructional relationship' is an important first step. Within this the advocate can identify facts, options and remedies but will listen for the client's instructions.
3   Keep the client properly informed. The client must know all essential facts related to her or his situation without being deluged by information. Equally the client must be kept informed of all actions taken on their behalf. Accountability is impossible otherwise.

4   Carry out instructions with diligence and competence. If you offer to do some-
     thing make sure you do it – but know your limits and do not undertake that for
     which you are not prepared or competent.
5   Act impartially and offer frank, independent advice. This means being able to say
     uncomfortable things to representatives from other organisations (or your own)
     and not being beholden to the other side. A co-operative relationship based on
     partnership with the other side is not appropriate and can lead to a breach of
     advocacy principles.
6   Maintain the rules of confidentiality. Clients must feel completely secure in the
     knowledge that what they say remains confidential. (Bateman 2005: 66–8)

ACTIVITY 2.6: ACTING AS ADVOCATE

A worker in an advice centre sees Mrs Ullah. She says she would like some help
in finding somewhere else to live. She describes the family circumstances and
adds that the maisonette where they currently live is damp and the stairs are
very difficult for her husband to negotiate. The Ullahs have found the housing
association officer extremely intimidating and do not want to upset him. After
she leaves, the advice worker concludes that the local authority would never be
able to re-house them and writes a stinging letter to the officer of the housing
association, in effect delivering an ultimatum about the damp and threatening
pursuit of compensation.
     What principles of advocacy has the worker violated?

Community development work

A range of practitioners, activists and volunteers now engage in community development work at least as part of their role, including community support workers,
community development workers attached to children centres, local social care initiatives, health promotion initiatives and youth and community workers. A stream of
guidance from central government stipulates that all public services should have
community development strategies as an important arm in service delivery in response
to central government requirement. Effective solutions to social problems, particularly those arising from social disadvantage, can be developed only through a change
of culture in public agencies that embraces some dimension of community development or capacity building (Home Office and Department for Communities and Local
Government 2005; Department for Communities and Local Government 2006).
     Social services have had some difficulties in responding to this agenda for the
same reason that it finds preventive work difficult, principally because the urgent work
responding to specific crises dominates local authority social work. But that is not the
only reason. For some years social work training programmes have shown less interest
in community practice and no longer promote it as a social work approach. Dixon
and Hoatson (1999) describe how community work has been marginalised within
social work training in English-speaking countries since the 1980s. This has produced

a paradox whereby social work committed itself to combating oppression in its value base at the same time as dispensing with the one important element needed to bring that work into focus: skills for community and neighbourhood engagement.

Dixon and Hoatson are very clear as to what has been lost. Community development work provides:

- Effective strategies for creating personal change through social action by bringing people together to support each other, to identify need, educate, build skills and confidence. The practitioner needs skills that take up individual troubles and link them to community problem-solving.
- Skills and frameworks to strengthen networks of residents, service providers and interest groups in the locality.
- Means for building locally based 'communities of interest' around service provision, based on values of participation and collective practice.
- Knowledge about how to mobilise numbers of people whether through social action campaigns or social movements.

(Dixon and Hoatson 1999: 4)]

Community development work has a long association with working for groups that are disadvantaged and contending with discrimination. It does this by:

- Seeking to create links and liaisons between groups and individuals within a locality, around issues of common concern on a basis of mutual respect, whilst recognising diversity and differences.
- Promoting the development of alliances and the recognition of collective action by encouraging people to reflect and act together in order to achieve common goals, and influence decision-makers.
- Acknowledging the specific experience and contribution of all individuals in communities, to enable people to enhance their capacity to play a role in shaping and determining the society of which they are part.
- Recognising that the unequal distribution of power is both a personal and political issue, and that community work has a responsibility for linking the personal learning which empowers people to the collective learning and action for change which empowers communities. Community practice is important because it generates the skills in working with people collectively and sees strengths where others would see needs and deficits. This is quite simply because in seeking to mobilise and empower local groups, train their leaders and build local organisations, community practitioners must start with assets and local capacities.

Because of the emphasis on locality, the broader concept of 'community practice' which combines some community work approaches with work with local groups such as residents' associations or disability action groups has become more prominent. Community practice centres on engagement of local citizens and working to increase levels of participation whether in defining problems, shaping solutions and having say in how services are delivered. It includes services aimed at the community as a whole – *community level services* – and services that are decentralised and locally provided – *community based services*. The former aims to improve wellbeing for all members of the community while the latter aims to bring specific services closer to the community.[1]

KEY POINTS

The chapter explores values, approaches and skills needed to tackle social exclusion.

❑   The impact of values – both personal and professional – is deep and lasting. With regard to poverty, social work has long been ambivalent: it has always worked closely with poor people but tended to see their poverty either as a result of personal weakness or part of the user's background which it can do little about.

❑   Anti-oppressive practice, the ecological approach and community social work each in their own way guide the practitioner both to a better understanding of exclusion and more effective practice.

❑   Key skills for redressing exclusion include listening and communicating, negotiating, advocacy and community practice.

KEY READING

Chris Clark, *Social Work Ethics: Politics, Principles and Practice* (Macmillan, 2000). Clark stresses the contingent, evolving nature of values rather than as fixed dogma.

Pamela Trevithick, *Social Work Skills* 2nd edn (Open University Press, 2005) is the standard text.

Margaret Ledwith, *Community Development* (Policy Press, 2005) and the Department for Communities and Local Government report on *Community Development Challenge* (DCLG, 2006) both make a convincing case for the broad purposes of community practice.

---

1   There are many kinds of communities – geographical communities such as specific neighbourhoods, communities of interest where members share a common commitment, interest or passion, communities of faith or ethnicity.

CHAPTER 3

FIVE BUILDING BLOCKS FOR TACKLING EXCLUSION

OBJECTIVES

By the end of the chapter you should:

- Be familiar with the building blocks for a practice that tackles social exclusion and promotes inclusion.

- Be able to review your own role and responsibilities in light of that practice.

- Be able to build your own knowledge base around concepts crucial to understanding social exclusion such as the importance of neighbourhood and social networks.

This chapter introduces the building blocks for practice which social workers need in order to work with socially excluded individuals, groups and neighbourhoods. The building blocks are generic; they apply to all forms of social work. Some may be familiar to you, others will be new and require you to think creatively about your role and responsibilities; still others have emerged from recent initiatives by government and non-governmental bodies, and from research about how the process of social exclusion works. In brief the practitioner tackling social exclusion is flexible, locally focused and willing to collaborate with other services. This ensemble of practice approaches and an advancing knowledge base, when combined with some of the skills described in the previous chapter, creates a new perspective linking social work with social justice.

The five building blocks are:

1   Maximising income and securing basic resources for users and their families.
2   Strengthening social supports and networks.
3   Working in partnership with agencies and local organisations.
4   Creating channels of effective participation for users, local residents and their organisations.
5   Focusing on neighbourhood and community-level practice.

MAXIMISING INCOME AND WELFARE RIGHTS

In this section we look at different strategies for maximising the income for the people you work with through benefits or advice on employment and skills acquisition. As explained in Chapter 2 the majority of those who use social work services are in poverty; any practitioner aiming to tackle social exclusion has to focus consistently on maximising the income of those with whom they work. Social workers are in as good a position as any to assist users and local people in examining at regular intervals the various means to improve their income levels. Practice begins with this realisation and commitment.

ACTIVITY 3.1:   WHAT DO YOU AND YOUR TEAM KNOW ABOUT MAXIMISING INCOME OF USERS?

At a team meeting run through this checklist on the state of your current preparation for maximising income.

- Does your team – and do you individually – focus on the income of users and consider with them at regular intervals options for how they might raise the level of that income?
- Do you have an up-to-date reference book on benefits such as the Child Poverty Action Group's *Welfare Benefits and Tax Credits Handbook*?
- Is money advice provided to users through another agency or by a member of staff such as an advice worker who is not part of your team?
- Who in your agency is responsible for discussing money matters and benefits with users?
- If you are in a local authority social services department, how do you implement your department's charging policy? Do you routinely consider user eligibility for other benefits?
- Do you consider yourself well informed on the range of benefits that users might claim?
- Does your agency have an anti-poverty strategy? Has it joined a benefits take-up campaign with other agencies?

Knowing the benefits system

People do not need a social worker in a formal capacity to obtain benefits or tax credits, but when in contact with families and individuals social workers should be able at least to review what benefits they are receiving and any further support they may be entitled to. The benefits system is complicated with annually changing rates and the regular introduction of new, often specific and targeted benefits but this should not deter practitioners. Broadly the rule should be: social workers should know in general terms the various sources of support and be able to help users to get what should be their entitlement – but need not be expert at the level of detailed knowledge (Thomas 2001). They do not, for example, need to have the knowledge necessary for appearing at tribunals: realistically this role could only be expected of a full-time welfare rights officer. But they should be able to recognise when a focus on a user's income level is essential and to know enough about the benefits system to be able to:

• Go through the range of the user's possible entitlements to determine whether they are claiming all that they can.
• Secure back payments of principal benefits if it can be demonstrated that a claimant should have had a benefit earlier.

The reasons why benefits are abruptly stopped can be intricate: because of an alleged failure to disclose a 'change of circumstance', non-attendance at medical examination, alleged cohabitation or uncertainty over immigration status. In such instances referral to specialist advice is essential when in doubt about an individual's eligibility.

The structure of benefits is explained in several excellent handbooks which you are strongly encouraged to consult. These include the Child Poverty Action Group's annually updated *Welfare Benefits and Tax Credits Handbook* and *Welfare Benefits and Tax Credits* by Keith Puttick both of which are clear and well laid out for quick reference. Both the Department of Work and Pensions and Her Majesty's Revenue and Customs run effective on-line services providing eligibility criteria and up-to-date rates for different benefits and tax credits.

The welfare reform programme instituted by central government since 1997 has dramatically changed both the kinds of benefits available and the relationship between benefits and work. In general many more benefits are now based on 'conditionality' that is, come with provisos attached requiring the claimant to look for work or seek training in preparation for work. The aim is to ensure that as many people as possible, including those adults with disability and mental health problems and parents with young children, join the work-force or prepare for work. Tax credits, jobseeker's allowance and employment support allowance and other employment-related benefits have in some cases drastically reduced access to the once dominant safety net of income support.

From January 2009 income support was progressively phased out in stages, with key groups previously reliant on it such as lone parents expected to switch to jobseeker's allowance or, if they have an incapacity, to employment support allowance (ESA).

Receiving ESA is conditional on searching for employment or training and such policies tying benefits to employability through the benefit system have aroused different opinions as to their consequences. One argument maintains that *only* by holding a job can a person avoid exclusion and conversely if a person is *not* in work that is a matter of personal choice and a form of self-exclusion. Another holds that the job market is highly unpredictable and is itself often exclusionary in the way it operates in relation say to ethnic minorities, women and people with disability or long-term health problems. What is certain is that the kind of work that people on benefit usually move into is low wage, temporary and part time. Work of this kind does not produce the pathway out of poverty as hoped. Even before the economic downturn of 2008–09 the proportion of working adults in low income households exceeded those in workless households in 2007 (Palmer *et al.* 2008: 68).

WHAT IS A TAX CREDIT?

One of the chief tools in linking the benefit system to work is through tax credits. A tax credit is, despite its name, essentially a means-tested benefit, although its effect is to off-set a tax liability *if the claimaint pays tax* (Thomas and Puttick 2009). Tax credits are determined and paid to claimants by Her Majesty's Revenue and Customs. Whether a claimant is eligible for a tax credit is determined by their level of income and not on any capital they might have – although income from capital of course counts as income. Child tax credit is paid on top of benefits including child benefit, income support and income-based jobseeker's allowance. It can also be paid along with working tax credit to claimants with children. However, while child benefit and other income such as child support is disregarded as part of income in calculating tax credits other benefits are not.

Working tax credit (WTC) supplements the earnings of low-income workers and is paid to a person if she or he works 16 hours or more a week. Additionally to be eligible the applicant must:

• have responsibility for a child
• *or* have a disability that puts them at a disadvantage in getting a job.

WTC can also be received by employees who

• are over 50 years old
• *or* work 30 hours a week or more, are over 25 years old and are not responsible for a child.

Child tax credit is income based and paid to low- and middle-income families, whether in or out of work, to those who have responsibility for a child under 16 or the main responsibility for a child in shared care arrangements. Couples must claim for a tax credit jointly; an individual who is part of a couple cannot decide to claim individually. (For guidance and worked examples of how WTC and CTC is calculated see CPAG 2009 and www.hmrc.gov.uk/tax credits/.).

Means-tested benefits

To be entitled to means-tested benefits a person does not have to have met any conditions on contributions but simply to satisfy eligibility criteria in relation to income and capital, including 'notional capital'. Eligibility is established through a detailed comparison of a claimant's needs (referred to often as the 'applicable amount') and weekly income. There is a long historical association with intrusive methods for determining financial status developed under the Poor Law with its bias against providing any form of financial support except in the direst of circumstances. While no longer so associated in the public mind means-tested benefits do require the user to declare all income as well as any savings they might have. In some circumstances, for example, when facing allegations of living together as a couple or working while claiming, claimants may be expected to attend interviews under caution and be subjected to other robust investigative procedures (Thomas and Puttick 2009).

The main means-tested benefits are:

- income support
- income-based jobseeker's allowance
- pension credit
- income-related employment and support allowance, all of which are paid through the Department of Work and Pensions and,
- housing benefit
- council tax benefit, which are paid by local authorities.

Income support and income-based jobseeker's allowance

Income support (IS) provides a minimum source of income for adults over 18 who are not required to be available for work and whose income, including that from other benefits, is below an officially defined minimum. Those who may claim income support include lone parents with children under a certain age, carers, students and others on training courses subject to some restrictions. IS can also be paid to some 16 or 17 year olds in their own right in certain circumstances. However young people of that age do not qualify if: (a) they have been looked after by the local authority – in which case their local authority should both support and accommodate the young person, depending on their status under the Children Act 1989 (Thomas and Puttick 2009) or (b) are counted as in 'relevant education' but are a child for whom someone is claiming child benefit or income support.

Because it is geared to cover certain designated 'needs' income support varies from person to person depending on what these needs are. Those eligible for IS include:

- some disabled claimants
- carers temporarily looking after children or family members
- lone parents
- 16 and 17 year olds in full-time education or work training schemes and not living with their parents.

For the purpose of determining the level of income support any income is taken into account including earnings and other benefits, such as child benefit, and child maintenance. Certain benefits are ignored in this calculation however, such as housing benefit, council tax benefit, attendance allowance and disability living allowance. As mentioned, part-time earnings from work of up to 16 hours a week are permitted for those receiving IS but those earnings are still treated as income in calculating benefit subject to modern disregards (Puttick 2006).

If a person is eligible the amount of IS payable depends on two variables. The first of these is the 'applicable amount', that is the aggregation of formal 'needs' which the claimant has. The applicable amount is arrived at by combining personal allowances, any housing costs (that is, mortgage commitments but not rent, which is covered by housing benefit) and any premiums for further specific needs. The latter includes a family premium paid to couples with at least one dependent child. Other premiums are available for disability, severe disability, a disabled child, pensioner and carer. The impact of such premiums can be difficult to work out since some can be paid jointly while others cannot. Child-related additions to IS were replaced by child tax credit so that IS is now an adult-only benefit.

As of 2009, for every £250 above the threshold of £6000 in capital or savings a claimant will lose £1 in benefit for both jobseeker's allowance and income support. With capital or savings over £16,000 claimants cannot receive any income support or jobseeker's allowance. If the claimant lives in a care home, and has capital between £10,000 and £16,000 for each £250 or part of £250 of capital you have, benefit is also reduced by £1 a week. With savings or capital over £16,000 would-be claimants cannot receive either income support or jobseeker's allowance unless they can take advantage of certain 'disregards' (DWP 2009).

For those who are unemployed and are required to be available for work, but have not previously made sufficient contributions to be eligible for contribution-based jobseeker's allowance (JSA), the claimant may apply for the 'income-based JSA' rather than IS. The 'income' in this case refers to the same sources of income that determine eligibility for IS. Income-based JSA is similar to IS in the form of means testing and in many respects the system is almost identical.

MEANS-TESTED BENEFITS

The major means-tested benefits include income support, income based jobseeker's allowance, income based employment support allowances, council tax benefit, housing benefit and pension credit. If one member of a family is claiming a means-tested benefit usually no other member can claim the same benefit for the same period and partners must choose which one will act as claimant. This rule applies to pension credit also with the additional requirement that the claimant must be over 60 years old.

For the purposes of means-testing 'a couple' now include these four relationship arrangements:

- both partners are over 16, married and living in the same household
- *or* are not married but 'living together as husband and wife' in the same household
- both partners are of the same sex, registered as civil partners and living in the same household
- *or* are of the same sex, not registered as civil partners but 'living together as if you were civil partners' (CPAG 2008: 713). A couple, as defined above, must claim as a couple, with their combined income and capital taken into account, and will receive any benefit due for the couple.

The notion of 'household' is flexible but left undefined. Whether two people should be considered a couple living in the same household depends on various circumstances. A house, that is the physical structure, can contain a number of separate households – for example a person living in exclusive occupation of separate accommodation, say in a self-contained flat, will generally be regarded as a household. Nor is physical presence always essential: there must be a 'particular kind of tie' binding two people together in a domestic establishment – which may include a household in lodging house or hostel. But the two or more people forming the household must be living together as a unit and show that they have a certain level of independence and self-sufficiency. For example a couple sharing a room in a residential home, because they need assistance in organising their personal care have been found not to constitute a household because of this arrangement (CPAG 2008: 714).

On the other hand benefits for an individual who regularly stays overnight in accommodation of another person may be treated, rightly or wrongly, as cohabiting and their benefit stopped. This can happen even though they have no sexual relationship with or long-term commitment to that person. People sharing a flat or who are offering mutual support to each other, or simply a tenant or lodger living in the same accommodation as their landlord fall into this category. Such a decision can and should be challenged by showing that the arrangement is in fact one of separate households where the requirements of 'couple status' are not prseent (Puttick 2006). Separate household status is established by showing that there are:

- separate arrangements for cooking and eating
- independent financial arrangements
- separate arrangements for meeting housing costs
- and, critically, that there is no evidence of family life (CPAG 2008: 715).

Couple status is established through:

- shared financial responsibility
- stability in the relationship
- shared residence

(For a useful guide on these difficult issues see DWP 2009.)

Non-means tested benefits

There are also a number of non-means-tested benefits that can be placed in two broad categories – contributory and non-contributory benefits. Among the first group are the jobseeker's allowance, employment and support allowance,[2] maternity allowance, bereavement benefit and retirement pension. Contributory benefits are partially funded by the National Insurance contributions a person pays while at work or which may be 'credited' or deemed paid for certain periods of time. Non-contributory benefits are paid out of general taxation and there are no contributory conditions that individuals need to establish in order to receive them. The main non-contributory benefits are: carer's allowance, disability living allowance, attendance allowance, child benefit, guardian's allowance and industrial injuries benefit.

Working with users

It is important to hold on to three objectives in working with any users and families to maximise their income. The first is to be able to look across the whole benefits system so that you can pick up linked entitlements. People can qualify for some non-means-tested benefits and as a result then be eligible for means-tested benefits. For example, if a young mother is under 16 she cannot claim IS or an income-based JSA but she can claim child benefit if she has responsibility for her child, as well as exemption from certain health charges such as prescriptions or dental work. If that young mother's parents include her in their family for their own benefit claims her infant can then also be included (CPAG 2008). A claimant's eligibility can act as a 'passport' to further entitlement. For example, a lone parent on IS will automatically receive maximum child tax credit, housing benefit and council tax benefit if she rents her accommodation.

The second objective is to help the user look closely at the interrelationship between benefits and work. For example, if a person increases her work to 16 or more hours a week on average and has child care responsibilities she will normally cease to be eligible for income support but would qualify for working tax credit. However this may raise difficult issues in turn – such as whether to encourage a person to take up employment when they have caring responsibilities for young children which could be undercut by that employment. Intangible matters, such as the social contacts outside the home that a job might bring, also have to be weighed against the caring responsibilities. They may benefit from 'better off/worse off' advice from a specialist adviser in welfare rights.

The third objective is to recognise that access to benefits and tax credits is increasingly linked to 'status' in the eyes of the authorities. For example, a person who is 'subject to immigration control' or who does not have a 'right to reside' is barred from most forms of support.

As a social worker who may be advising users on whether or not to seek work, you will have to know the direction that these reforms have taken in recent years. The core of the active benefits regime is the jobseeker's allowance for the unemployed which

---

2   Employment and support allowance effectively replaced incapacity benefit in the latter half of 2008.

combines benefit payments with job search or training and skills acquisition. This group of claimants will rapidly grow as lone parents are transferred from IS. All JSA recipients have to demonstrate they are actively seeking work although claimants can assert that for physical or mental disability, care responsibilities or religious conviction, certain kinds of work are not appropriate for them. The implications of constricting eligibility for income support, for attaching work conditions for lone parents who receive JSA (and lowering the age of their children where those conditions apply), the employment and support allowance for many claimants previously on incapacity benefit and the work capability assessment both introduced in 2008 are discussed in the next three chapters.

ACTIVITY 3.2: THE FRANKLINS

Mr and Mrs Franklin have three children: Bobbi, 14, Stu, eight, and four-year-old Carol-Ann. Mr Franklin, a tool machinist, has just been made redundant and Mrs Franklin has a casual part-time job as a school dinner server.

The family are buying the three-bedroom house where they live. Stu, their eight-year-old, is disabled. Mr Franklin is paying off a fine for a conviction for breach of the peace. He keeps a greyhound that he sometimes races. Both the Franklins smoke.

You are interested – as they are – in maximising their income. What benefits are the Franklins entitled to? Do a check on the specific amounts the Franklins might receive by consulting the DWP and HMRC websites for current benefit rates.

Take-up campaigns

Take-up campaigns seek to maximise benefit claims across a whole area through a concerted effort to remind those eligible for particular benefits to claim them. Organising take-up campaigns is generally productive both for the user and local authority social services departments. Requests for community care assessments are a logical place to start, ensuring that those approaching a social service department – carers, older people or disabled people – have had the opportunity to review the range of benefits for which they may be eligible. The new collaborative arrangements in the provision of benefits advice have proved productive in generating take-up campaigns often involving the local council, a social care provider, the Citizens Advice Bureau and the government's Pension Service.

- Housing benefit records provide another source from which to predict and pursue further claims.
- As young people with physical or learning disability reach the age of 16+ in schools and colleges the nature of previous contact that social workers have had

with them changes, but knowledge of their situation may prove instrumental in securing extra resources.

- Publicise widely. Ensure that notices of entitlements and of the campaign itself are placed in locations where people will encounter them – schools, day centres, surgeries, libraries and other public places. Small or infrequent notices simply will not suffice at a time when people are bombarded by all sorts of information and advertisement.

CASE STUDY 4: HARROGATE TAKE-UP CAMPAIGN COUNCIL TAX BENEFIT

In Harrogate the local council became aware that only six out of ten people eligible for council tax benefit were claiming it. It mounted a collaborative campaign in 2007 with near by district and borough councils to encourage higher levels of take up, particularly among older people who were disproportionately among those not claiming the benefit. The campaign worked closely with the Welfare Benefits Unit based in York which provides advice and training service to the voluntary and statutory sectors who deal directly with individuals claiming benefits. The campaign targeted those who tend not to claim this help including those:

- aged over 60
- carers
- larger families
- people with disability
- families with a disabled child
- part-time workers
- those on a low or modest income.

(Harrogate District Council 2007)

The mismatch between local authority administered benefits – council tax benefit and housing benefit – and national benefits such as jobseeker's allowance administered by the Department of Work and Pensions can cause significant confusion for users particularly as welfare-to-work measures become more exacting. Both sets of benefits generally use the savings threshold of £16,000 (in 2009) above which individuals receive no benefit. Changes in matters like hours worked, levels of income and capital and changes in household composition must be reported on a weekly basis by claimants to the local authority. To retain both council tax benefit and housing benefit requires regular resubmission of forms and checks that are complex and time consuming to complete.

UNDERSTANDING AND STRENGTHENING NETWORKS

A social network is the web of relationships through which people are connected. A network may be supportive or destructive, plentiful or virtually non-existent, close and intense or far-flung and distant. An essential element of social work is promoting the development of dependable social networks that fulfil certain functions for people. When thinking about networks it is important to remember that they can include individuals, families and neighbourhoods, as well as comprise specific groups of people, for example around types of work or shared interests or predicaments. Moreover, since people interact with institutions, organisations and services, networks include these relationships as well. The quality, purpose and functioning of networks varies dramatically: in terms of the numbers of people involved, the degree of interconnectedness and frequency of contact, the quality and duration of the relationships and the degree to which they are supportive or undermining (Jack 2000: 328). Networks are not confined to close personal relationships; in Chapter 1 for instance we made the distinction between networks for getting ahead and getting by – two very different types, with the former based on dispersed, more distant relationships.

There are advantages in using a simplified network map in cooperation with users which could prompt further information on their connections and supports as well as day-to-day contacts with agencies and other organisations – or the absence of these. The importance of networks should not lead practitioners to regard the business of putting such a map and grid together in an overly formal way. Remember the aims of network mapping: drawing on strengths, getting the big picture, encouraging family members to tell their story and reflect on their perspectives on their current circumstances. It provides a basis for both practitioner and family to discuss the specific nature of a family's networks and highlights potentially useful resources.

There is also reason to develop more sophisticated network mapping techniques whether they centre around a single person or family (often called 'ego' networks in social networking analysis) or around a multi-agency project (or 'complete' networks). Networks can be more hidden than one might suppose. In assessing the strength or weaknesses of networks our techniques for mapping have moved well beyond the conventional eco-map or other forms which proved so useful to social work in the past.[3]

In mapping a network it is useful to think of *nodes*, that is the persons, organisations or teams and *links* as the relationships and interactions between the nodes. *Hubs* are those nodes, whether persons or organisations, that have a far greater number of links than the average for the rest of the network participants. Mapping these connections exposes patterns of interaction and activity that otherwise would not be apparent. From such mapping it is possible to determine the 'role structure' within a network, that is, the functional, logistical and hierarchical nature of the relationships between the links.

---

3   Social work can fairly be said to have developed the idea of the 'eco map' which has a long and honourable history. However social network analysis has moved ahead in leaps and bounds in the last decade with more complex and powerful ways of mapping them visually. A range of software is available to accumulate data and map networks. The qualities of networks are crucial to individuals and families in their struggle to overcome exclusion.

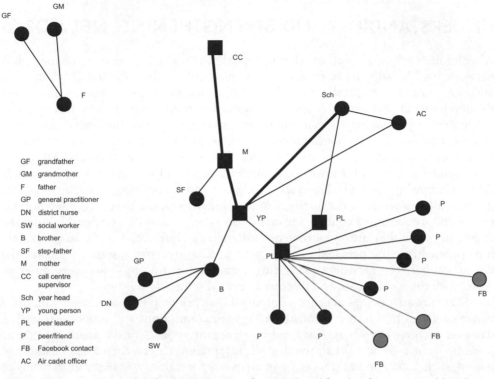

GF grandfather
GM grandmother
F father
GP general practitioner
DN district nurse
SW social worker
B brother
SF step-father
M mother
CC call centre
   supervisor
Sch year head
YP young person
PL peer leader
P peer/friend
FB Facebook contact
AC Air cadet officer

FIGURE 3.1   Example of a network map of a re-ordered family of a 16-year-old male
                 with attention deficit hyperactivity disorder. Father is estranged from the
                 family; younger sibling has a disability; mother works at a call centre and
                 the 16-year-old's peer group is highly influential

A number of structural factors dramatically affect the kind and quality of networks
that a person has; income, educational background, age, gender, disability, ethnic origin
and employment all shape the kinds of networks available to people. For example,
those who are older or in poor health tend to have less robust networks, with those
aged 85 and over having much smaller networks than those who are younger. On the
other hand those in higher income brackets, in employment and who attended university tend to have more extended social networks (Keating *et al.* 2003).

In particular it is important to map types of social assets: material support, emotional
support, advice, esteem, closeness, reciprocity and durability (Pinkerton and Dolan
2007). Visualising networks of individuals and families is a co-constructed activity
with users to produce a map of contact flows and to identify important sources (or
their lack) of specific support functions whether for getting by, such as care, emotional
support, friendship, or getting ahead, such as role modelling, mentoring, information
on training or jobs. Visualisation can also identify sources of income, contact with
voluntary or public agencies. The wealth of data in the visualisation of network maps
is enormous and can be applied to decision making and presentation at case conferences, or in appraising a family's resources with users themselves.

Once visualisation of the network begins to emerge practitioners can ask further
questions regarding the nature of the relationships. These cover the types of support
available; for example whether they provide information or emotional support, how
critical a member of the network might be, the closeness or intensity of the relationship

or other features such as frequency of contact and length of relationship. Although any one map is constructed from the point of view of a single family, through use practitioners will become more familiar with the different characteristics of families' networks. These include the size, perceived availability of different types of support through the network, the degree of criticism and attack that networks contain and the extent of reciprocity.

BUILDING PARTNERSHIPS

A partner may be defined as 'one who has a share or part with others' implying that there is an overall goal or organisation of which individual partners are aware. Partnership means joining the efforts of public, voluntary and private organisations in formal or semi-formal arrangements in which goals are agreed upon, some resources are pooled and common strategy planned though each partner may be responsible for implementing a different part of that strategy. The many sided nature of social exclusion and interlocking social problems that forms it require coordinated, joint approaches across a range of services.

Because the problems associated with social exclusion are deep-rooted and complex a single agency cannot resolve them on its own. The objective is to develop integrated programmes at all levels of practice from working with families, to work with whole neighbourhoods and local communities. Partnership makes holistic solutions possible, providing the means by which practitioners can move beyond the specialisms of social work such as care management or protecting children.

To understand the importance of partnership for reversing social exclusion it helps to conceive of the major services – health, education, housing, child protection and social services – as 'silos'. You may recognise the image: a silo is a large, tall structure found on farms for storing foodstuffs. They are self-contained and immovable, with no access between them. Major services are constructed like that: huge, immovable and interested only in what goes on inside themselves. As a result people are often 'dumped' – excluded – outside one or more service silos and receive no service at all. The rising exclusions from school of hard-to-teach pupils are a perfect example of dumping. Because of school performance tables, disruptive, hard-to-teach pupils are unwanted by any school and often there is only a token service available to provide them with a small amount of home schooling. In social work we can point as an example of dumping to the shifting back and forth between hospital care and long-term residential care of older people who have suffered a fall or stroke – with neither service wanting to absorb the cost of that care. Professional discretion in decision making and the growing culture of managerial focus on 'core' responsibilities and competencies has only reinforced the problem of dumping.

Alternatively users may have several different services circling around them each claiming a need for information particular to them and each wanting to collect and assess their own information. Attempts to resolve this problem have not necessarily produced the desired coordination among agencies. For instance, the common assessment framework is now available for different services to use – such as schools, social services or primary care trusts – to pool information about a particular child. Yet it is proving time consuming to fill out and other information channels have been established to circumvent it (see Chapter 4). A similar move to pool information on older people in need has not generated the closer collaboration among agencies that was sought.

Building effective partnerships

There are several principles to follow in establishing effective partnerships:

- develop standards of success that relate to creating awareness and supportive local attitudes (although relatively intangible) rather than tangible units of service
- choose a base for organising efforts – a neighbourhood, demographic group or profession cluster
- balance this organising with service delivery demands and opportunities and do not let the latter drown out the former
- share leadership and roles of influence as the collaborative constituency building evolves
- bridge class, racial and ethnic divides (Briggs 2002: 21).

Communication, cooperation and coordination are crucial to success. Differentiated tasks can be allocated among individuals with the various skills to contribute. Sometimes collaboration means recognising differences and finding ways to accommodate those differences. Each partnership should undertake a self-study of preferred styles – reflecting on their own styles and what, as a collaborative, they feel most comfortable with.

EXAMPLES OF PARTNERSHIPS

Increasingly, practitioners have become familiar with the new generation of initiatives based on partnership that have arisen to tackle social exclusion. These include:

- Youth inclusion and junior youth inclusion programmes working to overcome the exclusion of children and young people between the ages of 9 and 16.
- Healthy Communities involve collaborative efforts to reduce falls among older people.
- Mentoring schemes put young people in touch with an older adult for guidance, support and to act as a role model.
- School-based projects to prevent truancy, bullying and school exclusions.
- Children's centres are community-based combining health, early education and child development guidance both in the centres and on out reach.
- Intermediate care for older people leaving hospital involving health and social services.

Partnerships do not of course guarantee successful outcomes and at times they may be worse than no partnership at all. For example they may exist only on paper simply to provide a smokescreen for capturing resources. Or the individual organisations in a partnership may have vastly different levels of influence allowing dominant agencies to smother the interests of smaller, often community-based organisations. Centrally imposed conditions for competitive bidding carry their own drawbacks. They often stipulate a short time-frame for submitting applications giving considerable advantage to those major agencies with a specialised work-force and the capacity to do the hours of necessary planning and report writing. Local organisations, users and residents usually have no such resource to fall back on so for them to enter into a partnership on equal terms is difficult.

LEARNING WITHIN PARTNERSHIPS: A KEY TASK

- A stronger learning culture with agencies and particularly within government should be more openly acknowledged and sought.
- There should be widespread discussion about conflicting interests and competing philosophies, and how these influence the knowledge building process.
- More efforts should be made to promote shared learning and organisational change at national and local levels.
- Sustained investment is needed to develop ways of facilitating peer-to-peer and organisational learning, and to bring them into the mainstream.

(adapted from Coote *et al.* 2004: xiv)

In working to create effective partnerships there are a number of things for practitioners to think about:

- Make sure that any issues from past activity are aired among would-be partner organisations. From these discussions you can begin the process of identifying future positive behaviours, redefining roles and changing the language from the politics of agency self-interest to the mutual responsibility of partnership. The biggest gap to be bridged in any partnership involving local people is between the professionals' and local people's interests.
- Familiarise yourself with the 'turf' and core interests of would-be partners; few partnerships are agreed without some losses as well as gains for all parties.
- Establish a number of joint problem-solving teams to identify solutions. While holistic or joined-up services are the aim, the path is strewn with practical difficulties both small and large. The advantage of smaller problem-solving teams is that in the more informal atmosphere the 'sacred cows' can be discussed and all parties become involved in the identification of problems and in generating the solutions to overcome them (Anastacio *et al.* 2000).
- Joint problem solving provides the ability to debate the issue in purposeful ways without resort to traditional blocking-type tactics.
- Action learning – an action team of a dozen people can be useful in exploring complex problems. It may choose to acquire expert assistance and policy specialists or conduct study visits and seminars.

- Partnerships reflect a state of mutual trust and respect that has to be earned. The behaviours, language and spirit of the new relationship emerges and the competence of each participant is tested and established. To create a partnership without strong foundation is merely a declaration of friendship, or a short-term measure that will struggle to survive the challenges facing it (Sabel 1993).
- Developing working relations takes time among agencies who may have competing interests. Collaboration is not easy for competitors. The single biggest drawback to the partnerships demanded by government initiatives is the short time-frame for forming partnerships which must be done before proposals can be submitted.

ACTIVITY 3.3:   PARTNERSHIP – WHO HAS INFLUENCE?

Think of a partnership in which your agency is involved. Write down all the agencies and organisations which make up the partnership and, on a scale of 0 to 5, rate the degree of power that each holds within the partnership (with 5 as the highest). After you have done this reflect on three issues: What are the reasons and what is the basis for the degree of power that each organisation holds? Have the power relationships changed over time and if so why? What are the key characteristics of the power relationships of that particular partnership?

ACTIVITY 3.4:   PARTNERSHIPS – A COST–BENEFIT ANALYSIS

Using the same partnership that you chose above assess the costs and benefits involved for your agency in joining the partnership for each of the areas listed below:

- funding
- staff time and other non-monetary resources
- aims, goals and missions
- personal values and beliefs
- reputation of your organisation
- local community needs

For each of the above what do you think are the risks that the costs of the partnership will outstrip in benefits? How do you think those risks could be minimised?

PROMOTING PARTICIPATION

Ensuring the participation of users and citizens in discussing, planning and arranging the very services and programmes that will affect them is the fourth essential element in any practice aimed at reducing exclusion. Historically both central and local government have designed top-down service programmes relying on notions of infallible professional expertise and bureaucratic procedures. Their ways of doing things only created further stigmatisation and powerlessness. For citizens not to be involved is itself exclusionary: not only are users' views not taken into account but their sense of powerlessness is also reinforced. Now government acknowledges that citizen involvement at many levels of policy and service delivery is a necessary pre-requisite if major social problems are to be solved (Home Office and Department for Communities and Local Government 2005).

Social workers and their agencies have long recognised this influenced in part by the groups of users they work with. Movements for a greater voice for users began in the late 1970s with disability advocates calling for a wider range of service choices, normalisation and community participation. Child-care practices in the mid 1980s were found to freeze parents out of the decision-making process when the local authority social service departments were considering taking their child into care. Adults needing some form of social care – whether a place in a residential home or home care – have fought to establish means of giving opinions in decisions affecting them (Braye 2000).

Successive pieces of legislation also began to re-shape user participation in the assessment and provision of their own service. The Children Act 1989, the NHS and Community Care Act of 1990 and the Disabled Person's Representation Act in 1996, among others, require local authorities to consult closely with users when they undertake assessments and devise care plans, and in the follow-up reviews of how those plans are actually unfolding. The Local Government Act 2000 strongly signalled community participation in local partnerships in general while the phrase 'community engagement' considerably widened the scope for involvement of users in decisions that affect them as well as consultation with local people and community groups across the entire range of public policy.

Yet the degree of influence on social work decisions that a user and his or her family will actually have varies considerably and often depends on the attitudes of the particular practitioners and agencies involved. Genuine dilemmas arise when local authorities have statutory obligations to exercise authority and provide a service which users have little choice but to accept, for example in cases where parents are strongly suspected of child abuse or in instances concerning young offenders.

Advocacy and pressure groups for users have accelerated this process and provide an important recent lesson as to how participation and empowerment is actually achieved. A new development is that of user-led services which are independent of the local authority and organised by committed advocates with a clear view of how society excludes users of mainstream services. Not only do they provide distinctive forms of support but they offer powerful examples of flexibility, choice and involvement which itself exerts wide influence (Braye 2000).

Social work and the broader world of social care has for two decades and more explored ways of empowering service users, whether individuals or in groups. Across that time there have been bold explorations as to what empowerment means, particularly in relation to people who are oppressed, whether through racism, domestic violence, barriers for disabled people, or all forms of keeping certain groups of people subordinated and intimidated (Dalrymple and Burke 2005).

Alongside this exploration of empowerment there has been healthy scepticism within the profession as to what the concept actually means in the context of social service. 'Empowerment', Mullender and Ward wrote, 'is used to justify propositions, which at root represent varying ideological and political positions ... which lack specificity and gloss over significant differences' (Mullender and Ward 1991: 1). The ambiguity of meaning for terms like empowerment and participation has become even greater in the era of partnerships and collaborative working where local people are being invited to take up positions of influence in the face of multi-disciplinary cross professional networks.

Arnstein's ladder

Sherry Arnstein developed her ladder (Figure 3.2) as a way of mapping out the different gradations of what 'participation' can mean (Arnstein 1969). Although it has often been adapted it has never been improved upon and is still referred to regularly in discussions on participation. The higher up the ladder you go the more control citizens exert over the initiative or service.

While practitioners may be individually committed to maximum levels of user participation, they will often find that legal obligations, agency policy and user expectations all constrain participation. Each project you engage in should be looked at carefully to determine what level of participation is both desirable and realistic. For example, in working with advocacy groups on developing local mental health services or with community groups in developing a family centre, levels of user participation are likely to be high and encouraged by social work agencies. By contrast, developing appropriate forms of community care for older people in a particular area could well have less intensive user involvement.

Participation: deeper, wider, longer

The nature of social exclusion requires complex programmes with new ways of involving diverse groups of people dealing with difficult and conflicting issues. Thus participation as a concept can no longer be confined to users and to a particular service. Virtually all projects, whether originating with government, community groups or practitioners and their agencies themselves, need to think hard about what kind of participation they seek and what approaches they should use.

Information

Giving information to people is fundamental to effective participation; people need to know the specific details of a project or service that is going to affect them. However, if practitioners are providing information only, there are some drawbacks: this is a

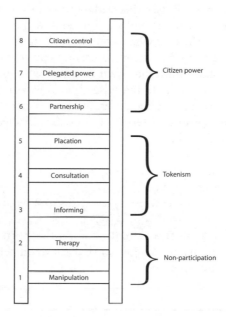

FIGURE 3.2   Arnstein's ladder of participation

take-it or leave-it approach which may prompt those affected to wonder whether there really is no alternative to the approach being put forward. You may get more vocal feedback than you anticipated. 'Information only' is appropriate if you have no room for manoeuvre and must follow one course of action or if it is the start of wider consultation with the opportunity to participate later (Wilcox 1994).

It is important to know your target audience: what do they know already and what might they expect? Make sure your audience will understand your ideas and language. Be clear from the start about why you are just informing rather than consulting.

Ways of providing information include the following:

- leaflets, newsletters, posters and other printed material
- presentations at meetings
- briefing the media with press releases and conferences
- advertising
- exhibitions
- using a short video.

Consultation

Consultation, in effect, gives people a limited role and choice in devising a project or service outcome. You offer some options, listen to feedback and comment and take these into account before proceeding with your action. You are not looking for involvement in implementation, although you hope it will enjoy the consent of those you have consulted. Social work uses this widely to obtain feedback on services and to win support from users when options are limited and the overall aim is already in place. Consultation is not sufficient when you are seeking to empower local interests or you are not in a position to take up the suggestions put forward.

Make sure you are clear about your own role and who ultimately will take decisions and how this will be done. Offering false choices is worse than offering none at all. Also be clear about how realistic the different options are; if you form a task force, local forum or committee, be sure its terms of reference are clear (*ibid.*).

Methods for consulting include:

• carrying out local surveys and questionnaires
• forming consultative committees
• consultation days with presentations, scenarios and feedback built in.

Try to found out in advance what information and other forms of support should be given to those whose opinions are sought so that they can reflect, discuss, learn and deliberate before giving that opinion.

ACTIVITY 3.5: CHECKLIST FOR CONSULTATION

To think in a structured way about the participation of users or local residents in a project you may be working on, run through the following checklist:

• Make sure you clearly define the different interests and groups to be consulted, whether based on gender, income, age, disability or ethnicity. Are they likely to have different perspectives and will you need to consult with each to be certain you have the whole picture?
• Ask yourself if they are likely to be satisfied with consultation.
• Can you present your vision and options for achieving it in a way that people will understand and relate to?
• Have you identified appropriate means for communication for the time available and the likely participants? (It is important to remember the power of visual representation and concrete examples.)
• Have you and your colleagues decided how to handle the feedback? By what means will it be logged or recorded? Have you arranged to report back to those you have consulted?
• Are you really just seeking endorsement of your plans or are you prepared to change your position?

Joint action

Joint action means accepting other people's ideas, working through decisions together, and having the time to engage in lengthier deliberations. Joint action is appropriate when users and residents need to own the solution, when fresh ideas are needed, when you need help in implementing your project or when empowerment and building capacity are themselves the objective. Make sure you plan the process before you start and allow plenty of time for its development. Make sure that roles and responsibilities are clear and that different interests are recognised. Acting together may take you into partnership, as discussed above, but equally you may remain on an informal level using temporary structures such as working parties, steering groups or small teams for overseeing and implementing decisions.

The means for generating joint action are more open-ended and require time for trust to build up between parties. They include:

1   Team-building exercises.
2   Working through scenarios.
3   Running exercises based on three-dimensional models of a local community (see Chapter 7).
4   'Future search' conferences that revolve around four key points:
    - get all parties in the room so that all aspects of the system are represented
    - think globally and act locally
    - focus on common ground and desired futures rather than problems and conflicts
    - allow discussion to be self-managed and take personal responsibility for implementation.
5   Citizen juries.
6   Community visioning.

Winning the trust of the community for joint action is difficult but essential for facilitating participation. Low-income urban neighbourhoods have seen service providers periodically gripped with a desire to get 'close to the people': they come, promise the world and then leave when funding runs out. Community trust is not automatic and must be earned too.

Citizen power

At the top end of the ladder – citizen power – the look and feel of work changes significantly. Practitioners should endeavour to act as convenors, catalysts and facilitators enabling local people to generate their own problem-solving capacities. Local people do their own investigations, analysis, presentations, planning and action; they own the outcome and share their knowledge. They do the mapping, diagramming, listing, sequencing and analysing. This is discussed at greater length in Chapter 7.

WORKING IN THE NEIGHBOURHOOD

Neighbourhoods are the critical level at which people engage. *Citizen Engagement*, the key strategy document from the Home Office, makes clear that successful outcomes depend on a culture change at the centre of the public agencies involved in combination with strong political leadership from the responsible local authority. Participatory approaches need to be fit for systematic, long-term participation in neighbourhood structures; these structures need to be efficient – so that local residents make a maximum impact from their involvement (Home Office 2005).

We have come to know much more about how powerful the social and organisational characteristics of neighbourhoods can be in the lives of people who live there. These 'neighbourhood effects' can be positive by providing resources and strengths that far outstrip anything that professional services could offer. Neighbourhoods with high levels of civic activity such as volunteering, supporting parents–teachers associations, running community halls or participating in neighbourhood watch schemes are likely to participate in projects at higher rates with, for example, greater willingness to serve on management boards and committees.

Neighbourhood effects can also be quite destructive, presenting people who live in them with challenges such as high rates of crime, non-existent job opportunities and poor schools that very few individual families could surmount (Wilson 1996; Sampson 1999). Neighbourhoods can also be 'closed' in their affiliations, hostile to diversity, and a seedbed for hate groups and physical attacks. But either way the importance of neighbourhoods cannot be ignored. Government has recently come to understand this very fact, which is why many programmes tackling social exclusion, such as Sure Start children's centres, health promotion and neighbourhood renewal have an area focus. The spread of 'locality teams' and neighbourhood-based teams within local government service provision is further recognition of the importance of neighbourhood.

Neighbourhoods may have definable features – railway tracks, highways, rivers or a specific type of housing, but although they may have geographical features neighbourhood remains a flexible and diverse concept. If you rely on 'walkable distance' as a criterion, for instance, people with disability could well take a different viewpoint. Political entities such as wards or constituency boundaries can be important but so can attendance for specific churches or mosques. Neighbourhoods may or may not have a common feeling of 'community' in which residents perceive certain common interests that arise because of their relative proximity.

'EYES ON THE STREET'

A good example of 'neighbourhood effects' is highlighted by the strength of informal mechanisms by which residents achieve some degree of informal social control. These include the monitoring of spontaneous playgroups among children, a willingness to intervene to prevent acts of intimidation by teenage peer groups and confronting persons who are exploiting or disturbing public space. The capacity of residents to control group-level behaviours is an important dimension to the social environment.

In her classic account *The Death and Life of American Cities*, the late urban specialist Jane Jacobs coined the phrase 'eyes on the street' to summarise this capacity of informal local control and how it could easily be disrupted by the poor planning of unthinking bureaucrats (Figure 3.3). Older neighbourhoods that had physically developed over time presented far greater opportunities both physically and socially for the public to stay involved in the social life of the neighbourhood.

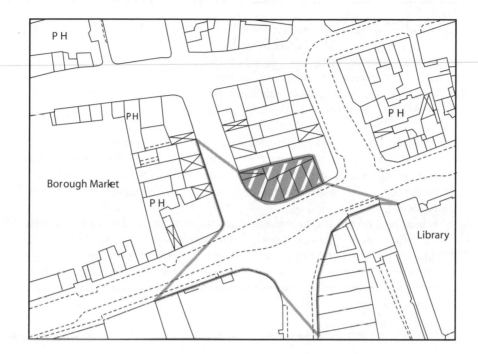

FIGURE 3.3   'Eyes on the street': the street map indicates how, in an older, physically
diverse neighbourhood, large areas of public space (outlined in grey) were
watched over by residents from just a few houses or shops

Whether in service plans, in central and local government policy documents or in social
workers' own discussions, too often the assumption is that 'the community' exists as
a single entity. The consequence can often be practical: a poorly arranged effort at a
consultation meeting for 'the community' or a single service plan that assumes the
community is a homogenous entity.

There are two different approaches for structuring neighbourhood oriented services to consider:

- The neighbourhood as the basis for the local delivery of services – this includes
moves to decentralise in common with other services, and the concept of the
neighbourhood management team. This can be referred to as *neighbourhood-
based services*.
- Community development – this means working to capitalise on existing strengths
and to enhance the capacity of the neighbourhood itself to solve problems and
accomplish tasks such as the social control of young people. Community development encourages individual and collective action allowing people to identify
their own potential, understand the processes of disadvantage and exclusion
and participate in the mainstream of their community, not on the margins. This
can be referred to as *neighbourhood-level services*. Both of these approaches are
discussed further in Chapter 7.

ACTIVITY 3.6: IDENTIFYING THE DIFFERENT COMMUNITIES IN YOUR AREA

Consider the different kinds of communities that may be found in your local area. From the list below check which you think are the most important for (1) your work and (2) for the area as a whole.

- Geographical communities – where at least a sense of common boundaries and certain common interests are widely if not universally acknowledged.
- Communities of interest – in which strong affiliations emerge from shared culture or similar social attainments; examples include communities around schools.
- Ethnic and religious communities – around culture and place of worship.
- Communities of identity drawn from shared social identity (gender and disability apply here) or of sexuality, such as gays or lesbians.
- Workplace communities – a large hospital will have an important presence in the locality, as will a large industrial enterprise such as a car factory.
- Service users.
- Age-based groups.

ACTIVITY 3.7: FINDING OUT ABOUT THE LEVEL OF LOCAL ACTIVITY

If you are serious about focusing on at least one neighbourhood in your work it is essential to know the current levels of activity as a baseline. Burns and colleagues (2004: 12) have developed this mapping exercise to establish such a baseline. They suggest several categories to examine, which are listed below. Using these categories map the baseline of activity for the neighbourhood you work or live in.

- individual contributions – for example, keeping gardens tidy, volunteering
- individual involvement in community activities – such as local football teams, lunch clubs
- informal mutual aid – such as child care, looking after neighbours
- organised mutual aid – credit unions, neighbourhood watch schemes
- participation in local networks and associations – tenants' and residents' groups, community associations.

KEY POINTS

The chapter has explored the five building blocks for a practice that aims to combat social exclusion. It covers:

❑   The importance of focusing on income and of having a broad working knowledge of the benefits system as a whole.

❑   The contribution that networks make both as a professional tool and as a source of social support for users.

❑   Partnerships with other service agencies and local organisations through which holistic, 'joined-up action' is delivered on the ground.

❑   Some of the benefits and difficulties in building high levels of user and resident participation.

❑   The importance of 'neighbourhood' and strengthening local capacity through service approaches to community development.

KEY READING

Child Poverty Action Group *Handbook on Benefits and Tax Credits* (latest annual edition CPAG).

Burns, D., Heywood, F., Taylor, M., Wilde, P. and Wilson, M., *Making Community Participation Meaningful* (Policy Press, 2004).

Pierson, J., *Going Local: Working in Communities and Neighbourhoods* (Routledge, 2008).

CHAPTER 4

WORKING WITH SOCIALLY EXCLUDED FAMILIES

OBJECTIVES

By the end of the chapter you should:

■   Understand how social exclusion impacts on the lives of young children and their families.

■   Know the gains and losses, particularly for lone parents, of linking benefits to work in maximising family income.

■   Be familiar with the outcomes in the *Every Child Matters* and Change for Children agenda for families with multiple disadvantages.

■   Be able to engage in family support initiatives such as parenting groups and family learning.

The purpose of this chapter is to guide practitioners through applying the building blocks for tackling exclusion to work with young children and their families. We suggest a number of approaches and ideas to address some of the components of exclusion as experienced by families with young children: low income, powerlessness and poorly performing social networks. We also examine innovative projects that focus on achieving the important outcomes stipulated in *Every Child Matters* and Change for Children agenda.

SOCIAL EXCLUSION AMONG FAMILIES WITH YOUNG CHILDREN

The consequences for children living in poverty and social exclusion are immense – for them, their families and the country as a whole. We know that social exclusion experienced in childhood is likely to ripple throughout that person's life. Children brought up in poverty tend to:

- Be socially excluded as adults and in particular to remain on low income throughout their lives.
- Incur health penalties at every stage of their life cycle with tendencies to low birth weight and respiratory diseases, and with obesity, heart disease and diabetes in later life.
- Be more likely to have mental health problems.
- Experience educational disadvantage where the accumulative effect of poverty on schooling widens the gap between the excluded child and the rest year on year (Hirsch 2008: 4-5).

Part of this effect comes from the stress that disadvantage places on parents. Economic stress exerts a disruptive effect on parents. When combined with changes in family structure and the physical concentration of people living in poverty, that poverty limits the range of choices available to parents in raising their children. For example low income negatively affects the extent of parental supervision of children and engagement with their child's school. Parents in disadvantaged neighbourhoods may rely on erratic forms of discipline, moving between harsh forms of punishment in an effort to keep their child safe and disengagement as those efforts prove futile; psychologists have long identified that inconsistency as contributing to anti-social behaviour (Weatherburn and Lind 2001: 77; Griggs *et al.* 2008). Families which sustain economic stress often cope also with social stress – social isolation, over crowded households, children's difficult behaviour, drug abuse and psychiatric disorder (Weatherburn and Lind 2001).

While lone-parent families are often viewed as vulnerable, particularly in relation to poor supervision of their children, all the evidence suggests that it is not family structure that is critical but the level of income poverty that the family experiences. Jonathon Bradshaw's exhaustive study of child wellbeing across the developed world clearly shows that the number of lone parents in Sweden for example is equally large as in the UK but that levels of child wellbeing are far higher, largely because of the quality of services available and the higher levels of income lone-parent families receive (Bradshaw and Richardson forthcoming).

The financial costs of child poverty to society as a whole are also enormous: one recent estimate has calculated that the public spending required to deal with the fallout from child poverty is about £12 billion a year much of which goes to social services, education and criminal justice to which can be added the low earnings of adults who had been excluded as children (£8 billion) and the extra benefits and lower tax revenues (£5 billion) to support them (Hirsch 2008).

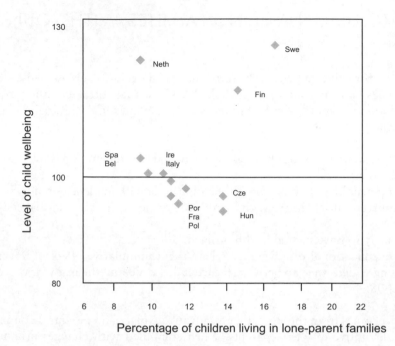

FIGURE 4.1   Wellbeing of children in lone-parent families. (Data drawn from *Progressive Inequality? Difficult Questions for the Next Decade*, Jonathon Bradshaw Conference presentation 16 February 2007)

ACTIVITY 4.1   COMPARATIVE LEVELS OF CHILD WELLBEING

This scatter plot summarises Jonathon Bradshaw's research into the relative levels of wellbeing of children and young people of lone parents across the developed world. I have deliberately omitted both the US and the UK. Where do you think they would each be located?[4]

Historically the number of children in the UK affected by poverty and social exclusion has been among the highest in the developed world. In 1998–99 a record four and a half million children were living in households with less than half the average national income after housing costs. By this standard one in three children were living in poverty at that time, twice the rate in France or the Netherlands and over five times that in Norway and Sweden (Piachaud and Sutherland 2001).

4   Both the US and UK are statistical 'outliers' when compared with other European countries and are to be found in the lower right hand corner. The level of wellbeing for children and young people in the UK is 84 with some 17 per cent living in lone-parent families while in the US the level of wellbeing is 82 with 21 per cent living in lone-parent families.

Reducing child poverty was a major objective for the incoming Labour government in 1997. It declared that it would seek to cut the number of children living in poverty by half by 2010 and abolish child poverty completely by 2020. To do this government introduced several important initiatives such as child tax credit, working tax credit and the new deal for lone parents, which aimed to raise the living standards of those parents on low income. Such measures have had some effect with the number of children in poverty having fallen approximately by half a million (Knight *et al.* 2006, see Chapter 10). Yet the number of children living in poverty remains stubbornly high – in 2006 just under four million children.

There has also been a modest fall in the number of children living in households where no one is working to 1.8 million children in 2006, some half a million fewer than ten years earlier. This is still the highest proportion of children living in 'workless' households in Europe, fully two-thirds higher than in France or Germany (Palmer *et al.* 2007: 55). To reach its target of halving the number of children living in poverty in 2010 a further 1.8 million children need to be taken out of poverty.

INDICATORS FOR CHILDREN IN POVERTY AND SOCIAL EXCLUSION

The New Policy Institute developed the following indicators to track the number of socially excluded children year on year.

- Children living in workless households – indicating the extent of polarisation between families with and without work.
- Children living in households below 60 per cent of average income – a standard threshold for determining relative poverty.
- Low birth-weight babies – reveals the persistent inequalities in health.
- Low attainment in GCSE results – educational attainment is strongly associated with social deprivation or affluence.
- Permanent school exclusions.
- Children whose parents divorce – a number of adverse outcomes are associated with divorce and separation.
- Births to girls under the age of 16 (adapted from Palmer *et al.* 2008).

Remember, each of these indicators is precisely that – they help us calculate the number of socially excluded children in Britain. They are *not* causes of exclusion.

ASSESSING SOCIAL EXCLUSION AND NEED

Children in need

The concept of 'children in need' has been fundamental to social work with families since the implementation of the Children Act 1989 and has much in common with children who are socially excluded. Both concepts draw attention to the wider environmental, economic and ecological dimensions in which the child is being raised. Both focus on material poverty, the quality of housing, the child's relationships outside the home and the impact of any disability. Understanding how these two basic concepts relate to each other makes a good starting point in developing approaches to practice that tackle the exclusion of families with young children.

There have been efforts to harmonise services for children in need and to understand service provision in light of what we know about social exclusion by focusing on the child within an ecological context. The Department of Health (DoH 2000a) explicitly adopted an ecological model as the basis for assessing children in need which asks practitioners to consider the wider environmental, social and economic components of exclusion. The familiar 'triangle', published in *Assessment of Children in Need* captures the range of individual developmental needs of the child, parental capacity to care and wider environmental influences that the Department of Health want social workers to consider when assessing children in need (Figure 4.2). The *Framework* in effect brings together theories of child development such as attachment with heightened awareness of impact of social and neighbourhood environments. While social workers have felt competent assessing the first two domains – developmental and familial factors – the third poses a significant challenge to traditional assessment perspectives. This requires practitioners to look at:

- the level of local resources and whether the family can access them
- the extent of the child's social relationships outside the family
- the impact of housing, parental employment and income level on the child's well-being and the parents' capacity to parent.

Jack and Gill have prompted social workers to explore this 'missing side of the triangle' more thoroughly (2003) and to pay greater attention to the role of local environment in child assessment. They have laid out the key areas that social workers should pay close attention to. First is the interaction between a family and available community resources, and the factors that may limit the family's use of those resources. Practitioners should consider the availability of local resources and the way an individual family is or is not able to access them. To do this social workers need to know the range of resources available in that neighbourhood – local play facilities, child care provision, open access schools and youth centres.

Second, is the extent of the child's social integration in terms of local relationships and the degree to which the child has been able to develop significant relationships outside the family. Such relationships especially as the child begins school and engages in neighbourhood peer groups, depending on their degree of supportiveness or rejection, play an important role in the child's emerging identity and behaviour. The practitioner must bear in mind that housing location, income level and family finances, and parental

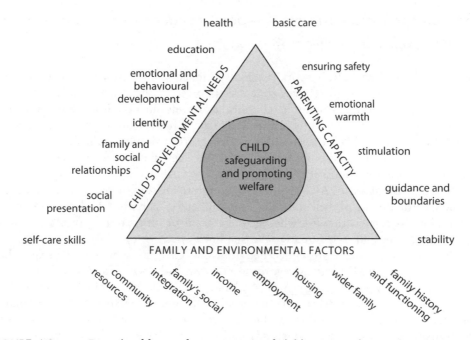

FIGURE 4.2   Triangle of factors for assessment of children in need

employment all shape the degree of integration a child and its family enjoys locally. While social work is not responsible for developing interventions on its own, full consideration of the child's wider environment prompts planning, in conjunction with other agencies and community groups, to tackle the particular stressors facing a family.

ACTIVITY 4.2   THE 'MISSING SIDE OF THE TRIANGLE'

Jack and Gill (2003) ask social workers to consider the following assets among others in a child's wider environment when assessing children in need:

- the employment and income of the parents
- availability of transport
- the extent of reciprocal helping relationships in the community and neighbourhood
- the degree to which parents feel supported in bringing up children
- expensive credit facilities
- the availability and cost of child care
- whether parents feel safe in their neighbourhood.

In assessments of need and in your tacit judgments about a family, which of these factors do you take into account and which do you ignore?

Common assessment framework – does it undermine or promote efforts to tackle exclusion of children?

The common assessment framework (CAF) is designed to provide a 'front-end' process for practitioners across all services that are involved with a particular child about which there are concerns whether behavioural or developmental. It is intended for use when there is an early sign of difficulty and to identify further supports where these are needed. The intention is that it should move away from simply establishing eligibility for a particular service and point toward those services that will help the child attain the outcomes identified in *Every Child Matters*. The CAF – and the linked comprehensive electronic database, eCAF – requires logging information on aspects of the child's life, such as the quality of the child's early attachment to parents, whether children are clean and appropriately dressed, whether there are difficulties in the parents' relationships and the type and style of parental discipline.

There are those who are concerned that the CAF constructs a database that breaches long established ethics regarding consent and privacy and will hurt those who are in poverty and in poor health (Anderson *et al.* 2009). Other critics argue that talk of a 'common' framework can marginalise dissenting perspectives, particularly those that focus on power, poverty and inequalities in wealth and in so doing promote a centralising and disciplinary consensus within a broader but hidden policy context oriented towards getting both parents (and their child) into the labour market. Axford et al. (2006: 174) argue that the 'objective of smooth, speedy and inter-disciplinary decision-making may seem to parents and children to be a "ganging up" of agencies against them, with matters substantially agreed between professionals before a joint meeting'.

A conflicting perspective emphasises that the CAF encourages a dilution of previous service mandates on child protection, leaving children more at risk rather than less. Munro and Calder for example assert that 'The very words of child protection, child abuse and risk have virtually disappeared from the language, within this agenda victims of abuse are in danger of being lost... they are being merged with all other groups of children in need' (Munro and Calder 2005: 439).

ACTIVITY 4.3   ARE CHILDREN MORE AT RISK?

Reflect on the common assessment framework, on what Jack and Gill are saying about more emphasis on social conditions in assessing need, and on the views from Axford *et al.* and Munro and Calder above. Which viewpoint do you think corresponds most closely with your experience either on placement or in your work?

ACTIVITY 4.4: A CHILD IS ILL

Doreen lives with her three children in a high-rise block of flats which she rents from the local authority. Her partner moved out some months ago. She has no car and works for 12 hours a week at a local shop. She relies on her mother and friends to provide child care for that time and often depends on last minute calls on her mobile to make care arrangements. Her three children are eleven months, three years and six years.

Alex (for Alexandra) lives in a three-bedroom house which she owns with her three children who are also eleven months, three years and six years. Her partner also moved out some months back. Alex drives to work each day to her office and has full-day child care for the younger two starting at 8 a.m. and finishing at 5.15 p.m.

Both families wake up one morning to find that their toddler is running a high temperature and they need to see a doctor. What different experiences will they have in getting to see a doctor? Think about these differences in relation to the following decisions that each family has to make: making an appointment with the doctor; arranging child care; getting to the surgery; talking to the doctor; caring for the sick child, and administering any prescribed medicine.

MAXIMISING INCOME OF FAMILIES

Paying attention to sources of income whether from benefits or work is an essential part of any practice aiming to reduce social exclusion. For families this can be a complex task, particularly as a consequence of linking benefits to taking steps to improve employability. In brief the interaction between benefits, tax credits and being prepared to work is more complex than ever. While practitioners are not expected to have specialist knowledge they should be familiar with the major benefits linked to caring for children and the work requirements linked to these.

Tax credits for families

Child tax credit

Child tax credit (CTC), introduced in 2003, is paid to a child's main carer to help meet the cost of raising children. (From 2004 it was no longer possible to include children in new claims for income support or income-based jobseeker's allowance; the old family premium and premium for a disabled child available through IS were no longer available from that point.) It is an example of what government has called 'progressive universalism', that is it is widely available for families on a range of incomes but as a family's income increases the tax credit diminishes on a sliding scale. Nevertheless it continues to support families well above the poverty line of 60 per cent of average national earnings.

Working tax credit

The introduction of tax credits has introduced a new set of complexities into the tax and benefits system that parents of young children have to negotiate when they are returning to work or wanting to come off benefits in order to work. Claimants' own experiences have reflected some of the confusion arising from such complexities. Anyone working 16 hours a week or more with sufficiently low income can claim working tax credit (WTC). There is also a child care element within the WTC to help meet the cost of child care for working parents, whether provided by a registered child minder, day care or after-school club. It is intended to cover 80 per cent of such costs up to a maximum level. To be eligible for working tax credit a claimant needs to be working at least 16 hours a week (while an adult over 25 with neither a disability nor children needs to work a minimum of 30 hours a week).

Lone parents and predicaments for parents in low wage work

Working parents with young children rely on complicated arrangements that can vary depending on how many hours the parent works, the number of children in the family and the types of education and care services that are used. Working mothers often rely on a mixture of formal and informal services with a further layer of back-up and support to develop what for their children will appear as predictable and relatively seamless. Co-ordinating such arrangements is a skilled and time consuming activity, which parents – often mothers – have to take on. Full-time working mothers frequently had the least complex arrangements while part-time working mothers had the most complex (Skinner 2003). For example, moving a child between statutory part-time pre-school education and child care in a private nursery can prove particularly complicated because they are institutionally separate with different opening times and, for those without cars, no linked transport.

The work–benefit trade-off

From the late 1990s the introduction of tax credits and increase in income support for parents out of work led to some improvement in raising the incomes of lone-parents through the tax and benefit system. But among EU countries Britain still has the highest proportion of children living in lone-parent families with the exception of Sweden. It also has the highest proportion of children in lone parent families who are not in work (Bradshaw and Richardson 2009). Poverty rates of children living with lone parents remain stubbornly higher than for children in two-parent families with half of all lone parents on low income, some two and a half times the rate for two-parent families with children.

Lone parents face particular predicaments around whether to work and if they do so, for how many hours. In general they struggle to obtain child support from a non-resident parent, and wonder just how much to rely on family friends and neighbours to provide care and support. The new deal for lone parents, attempted to address

WHAT PARENTS REALLY WANT

Dex summarises from her research into what parents would ideally like from their work:

Mothers want fathers to work shorter hours; parents of both sexes – and their children – dislike weekend working, especially Sundays. Couples putting their own needs second to those of their children by working long or atypical hours may help to explain links between mothers' full-time work and divorce rates. The Government's target of tackling family poverty through work can also send a signal that only paid work is important – reinforcing the low value placed on unpaid work and care. The overlapping implication – that paid child care is better than parental care – runs contrary to the instincts of many parents.

Fathers in families from lower socio-economic groups are doing more child care than those from families with higher socio-economic status (La Valle *et al.* 2002). The paradox here is that these fathers often express more traditional views about families and the gendered division of labour. But in practice, they are more prepared to break the traditional division of labour by looking after their own children while the mother works. Some of the higher earning fathers expressed more egalitarian views but worked such long hours that this precluded them living up to their expressed values in terms of the time they could spend with their families.

(Dex 2003: 4)

these dilemmas and evaluations of the programme have established that the approach has been moderately successful. It was in origin a voluntary programme for those lone parents on income support and whose youngest child is over five years and three months old and offers the services of a personal adviser, help with job applications and CVs and rehearsals for interviews. Following the gradual transfer of lone parents to jobseeker's allowance, the new deal for lone parents has been recast and in effect extended to all lone parents. The government aims for 70 per cent of lone parents to be employed by 2010 compared to the 56 per cent in work in 2005. To achieve this it has gradually tightened the conditions that link the benefits for lone parents with work: from expecting them to go to work when their youngest child is 12 years of age, then 7, and possibly will go lower.

All parents with young children face variations of the same trade-offs, both practical and moral, between looking after their children and working, in regard to work but for lone parents these dilemmas are more pointed. Many parents must balance a number of realities: taking a low wage job without career prospects, how to respond to work-focused interviews when required, how much to rely on their relationships with family, friends and neighbours for child care. Other tasks include finding reliable child care and judging the trade-off between quality and higher fees. One trend is to take up a 'mini-job' – under 16 hours a week when children are very young (but of course not eligible for working tax credit).

ACTIVITY 4.5: LONE PARENTS AND WELFARE-TO-WORK

Willow is a 24 year old mother with a six-year-old daughter soon to be seven. She has no relationship with the father of the child who is also 24 and is paying small amounts of child support when he can. She is currently receiving income-based jobseeker's allowance and has been called for an interview to assess her prospects for working. Willow left the care of the local authority when she was 18. As her community support worker you have offered her a range of family support services, including child care, since she left care. What benefits, incentive or tax credits will she be entitled to? What other issues do you think might arise in your discussions with her?

EVERY CHILD MATTERS: SUPPORTING EXCLUDED FAMILIES

The concept of family support service covers a broad spectrum of practitioner activity and service provision, the aim of which is to help families contend with difficulties and overcome specific obstacles they face when bringing up children. Under the Children Act 1989 local authorities have a positive duty to provide a wide range of support services for families with children in need (DoH 1991). That act recognised that parenting is a difficult and at times onerous job. It sought to ensure that practitioners viewed parents' requests for help not as an expression of inadequacy deserving a paternalistic, grudging provision of service but a natural element of parenting. The support services mentioned in the Children Act include day nurseries and child minding, holiday activities and help with travel, as well as cash payments under Section 17 to cover financial emergencies and short-term local authority backed accommodation for children (*ibid.* 1991).

But we have moved a long way from the understandings that permeated the Children Act 1989. We are more aware now that an infant's cognitive development relies on parental wellbeing and parental capacity to provide stimulation and affection from inception onward. An array of research indicates that children's need for stimulation is wider and more complicated than was recognised in the 1980s when the Children Act 1989 was passed and that services have to be reconfigured to promote family wellbeing to ensure a healthy ecology for the child.

The significance of the green paper *Every Child Matters* and the associated Change for Children programme, originally launched by government in 2003, lies in the efforts to improve the wellbeing of children regardless of what service system they or their family are in contact with – whether housing, health, pre-school care and education or school itself. The five outcomes of *Every Child Matters* requires practitioners to think in terms of what all children need to secure a reasonable level of wellbeing, the conditions and resources that all parents want for their children. And it asks that social workers deliver for children in need those same outcomes that all children should enjoy universally. If children have good health, are safe from abuse and exploitation and show better behavioural and cognitive development than they would have otherwise had then children's services will have done what they are supposed to do.

The notion of specific outcomes for children means that the work of all public agencies and their partners coalesces around universal concepts of wellbeing and achievement, things that virtually all parents want for their children. The five outcomes for children are:

- being healthy: enjoying good physical and mental health and living a healthy lifestyle
- staying safe: being protected from harm and neglect
- enjoying and achieving: getting the most out of life and developing the skills for adulthood
- making a positive contribution: being involved with the community and society and not engaging in anti-social or offending behaviour
- achieving economic wellbeing: not being prevented by economic disadvantage from achieving their full potential (DfES 2003).

These outcomes have profound relevance for socially excluded children. To secure them requires a greater emphasis on community-level intervention. Services are asked to collaborate, particularly health and education, but so too are adult services. A key worker for specific children should be provided across adult and children's services. There are home visiting dimensions to this new orientation as well as intensive phone-based support services and specialist parenting advisers for families who are struggling with their child's behaviour. Additional outreach services are delivered from Sure Start children's centres while local authorities are issuing parents charters – calling attention to the services that are available from their local authority and giving parents an idea as to what support is available as their child develops.

'Hard to reach' families

Social work has for many decades worked with what it referred to as 'problem families', families that face a number of difficulties at the same time and seem able to recycle them through many guises. Within the context of social exclusion they are often recast as 'hard to reach' or 'families at risk' by government (Social Exclusion Task Force 2006), so designated because they appear to be immune to the range of initiatives since 1997 that have promoted inclusion. Government has recently estimated that around 2 per cent of families are continuing to experience multiple problems, despite the backdrop of rising prosperity, placing their children at risk of adverse outcomes. This formulation seeks to account for what government poses as a residual number of families who have failed, despite the progress in tackling poverty and improving children's outcomes generally since 1997 and whose problems are clearly more than just low income. The basket of disadvantages which government has identified as characteristic of such families are:

- no parent in the family in work
- family lives in poor or overcrowded housing
- no parent with a qualification

- mother with mental health problems
- at least one parent with a long-standing limiting illness or disability
- low income, ie. 60% below the national median income and cannot afford a number of food and clothing items (Social Exclusion Task Force 2008).

Some 2 per cent or 140,000 families are, government calculates, said to experience five or more of the above. This is the threshold, so government argues, at which children's outcomes are damaged and their behaviour suffers. Children at age 13 to 14, for instance, who live in families with five or more problems are, according to *Families at Risk*, 36 times more likely to be excluded from school. This notion of a quantifiable number of families resistant to services suggests a type of family that is somehow separate from the wider social processes with some of the characteristics of an 'underclass' referred to in Chapter 1.

To tackle multi-problem families government has launched 'Think Family' a multi-prong approach that extends the logic of integration of the Every Child Matters agenda beyond children's services to all services, including adult services, so that multi-agency working, information sharing and assessment are all focusing on these families with a 'shared script' (Social Exclusion Task Force 2008).

REACHING PARENTS

A study by the National Family and Parenting Institute found that reaching parents, especially those that have been excluded from services, depends on effective home visiting strategies. Universal visits to parents right across the local community, linked to supporting children's play at different stages of development, were seen as less stigmatising than a focus on parenting skills *per se* and help centres to identify families who needed more support. This approach was said to work for parents with multiple disadvantages that had tended to exclude them from services. The study concluded that 'access to "hard-to-reach families" often depended upon presenting services as an entitlement and as aligned to familiar health services'. Attention to particular details also made services more inviting. These included:

- regular, informal contact, for example through drop-ins and baby cafes, helped build trust
- dedicated staff and special programmes to attract minority families, fathers, teenagers and other groups of potentially excluded parents
- newsletters, flyers, local press and space in local publications all had their place in promoting services
- *but word of mouth was the most effective means* by which to win general acceptance of a particular programme (Apps *et al.* 2007: 6; my italics)

HomeStart and NewPin

These are both well-known programmes in England and Wales that use parents to support one another. HomeStart aims to help mothers of children under five restore control over their lives so that they can establish a positive environment for rearing their child. NewPin is similar in that it aims to relieve emotional stress, increase self-esteem, reduce depression and help create better parent–child relationships. Both schemes train women to provide emotional and practical support to new mothers who need it – whether in budgeting, cooking or coping with a crisis. Although referrals mainly come from health visitors, social workers may also refer. The lessons from NewPin and HomeStart are important: the programmes work with mothers on low incomes, living in poor housing, many of whom have suffered from domestic violence; some two-fifths have been lone parents and are socially isolated. The prevalence of depression among the mothers assisted was high. An evaluation of HomeStart has suggested that while mothers valued the service there seemed to be little significant difference between mothers receiving the service and a comparison group which did not. This however may have been because the service was not sufficiently intensive based as it was on one visit per family per week (McAuley *et al.* 2004).

Parent-support groups

Parenting is a difficult task at the best of times; under exclusionary pressures, whether these are high neighbourhood crime rates, local racist activity, low income, over-crowding or poor housing, that task becomes highly stressful. Whatever their circumstances parents often want to learn more about parenting and to share their experiences. Perhaps they want to break the patterns set by their own parents when they were young or to gain the support of other parents locally or to learn techniques that would improve their own parenting skills. One way you can help parents to achieve more confidence and mastery is through a parents' support group.

Parent-support groups vary widely in what they cover. The focus may be on helping parents change the behaviour of their children or on the self-esteem and social networks of the parents themselves. What a group covers is related to who comes and why, and this may well depend on what organisation you work for, for example, parents may have to attend as part of a plan for having their children back from the care of the local authority.

Grimshaw and Maguire (1999) interviewed a number of parents involved in parent groups (including those who decided not to attend). They found that:

- over half wanted to have access to a programme before the child reached the age of three
- a quarter were interested in children's behaviour, another quarter wanted information about child development and under 10 per cent were interested in educational issues
- most mentioned child care as a basic requirement before they could attend
- there was strong preference for a 'leader' to be a parent or a professional and a parent.

ACTIVITY 4.6: RUNNING A PARENTS' GROUP

Prepare yourself for running a group by asking these questions:

- Values: why am I doing this? why do I think this is a good idea?
- Goals: what is my vision? what do I want to see happen in the long term and short term?
- Parents: what do I know about parents and their issues? what do I need to find out?
- Allies: who can I talk it over with? Who has needed resources (able to free the time, provide seed money)? Who will be encouraging but realistic?
- What do I need to equip myself to do it – training, materials, money?

In planning what your group will do and techniques in running such groups you can receive powerful assistance from publications such as *We Can Work it Out: Parenting with Confidence* from Save the Children or *TIPS: Tried and Tested Ideas for Parent Education and Support* by Herbert and Napper. The important thing to remember is that you do not have to be a master of small-group work to start a group. Nor do you have to be an expert on parenting yourself. The qualities parents look for in a group leader are nearly all to do with being a good counsellor – the ability to communicate and listen, and to have patience, openness and compassion. You are first and foremost the facilitator of something extremely important to parents that will help them to regain a sense of control over their lives. As long as you have done the right ground-work with high levels of involvement the 'content' and the running of the group will emerge from that.

Whatever the approach parent support programmes have certain things in common. First the process of putting the programme together is more important than the content; the way relationships are developed, the positive and encouraging attitudes of practitioners and the way in which programmes have all been found to have an impact on the way parents view the effectiveness of any programme. Effective programmes are found to engage parents and children together, particularly when the children are young and to maintain continuous outreach work to keep parents engaged in the programme. Second in any locality there should be a range of universal, open-access services available for all parents in addition to the target services aimed at parents who need intensive support. Third, parents learn well from sharing experiences with other parents and programmes should build in time for peer support.

Early years

The Childcare Act 2006 makes accessible high-quality child care and services for children under five for all families. The act puts early childhood services into the mainstream of local authority activity the statutory duties of which include:

- improving the outcomes of all children under five and closing the gap between children in areas of the poorest outcomes and the rest through early childhood services that are integrated, proactive and readily available
- developing the child care market in their area to ensure that it meets the needs of working parents, especially those on low incomes and with disabled children
- introducing the Early Years Foundation Stage curriculum which integrates education and care for children from birth to five
- raise the quality of the pre-school care and education by reducing the regulatory framework.

Those children's centres arising from the former Sure Start local programme have gained wide legitimacy as a resource within the areas they serve. They offer a range of family supports: every three and four year old entitled to 15 hours free early education per week for 38 weeks a year – up from 12.5 hours in 2007. This extends up to 15 hours free education per week to 20,000 two year olds in the most disadvantaged communities. To help with the transition to primary education a school's Key Stage 1 teachers and early years practitioners jointly look at the progress on outcomes identified at a child's Foundation Stage Profile and plan for the next phase of each child's learning.

Family learning

Low achievement in education increases the probability of poverty and disadvantage later in adult life. But performing well in school is no longer regarded as the outcome only of the child–teacher relationship. Parental involvement in their child's education has been demonstrated to vastly enhance the attainments of that child.

One way of encouraging this is through family learning schemes. These involve family members in supporting the development of their child's reading, writing and talking. But they achieve more than that. They increase parental confidence and break a cycle of overly disciplinary styles of parenting through increased parental control and improved self-esteem. They also have been shown to break the cycle of disadvantage by removing some of the risk factors that may pre-dispose young males towards crime as they grow older (Crime Concern 1999a).

There is a positive correlation between levels of parental education and a child's proficiency in school. There is voluminous evidence to suggest that the involvement of parents in their child's education fosters that child's achievement. Yet children from poor and excluded backgrounds are less likely to have the advantages of living with highly educated adults and tend to perform less well on measures of reading comprehension (Handel 1999: 15). Literacy influence in families begins at the most basic level with children learning speech as their caretakers talk and interact spontaneously with them; later they watch their parents' and siblings' literacy behaviours and may use them as a model for their own (*ibid.*: 16).

Establishing family learning schemes emphatically requires a partnership approach. Youth offending teams, social service agencies and local voluntary and community groups will all have an interest in the benefits of such a scheme. Those schemes that take place within primary schools (as opposed to nurseries, playgroups or local colleges) have been judged most effective principally because of the involvement of the head who drives the project forward. While teaching staff may play a prominent part in selecting children, if the scheme is collaborative selection should be a joint process (Crime Concern 1999a).

Families that are most likely to benefit from a family learning scheme are those with:

* Children between 7 and 9 who show signs of school failure, particularly in literacy.
* Children who demonstrate emotional and behavioural problems.
* Parents who have low educational attainment themselves and may need help with literacy.
* Parents who are reluctant to become involved in school activity but do seem to value education.
* Parents who may benefit from advice on positive parenting (Crime Concern 1999a).

In most family learning projects, parents will play an active part by reading or learning to read themselves alongside their children, carrying out library visits and writing shopping lists and notes. Families can build up a fund of expectations and attitudes towards literacy in which family routines and resources of information are put into place. Of course practitioners will have to be extremely sensitive as to what is at stake for the parents themselves. It is easy for an initiative to slip into paternalist habits. Parents may associate school with failure and feel inadequate; you do not want them to repeat the experience. The use of volunteers, whether retired or from a different social or ethnic background, may lead to transactions that are perceived as condescending, while attempts to develop charts and targets could be misunderstood and resented as not adult-oriented.

CHILDREN WITH DISABILITY

With the arrival of a disabled child the family is suddenly exposed to the exclusion experienced by many disabled people: parents of disabled children report that the family is frequently marginalised and isolated by friends, relatives and customary social networks. They become used to being stared at in public and the topic of other people's conversations (Dobson *et al.* 2001). Their family no longer evokes positive feelings and warmth but becomes the object of pity. As Dobson and her colleagues write, 'By being treated as a "matter of regret" they [are] stripped of their family status and denied the same emotional and social worth as "normal" families' (Dobson *et al.* 2001).

Economic hardship for the family also often ensues since the costs of raising a child with a disability are more than twice those for a non-disabled child, with heavier expenditure on medical items and toiletries, such as nappies, creams and clothes, as well as items to amuse, occupy and stimulate. Parents' earning power is also more constrained as a result of diminished employment opportunities from having to provide greater amounts of direct care even for older children, while benefit levels do not meet the extra costs or loss of earning power. Of the families with disabled children that Dobson et al. surveyed parents were able to spend only half of what they felt was required to ensure a reasonable standard of living for their child; this particularly applied to children up to the age of five.

For social work the dominance of an individual rather than social model has prevented practitioners from recognising as clearly as they should these exclusionary barriers. The Children Act 1989 requires local authorities to provide services in their area designed to minimise the effect of disability on disabled children and to give disabled children the opportunity to lead as 'normal' lives as is possible (see Schedule 2, section 6). But services have not necessarily succeeded in this objective. Part of the difficulty has been professional detachment from the concerns and objectives that families with young disabled children have. Too often services for disabled children have been located with a risk and protection perspective thus marginalising services to promote inclusion (Oliver and Sapey 2006: 85).

The framework for assessment should help practitioners to focus more intently on the exclusionary social factors that thwart full development. As a consequence, since April 2001, social workers are required to adopt a child-focused model of assessment that will do away with the split between safeguarding the child and promoting her or his development (Wonnacott and Kennedy 2001).

Jack (2000) shows how an ecological approach addresses many of the multiple barriers experienced by families with disabled children because it encourages the practitioner to look at areas such as material disadvantage and local discriminatory attitudes within services. According to Jack, families with disabled children require:

- information on services and how to access them, particularly practical services such as child care, short breaks and help in the home
- changing local social awareness around discrimination in transport, recreation and leisure facilities
- focus on the strengths or weaknesses of social networks
- income maximisation.

To obtain these social workers should use their organisational roles to develop procedures, allocate resources and shape public attitudes that challenge the exclusion and discrimination disabled children face by explicitly adopting community-building strategies (Jack 2000).

Providing information is the essential starting point. Parents of disabled children advance strikingly similar criteria for good-quality information irrespective of the child's disability:

- The way in which information is presented and delivered and how it is organised is crucial.
- Information on the roles of all the different agencies involved in providing services for families with disabled children is needed.
- Books, leaflets and videos are not enough by themselves; all such formats need to be supplemented with personal contact and guidance from those giving the information.

(Mitchell and Sloper 2000)

Thus parents tell us there are three dimensions to useful information: (i) brief leaflets outlining services and benefits; (ii) longer booklets for more detailed understanding; (iii) a person with whom to interact. The role of a professional variously called 'key worker', 'link person' or 'facilitator' to guide parents through the maze of service provision is important here (Mitchell and Sloper 2000; Braye 2001). Braye suggests that there is potential for such a key worker to undertake holistic assessment of need and to co-ordinate any specialist health or medical involvement within the framework of the social model. To make the role work well for the family, family members have to be engaged from the start with the role negotiated and spelled out clearly. Set up in this manner the key worker can become effective in promoting inclusion (Braye 2001). Addressing the exclusion of disabled children requires the acknowledgement that institutional discrimination of disability is inherent in the systems that surround the child in ways similar to institutional racism. The need to develop materials, procedures and practices to enable non-verbal disabled children and those with complex health needs to participate in assessment and care-planning is pressing. Equally pressing is the need to adapt services to meet the perspectives of distinct ethnic communities. Some initiatives now underway – a Bangladeshi social worker in one London borough working with families, using local voluntary organisations to provide befrienders and advocates or an Asian Disability Training Team to influence the design and delivery of services in Bradford – offer useful examples of what might be done.

Short breaks

Short breaks for parents with disabled children are a crucial service for supporting those families within the community and expanding family networks (Social Services Inspectorate 1998). The Quality Protects programme also specifically mentions expanding short-break provision for families with disabled children as does Children First in Wales. According to the Social Services Inspectorate some 10,000 children use short-break services to have time away from home in new environments and the chance to develop new relationships and try new activities.

Short-break carers until recently have provided overnight services but are now expanding to include day care, sitting and befriending, and in home support for families (Prewett 1999). In her survey, Prewett found that most carers within short-break schemes had experience with disabled children, either through personally knowing a child who needed a short break or through working with disabled people professionally or as volunteers. Carers themselves reported finding a range of rewards and satisfactions for themselves in the work, with developed commitment to the individual children they cared for (ibid.).

While the gains of short breaks for disabled children are clearly established and address some exclusionary barriers, the biggest problem for social workers is having enough carers in local schemes to meet need. Prewett has summarised effective practice in boosting recruitment of carers for local schemes (1999):

- Use professional quality advertising with positive disability images.
- Highlight the enjoyment, satisfaction and rewards for short-break carers.
- Highlight the skills and experiences gained which are useful in other careers.
- Involve current short-break carers and users in raising awareness.
- Emphasise the quality training in preparation and the ongoing training and support that follows.
- Adopt a community-wide strategy:
  - give talks to community groups
  - ensure that specific groups – young people, black carers, lone parents, for example – are welcome
  - employ scheme managers and workers from minority ethnic backgrounds.

CASE STUDY 5: SHORT BREAKS

A seven-year-old boy, with autism, moderate learning difficulties and behaviour problems is one of five children. His parents are wary of the way social services arranges 'respite care' and choose not to use it. Their chief objection lies in the fact that they have no voice in the selection of any proposed carer. The organiser of a local parent support group, however, found a couple specifically interested in befriending a child with special needs. The social worker, in touch with that support group, encouraged the boy's parents and the boy to meet this couple at the local Saturday club that he attended with other children with special needs. They all met at the club and the beginnings of a relationship was formed which had the parents' confidence. The boy subsequently began short visits to the couple's home and these eventually extended into overnight stays (Jack 2000).

The way breaks are arranged is also important. The service-based model for respite care is usually triggered when a family makes a request for short-term care and a project worker identifies a suitable carer. But in what has come to be called a 'resource model' the social worker works with parents to identify and extend existing child care networks – whether babysitters, playgroups, childminders and family centres – and finds sources for short-term breaks within them and with the family's active collaboration (Jack 2000).

KEY POINTS

❑   There is a similarity between children in need and socially excluded children which prepares social workers for working with excluded families.

❑   A full assessment of excluded children and their families requires all dimensions of the assessment framework to be taken into account.

❑   The interplay between the benefits system and working, particularly for lone parents, raises many issues for both practitioners and parents. Maximising family income is a major objective for lifting children out of poverty.

❑   Many initiatives to support families have flowed from the policy agenda set by *Every Child Matters* and can be adapted to promoting inclusion – for example children centres, family learning projects and the provision of care and education for under fives. While there are different points of view about the direction of the Every Child Matters agenda it has revolutionised provision in Britain when compared with the middle 1990s when day care was extremely patchy at best.

KEY READING

Jacqueline Barnes, *Down Our Way: The Relevance of Neighbourhoods for Parenting and Child Development* (John Wiley and Sons, 2007). Barnes provides an expert and realistic look at the interplay between neighbourhood environments and children's development.

Gordon Jack and Owen Gill, *The Missing Side of the Triangle: Assessing the Importance of Family and Environmental Factors in the Lives of Children* (Barnardos, 2003).

Social Exclusion Task Force, *Think Family: Improving the Life Chances of Families at Risk* (Cabinet Office, 2008).

CHAPTER 5

REVERSING THE EXCLUSION OF YOUNG PEOPLE

OBJECTIVES

By the end of the chapter you should understand:

■ How exclusion undermines a young person's transition to adulthood.

■ The tasks and responsibilities that social workers have for young people leaving care or accommodation.

■ Approaches to working with excluded young people such as truants, teenage mothers, young offenders and young homeless.

■ The value of school-based programmes.

■ How to strengthen young people's networks through mentoring schemes.

Social exclusion as a process is grounded in poverty and disadvantage but works across several dimensions of social life, with lack of access to education and work, weakened social networks and loss both of self-esteem and influence over events. As a process social exclusion has a disproportionate impact on young people. This chapter explains why this is so and lays out a number of approaches that social workers may adopt, either on their own or in partnership with other agencies and local organisations.

Tackling the social exclusion of young people embraces work in four main areas:

1   Keeping young people in school since it is clear that the sense of disaffection from school is a major component on the pathway to exclusion.
2   Supporting parents facing behavioural difficulties and family conflict.
3   Addressing youth crime and anti-social behaviour.
4   Working with care leavers.

Each of these are complex areas of work; they require multi-prong efforts that interlink as they respond to the ecological domains that embrace family, child and neighbourhood.

EXCLUSIONARY PRESSURES ON YOUNG PEOPLE

In Chapter 1 we emphasised how certain key economic changes have made life choices more competitive, uncertain and skill-dependent than 20 or 30 years ago. The impact of these changes has only widened the inequality between different groups of young people in two ways. First, the labour market now places a premium on social skills, educational attainment and the ability to handle knowledge and information. Gone are the unskilled and semi-skilled manufacturing industries which paid young men reasonable wages, enough to establish a family on – shipbuilding, machine tools, mining, car and steel manufacturing and the like. Second, a results oriented education system that relies on testing has introduced a curriculum that, whether intended or not, diminishes the importance of trade skills. While government raised the school leaving age to 17 in 2008 this will not in itself alter the structural forces that drive a certain proportion of young people out of education and the labour market. For the roughly 11 per cent of young people who are alienated from school this more intensive, performance-related environment has made satisfactory attainment even more difficult to achieve.

The result has been a growing inequality within broad cohorts of young people with a substantial proportion finding it extremely difficult to get a start in the labour market. In 2006, some 250,000 16–18 year olds fell into a group labelled by government as NEET - 'not in employment, education or training', 11 per cent of that entire age group. This was the same number as ten years previously – and significantly more than 2001 – despite the number of initiatives flowing from government (Palmer *et al.* 2008).

For a substantial minority of those aged between 16 and 18, then, the high-skill economy leaves them poorly equipped to become independent. Their passage to adulthood is encumbered with personal or family problems, poverty and other kinds of social exclusion so that clear steps to independence are missing and their goals and transition points are confused. When leaving home is triggered by problems such as pregnancy, unemployment or family conflict they have to negotiate a number of risks with very few resources.

RECENT GOVERNMENT INITIATIVES FOR YOUNG PEOPLE

- Introduction of modern apprenticeships, which attempt to restore a system of on-the-job learning of specific skills.
- School-based programmes to strengthen emotional resilience.
- Introduction of outcomes for all young people in *Youth Matters*.
- Mentoring programmes to provide role models for young people.
- Citizenship programmes to promote civic understanding and encourage participation in local affairs.
- Personal education allowances for looked after children.
- The Education and Inspections Act 2006 which underpins the expansion of 'positive activities' for young people including both recreational and sports activities, leisure and cultural activities and educational activities such as clubs, coaching sessions, and volunteering.

ACTIVITY 5.1: PROGRAMMES IN THE AREA?

Government legislation, white papers and practice guidelines lay out general lines of approach to working with young people. But often they embrace aspirations that are hard to put into practice. For each of the programmes referred to in the box above find out whether they exist in your area and if not why not. If they do examine how they are being implemented.

Engaging young people

Before we look at specific kinds of work to tackle the exclusion of young people it is helpful to think about the barriers they think they face. Getting representative views and opinions from young people themselves is an urgent first step. There are to hand a range of options for channelling this opinion – whether through young people's parish councils, detached youth work, surveys in school or community or providing informal groups of young people with disposable cameras to take photos reflecting the way they see their neighbourhood.

As this opinion is assembled you may well hear distrust expressed regarding some of the very sources of support that professionals presume to be effective, but at least you have their direct opinions on their community, the adult world and issues of identity. You will also discover that young people regularly return to the same issues: drugs, the unfairness of particular teachers, experiences in school, uncertainties about training and employment, personal experiences of bullying and harassment, lack of money and debt, contraception and pregnancy and problems with the law.

From these conversations you get a different notion of 'community' – sometimes something that is limiting and intrusive, but sometimes also referring to anyone who helps out or listens (as among homeless young people). What comes through is the wish to be self-reliant, to get out from under rules, and feelings of alienation from the adult world. What young people want for themselves in the end differs little from what people in general want, but their perceptions about how to obtain these wants and what supports there are along the way differs significantly from what an older genera-tion of practitioners might have experienced themselves. Young people want:

- respect and understanding
- to be consulted and taken seriously
- accessible and affordable places to meet
- to share the aspirations of the rest of us: to have a job, a home and significant relationships
- to share concerns over environment and matters like personal safety, transport and leisure.

(Save the Children 1998)

Gender differences

Boys are more likely than girls to perform delinquent acts, engage in bullying, play truant, become permanently excluded from school or commit suicide. They are also more likely to engage in anti-social behaviour and abuse drugs. There is also evidence that boys are less likely to seek help or to talk about their problems with others. Girls are more prone to eating disorders, engage in more acts of deliberate self-harm and have a greater likelihood of becoming young carers. They may also have greater prob-lems with self-confidence (Madge *et al.* 2000). It is easy to develop stereotypes around such gender differences and to miss the fact that each set of behaviours can create a basis on which the young person is excluded from work and community, whether through poor educational attainment, anti-social behaviour or early pregnancy. But the differences in behaviour and in the ways that help is sought are sufficient to raise the question of whether different approaches to working with boys and girls are required (*ibid.*).

There has been much recent focus on the link between boys' behaviour and later involvement in crime. The pattern links lack of parental control and low educational achievement at a relatively young age with a later tendency toward 'anti-social behav-iour' and truancy around the ages of 12–14 with outright offending later in adoles-cence. In this field there are a number of competing points of view: from the proponents of moral discourse comes the argument that boys raised by lone mothers are lacking a male 'father' figure and are able to evade parental control. Feminists argue that the upsurge in anti-social behaviour is not the mother's fault but point to received messages on masculinity embedded in peer-group opinions, media imagery and corpo-rate marketing techniques (Harris 1995). Somewhere in between is an emerging third view – that young unskilled males are increasingly ill-equipped to cope in school (and the world of work). This view points to the fact vulnerable young men, from low-income families and with the prospect of few qualifications on leaving school, have particular difficulties. Opportunities for these relatively unskilled workers tended to be temporary and short-term based on sub-contracting or agency employment. They have few chances for training in these casual and insecure sectors and become trapped in precarious patterns that make it difficult for them to secure stable employment (Furlong and Cartmel 2004).

Communication and relationship building

Building relationships with many marginalised young people is not straightforward because of negative past experiences and perhaps constricted opportunities for personal and social development. Sometimes unresponsive in conversation, erratic in time planning, acting on impulse – these are in fact common habits among adolescents (Coleman and Hendry 1999). But it is important for practitioners to remember that despite the difficulties and feelings of not being able to build rapport, the young person's interaction with parents, teachers, friends, mentors and social workers is the crucial catalyst for marginalised young people overcoming those barriers and securing what they want. Often the number of adult relationships committed to the wellbeing of a young person will be very few in number – perhaps one, perhaps none.

ACTIVITY 5.2: TALKING TO A GROUP OF YOUTHS

A group of four 15-year-old boys is highly identifiable in the small town where they live. They publicly hang around together and are linked in the public mind to specific acts of vandalism in the area – breaking stained glass windows in the local church, pulling down fences, trashing the public lavatories, gathering on the local recreation ground and spreading their trash – cans of beer, cigarette packs, sweet wrappers. At the local youth centre they have a habit of intimidating younger, smaller boys; they do this by verbal intimidation, making raucous and abrasive noises, jabbing other boys with elbows, mock fight postures, and regular swearing.

    The youth centre is on one of your patches and the all-volunteer staff at the centre are asking you for advice on how to re-establish rapport. What would you suggest?

Much of a practitioner's work will be directly or indirectly involved in creating and strengthening such relationships. What they value above all is their relationship with the counsellor, social worker or youth worker who is attentive and available. This experience of safety, consistency, trust and acceptance may be their first. For some it may be a revelation: 'I'd never been taken seriously before! He didn't seem fazed! I felt like he was bothered!' (Luxmoore 2000: 74). This goes some way towards balancing previously hurtful and unsafe experiences with adults and gives the young person a broader emotional understanding for dealing with the dilemmas they face.

    One of the hardest things for a young person to learn is to distinguish between 'what's me' and 'what's not me' (*ibid.*: 75). The practitioner's skill in 'reflecting back'

– which means listening to what the young person has to say and then repeating it so that he or she can clarify what they actually feel – is an important tool. Luxmoore cautions against giving indiscriminate praise and admiration. A social worker or counsellor should be warm but remain non-judgemental so that young people can begin to discover their own sense of good and bad. He suggests, when talking to a young person who feels particularly helpless, asking 'who would understand how you're feeling?' or 'who could speak up for you in this situation?', helping them to identify who is an ally and on their side. What matters is that they consider the character 'good'.

There are ad hoc ways to elicit opinion as to how young people see their world. Drawing cartoons and other interactive art on smart boards, providing disposable cameras to photograph their neighbourhood, short questionnaires about specific issues or developments, or working on family trees are all possibilities to consider.

We now look at specific approaches to work with young people excluded by difficult transitions to adulthood: keeping them in school, providing mentoring and guidance, avoiding homelessness and preparation for leaving local authority care.

WORKING WITH SCHOOLS

Truancy and school exclusions together form one of the most visible indications of excluded or 'disaffected youth'. Compared with the late 1990s the number of permanent exclusions has declined by a fifth so progress has been made (Palmer *et al.* 2008: 95). There has also been improvement in the numbers of pupils out of school without authorised absence. Government points to a hard-core group of pupils – 6 per cent – as responsible for more than three quarters of all unauthorised absences (J. Shepherd, *Guardian*, 31 July 2008).

Numbers of 'out of school' pupils in any one neighbourhood constitute a significant source of peer pressure on others to abandon their education or engage in anti-social behaviour. The 2004 Youth Crime Survey showed that 45 per cent of young people in mainstream education who have committed an offence say they have been absent from school without their schools' approval. It also showed that 62 per cent of 10–16 year olds who have committed criminal or anti-social behaviour have also had periods of unauthorised absence. While rates of exclusion from school have fallen for black pupils they are still permanently excluded at over three times the rate of white pupils; a black Caribbean pupil is over two and half times more likely to be excluded (CRE). In justifying the concept of 'truancy sweeps' the Department for Children, Schools and Families cites the fact that 90 per cent of pupils with five or more good GCSEs have an average absence of 7.5 days per year or less but among pupils with 20 days or more absence per year 31 per cent achieve the same pass rates.

Poor behaviour and school exclusions

Pupils who underperform or fail at school are more likely to lose out in the job market and to face exclusion in adult life. Increasingly it is recognised that learning difficulties at school can begin a cycle of behavioural problems, school exclusion and crime (Barrow Cadbury 2005: 47). Reducing poor attendance, school exclusion and disruptive behaviour also reduces the risk of a young person becoming delinquent. Social workers make their contribution in relation to vulnerable children, mediating between schools and the child's family and in relation to non-academic aspects of curriculum.

ACTIVITY 5.3: SCHOOL DISAFFECTION

Bart, 15, has the habit of intimidating other boys at school. He is tall, wiry and strong for his age. He asserts himself by coming up fast to other boys in the corridors or on recreation areas gesturing with his fists. When teachers are not looking he will land a covert punch, trip a boy or belittle someone. He regularly uses bad language and can get very angry over the slightest provocation. Despite all this he has his likeable, even tender side. He dotes on his younger sister and was very upset when Madeleine McCann went missing because as he said it could have been his little sister.

Bart is on the verge of being excluded from school. As a social worker attached to the school what approaches and strategies would you adopt with him? Would you try to save his place at school? If not what would be the realistic alternatives for him? What do you think could be the long term consequences for Bart of your actions?

CASE STUDY 6: KEEPING CHILDREN IN SCHOOL IN BUCKINGHAMSHIRE

Two schools, Wycombe Grange in High Wycombe and Chess Valley Grange in Chesham, operate pupil referral units at Key Stage 4 and Key Stage 3 respectively. The units provide services that effectively support young people by working in partnership with them, their parents, the local education authority and an array of related professionals. The units provide education and support to pupils who have been excluded from school for all or part of the week, those who are out of school due to chronic illness, pregnant school-girls and young mothers. They also provide support for pupils who risk social exclusion because they find it difficult to cope in a 'school setting'. Both units are well resourced and help deliver all elements of the national curriculum, foundation subjects and an increasing raft of alternative provision. The teaching groups are small, very focused and therapeutic and they can address preventative work on request.

Schools as a partner in service provision

Schools have become important partners for social work underpinned by creating unified children's services, combining schools and social services, within local authorities. Capitalising on these assets government has shaped many initiatives for young people through schools which provide a ready channel for working with parents and 'whole family' involvement, helping parents manage difficult behaviour and boosting their knowledge of child development. As Pugh and Statham put it:

> A whole school approach which improves the emotional climate of the school and builds on relationships with families, is more likely to promote the wellbeing of all children *and to form a sound basis for more structured and sustained intervention for those children with particular needs*. (my italics; Pugh and Statham 2006: 288)

What Pugh and Statham have in mind are school-based interventions that enhance children's wellbeing by:

- increasing self-esteem, self-awareness and self-confidence
- promoting attachment and developmental catch up
- improving relationships and peer acceptance
- improving educational attainment
- bringing attention to bear on the needs of vulnerable children.

One of the ways of achieving these is through home–school link projects. They cover a fast proliferating cluster of service activity – providing home visits, parental support with children who engage in difficult behaviour, anti-bullying, mentoring, befriending and other forms of peer support. Promoting positive mental health is a thread common to many such programmes as they respond to complex links between rising mental health problems in children, problematic child behaviour and school exclusions. Nurture groups in primary schools, after-school clubs and homework clubs all feature in the extended school model (Boxall 2002).

An extended school essentially means using the school as the base for providing programmes for children and young people beyond learning in the classroom. While many activities may come under the concept, at a minimum it will offer:

- Child care provided through the school site or through school clusters or other local providers. The care provision may last from 8 a.m. to 6 p.m. all year round with supervised transfer arrangements where needed.
- A programme of activities such as homework clubs, study support, sport (two hours beyond the finish of the school day) as well as music, drama and the arts.
- Parenting support including information sessions on childhood transitions and parenting programmes run in collaboration with children's services.
- A swift and easy referral system to a wide range of specialist support such as speech therapy, sexual health, intensive behaviour support and child and adolescent mental health services.

Social worker relationships with schools have been partial and at times not easy. For social work, whose culture is wedded to the notions of the uniqueness of individuals and individual autonomy, the rule-based school system and authority of the headteacher can seem inherently antagonistic to working with troubled young people. To a certain extent the policy and practice outlined in the schools white paper of 2005 potentially aggravates this relationship further since it makes pupil selection and local autonomy for schools a priority (DfES 2005). Yet children's services need schools to play a key role in delivering the outcomes of *Every Child Matters* (ECM). In the Children for Change agenda government has given a clear indication that schools are the central institution with the capacity and the legitimacy around which to cluster the multi-pronged services to deliver ECM outcomes. This sometimes leaves the practitioner in the difficult position of drawing on facilitation and negotiation skills in order to hold schools to account on behalf of young people particularly with regard to the admission or exclusion of particular pupils.

A practitioner's attitude towards school is important because it influences how he or she develops relations with individual schools. In the past, social workers did not see schools as experts in problem children and believed that family support for children in need lay outside the education system (Vernon and Sinclair 1999).

ACTIVITY 5.4: YOUR KNOWLEDGE OF LOCAL COMPREHENSIVE SCHOOLS

With two or three colleagues pool your knowledge about the comprehensive school in your area. Run through the following checklist:

- Do you know the head and others in the school management team?
- Do you know any of the teachers individually, for example heads of department ments, form tutors or heads of year?
- What is the ethos of the school?
- What are its strengths and weaknesses?
- Are you familiar with basic school data such as GCSE results, GNVQ attainments, A-level and AS-level results?
- Do you know the attendance levels and the number of temporary and permanent exclusions?
- What is the school's disciplinary policy? What are the grounds for temporary and permanent exclusions?
- Do you know the incidence of bullying in the school and the school policy on it?
- How effective is the pastoral support programme in the school?
- What learning support is available for pupils in mainstream classes?
- How are the average attainments of children looked after by the local authority?

MENTORING

Mentor means 'a trusted counsellor or guide'. Mentoring is a consciously developed relationship that mixes an informal educative role with personal support and encouragement, together with the roles of change agent and advocate. Broadly any mentoring project will 'aim to connect two people in a one to one voluntary relationship, with one person being more experienced than the other and with the expectation that their skills and knowledge will be transferred' (Alexander 2000: 2).

Mentoring provides a young person with both a role model – that is, a successful example to follow in terms of a career path, personal conduct or in studying – and a source of instruction and guidance. The act of mentoring involves several roles – as good listener, critical friend, counsellor, network and coach. Perhaps one of its key assets for socially excluded young people is to provide a bridge to areas of life that have been habitually closed off. This may include useful prospective employment contacts, access to social networks and resources outside the neighbourhood, and guidance on how to make those contacts effective. Mentors are potentially a key element in what is called 'bridging social capital', assets stored in social relationships that are outside the young person's immediate neighbourhood, family and friends.

While all of us use the term informally ('she was my mentor' meaning someone you turned to, either colleague or peer, when you were learning the ropes at work) what is asked of mentors for young people is substantially more. There are three key features of a mentoring relationship:

1   It is a voluntary arrangement as required by the person being mentored and can be ended by either party at any time.
2   Mentors are equipped with the necessary interpersonal skills to manage and monitor the relationship.
3   Both those mentored and mentors understand the boundaries and purpose of the relationship.

Mentor schemes can assist in work with young offenders or those at risk of offending, poor school achievers, homeless young people and care leavers to name a few. In setting up a mentoring scheme you need to think about:

- Who the scheme is for: is it intended for pupils with a substantial record of unexplained absences, those aged 17 plus who are looking for work, for care leavers in the area or for those cautioned by the police? The group may be large or small, focused or general – but from the beginning thinking about who the scheme is for is closely linked to the purpose and the aims of the scheme. Be sure to collect data on how many young people are likely to be interested.
- Establish aims and objectives: the project needs to think through what its prime purpose is, what it is trying to accomplish, and what kind of achievement it wants to be known for. Its objectives are the more specific steps outlined to achieve those aims.
- Careful thinking around gender: will the scheme be for girls or young women only, for example? What will be the gender balance in the likely supply of mentors?

- Careful thinking around ethnicity: are shared cultural or religious norms between those being mentored and likely volunteer mentors important?
- Overlap: make an audit of existing voluntary and statutory services to ensure that what you want to achieve is not already being done in your area. Decide where the project will be placed within that map of current services.

Recruiting mentors calls for accurate judgement of people. Alexander (2000) lays out what interviewers should look for in prospective recruits:

- Perception of self: do they feel comfortable in front of others? Do they have the capacity to speak about their feelings and are they open about themselves and their experiences? Are they aware of their own prejudices and personal limitations? Do they have a sense of worth?
- Warmth and the perception of others: do they believe that people are responsible for their own destiny and that individuals can cope with difficulties when supported? Do they think all people are worthy of help? Are they easily threatened by others and can they challenge others when needed?
- Perception of purpose and task: do they believe that an individual's difficulties can be affected by both personal and environmental factors? Can they imagine themselves in others' shoes and perceive the mentor's role as enabling and not controlling? Do they respect difference and value freedom of choice?

YOUTH HOMELESSNESS

A recent survey estimated that some 75,000 young people experienced homelessness during the year 2006–7, (a figure that takes into account only those young people in contact with services; Quilgars et al. 2008). This figure includes 43,000 young people aged between 16–24 who were accepted as statutorily homeless in the UK and some 31,000 who were not deemed statutorily homeless but who used Supporting People services (Quilgars et al. 2008). Of those accepted for priority housing in 2006 by local authorities some 9 per cent were young people, including seven and half thousand persons aged between 16 and 18 and some 900 care leavers aged between 18 and 20 (Department for Communities and Local Government 2007).

A wide range of complex problems facing young people in their transition to adulthood contribute to creating the numbers of homeless. Family conflict, often long standing and involving relationship breakdown with parents, step-parents or a parent's partner is frequently the catalyst, often accompanied by trauma and violence. Roughly one-third of homeless young people have been looked after by a local authority, pinpointing the failure of local social services to assist appropriately the transitions for those young people in their care. Quilgars and colleagues found that young people from disadvantaged backgrounds and those who experienced childhood disruption and trauma (especially violence) were far more likely to be homeless than those who did not. They also found that homelessness can either trigger or reinforce mental health problems or drug misuse. Not surprisingly they also found a link between homelessness and withdrawing from education, training and employment as well as a record of comparatively poorer health than the youth population at large (Quilgars *et al*. 2008).

Policy and practice have acknowledged the importance of preventive work, within an overall strategy to combat youth homelessness. The National Youth Homelessness Scheme (NYHS) in England lays emphasis on the provision of mediation and supported lodging schemes. Scotland – where rates of youth homelessness are three times that of England, 15 per 1000 young people – has focused on reducing the high number of young people who run away from home while Wales and Northern Ireland focus on the social inclusion of all homeless persons (NYHS 2008; Pawson *et al*. 2007).

The Homelessness Act 2002 placed a duty on local authorities to accept homeless 16 and 17 year olds as a priority for re-housing. The development of youth homelessness strategies linking these with Supporting People Plans and Children's and Young People Plans are found more commonly now. Among the housing support options available for schemes responding to youth homelessness are: floating support practitioners, befriending and mentoring schemes to rebuild social networks have both proven effective as have schemes to guarantee rents and deposits in smoothing a young person's move into private rented accommodation.

Yet a Centrepoint survey in 2005 found that out of 100 local authorities 60 did not have, as part of their homelessness strategies, any plans for how they would house young people. In addition daunting assessment procedures, uneven mediation services, tension between mediation practitioners and public agencies and prolonged periods in temporary accommodation all contribute to the continuing difficulties that young people have in finding suitable housing (Quilgars *et al*. 2008).

The dearth of social housing has also severely hampered the development of wider strategies and a lack of clarity as to whether this accommodation should be 'temporary', that is moving young people on as soon as possible, or 'transitional' – providing an opportunity to assist young people in gaining life-skills. Moves between accommodation settings are common often driven by shortage of suitable units which only increased instability in young people's lives catching young people in what they themselves described as the 'homeless circuit' for years (Quilgars *et al*. 2008.)

DEALING WITH ANTI-SOCIAL BEHAVIOUR

The anti-social behaviour (ASB) of young people remains stubbornly prominent in the public mind, in government policy and it must be added in the media. In a sense it is both a product of social exclusion – young people alienated from school and at a remove from parental and neighbourhood norms – and a driver of exclusion, for example of older people who feel it is unsafe to venture out at night in particular areas.

The Crime and Disorder Act 1998 introduced a framework of powers for the police and the new multi-disciplinary youth offending teams to tackle street level behaviour that causes intimidation, fear or destruction of property. As defined in the Act ASB is 'behaviour that is likely to cause alarm, harassment or distress to members of the public not of the same household as the perpetrator'. Such a loose construction of what ASB is, dependent as much on the perception of behaviour as on its consequences, ensured that it would not be easily curtailed.

Anti-social behaviour is both a product of social exclusion and a force for exclusion. Behaviour such as shouting and verbal intimidation, fighting, public drunkenness, vandalism and graffiti, often intimidates local people and causes apprehension if not out right fear among residents. At the same time it is patchy occurring only in particular areas or neighbourhoods although the fear of young people in groups is often exaggerated in both the media and the public mind. This exaggeration effect can in the extreme lead to older people not venturing out or staying away from particular areas, to children not being taken to a playground where young people congregate. But there are two sides to this issue. A recent Audit Commission report, *Tired of Hanging Around* (Audit Commission 2008) interviewed young people about their congregating, often visibly and in public, and found that young people themselves viewed this as a way of creating space for themselves, out of reach of adult involvement, and as a way of structuring their own time.

When Millie and his colleagues probed more deeply into what people actually thought constituted anti-social behaviour they found there was concern with just three issues: general misbehaviour by children and young people, visible drug and alcohol misuse and 'problem families' and neighbour disputes (Millie *et al.* 2005). What the public were *really* bothered about was anti-social behaviour as a sign of social and moral decline. The public favoured more disciplinary solutions, while local agencies explained it in terms of social exclusion and deprivation and favoured prevention and inclusion strategies. As a kind of compromise in the three case study sites they investigated, each had local strategies in place to combat anti-social behaviour that were graduated and proportional and balanced preventive services with enforcement (Millie et al. 2005).

WHY ANTI-SOCIAL BEHAVIOUR?

Millie and colleagues found that when talking about the causes of local anti-social behaviour, local people advanced three different explanations or 'narratives' as to why it happens:

- social and moral decline: anti-social behaviour seen as a symptom of wider social and cultural change, and in particular a decline in moral standards and family values
- disengaged youth and families: anti-social behaviour arises from the increasing disengagement from the wider society by a significant minority of families and their children
- 'kids will be kids': anti-social behaviour is really the age-old tendency for young people to get into trouble, challenge public and parental boundaries and antagonise their elders (Millie *et al.* 2005).

Government has introduced waves of initiatives and statutes to attempt to stamp out anti-social behaviour. Anti-social behaviour orders, acceptable behaviour contracts, imprisoning parents of young people who persistently truant, dispersal orders used for congregating youths, the Anti-social Behaviour Act of 2003 requiring social landlords to have policies for monitoring tenant behaviour have all tried to damp down ASB. Clearly this was government attempting to respond to an issue on which sections of the public in certain areas felt strongly. Often there was a populist cue taken up by local authorities who have websites and help lines primed to receive notice of incidents from the public whether unwarranted noise, dogs fouling pavements, or threatening behaviour among others.

There are competing perspectives concerning anti-social behaviour. One locates it as a function of community pointing to the lack of informal social controls in a neighbourhood arising from widespread clustering of families on low income. This lack of capacity to uphold norms of behaviour produces a social vacuum which gives prominence to groups of young people – primarily but not exclusively young men – who in turn encounter no countervailing authority on the streets (Power 1997). A second perspective views anti-social behaviour arising from particular family dynamics: the lack of parental supervision, parental rejection, erratic and harsh discipline, marital conflict, parental criminality and weak attachment are all significant predictors of anti-social behaviours, including drug use and offending (Patterson 1985; Rutter *et al.* 1998).

Each is persuasive and each has provided the rationale for numerous programmes. The first utilises punitive responses such as anti-social behaviour orders, disperal orders, or imprisoning parents for allowing their children to truant. The second develops intensive family interventions such as the Family Intervention Project, Think Family, parenting programmes and programmes for multi-systemic therapy. In the middle are mentoring schemes, car repair schools, football in the community and other efforts to engage and inspire young people in order to lead them to pro-social behaviour.

Anti-social behaviour is undeniably linked to disadvantage and the way poverty constrains individuals' choices and reshapes their estimation of their future and the day-to-day calculations needed to realise that future. The authors of an Ipsos Mori survey found that it could predict how anti-social behaviour would be perceived by residents in a given area by its level of deprivation, population density, recorded level of violent crime and the proportion of residents aged 25 years and under (Ames *et al.* 2007). Protective factors such as smaller families, good maternal health, good home care and parental employment provide sources of resilience even in high-risk neighbourhoods (Haines and Case 2005). Whereas inconsistent discipline from parents, family conflict, and low parental involvement in their child's school are factors in the life of a young person who engages in anti-social behaviour.

Recent initiatives concerning anti-social behaviour

Practitioners, as so often when dealing with the excluded and marginalised, are in fact pulled in two directions. On the one hand they are involved with families who have parenting orders, curfew orders and anti-social behaviour orders served on family members. On the other they have obligations to provide services for 'children in need' (including of course young people under 18) which, under the Children Act, includes children at risk of abuse and neglect, children who are delinquent or at risk of becoming so and children with serious family problems or whose home conditions are unsatisfactory.

Perhaps this chasm between approaches will not be as wide as in the recent past. There is growing realisation across professional and policy circles that anti-social behaviour and the challenging behaviour of the younger child are inter-linked. This awareness makes responses to ASB all the more complex. Clearly damping down ASB is more difficult than simply instituting a disciplinary legal regime that in one form or another attempts to control or punishes ASB. A recent rethink, reflected in government policy, has begun to point to a different response, one that pays more attention to needs, to family dynamics and adverse neighbourhood and environmental factors. Programmes in schools such as social and emotional aspects of learning (SEAL) have combined with multi-systemic family therapy to address an entire spectrum of difficulties across the young person's ecology.

CASE STUDY 7: SHOULD WE ACTUALLY REWARD YOUNG PEOPLE?

Joseph Rowntree Housing Trust wanted to see whether rewarding young people for positive (pro-social) behaviour was a workable approach. In 2004 it set up a project to reward those young people who made a positive contribution to their city. It instituted a scheme in which points were obtained by individuals who undertook certain community activities such as dog walking, litter collecting, giving assistance at community events, removing graffiti and planting trees and bulbs. The points were then used to claim certain rewards – dinners out, trips to the cinema. In close association with the Royds Community Centre it established a similar scheme in Bradford.

The scheme in Bradford was notably more successful than in York. The level of reward was significantly higher (roughly equivalent to £5.00 per hour) in that scheme and the level of staffing also higher with two project workers working 15 hours per week each.

There are issues for reflection arising from the schemes. (1) While the details of the schemes were clear, the broader philosophy behind the idea was less clear and had not been jointly worked out with participants. Who were the target groups of young people to be and why? (2) Fifteen years of age became a kind of cut-off point – with those younger than that more willing to participate and those older having nothing to do with the scheme, viewing it as 'geeky and boring'. Boys were more difficult to recruit than girls. (3) What actually was the function of the reward? As an incentive to join the scheme it became less important as participants developed interest in the activities for themselves, whether gardening, increased environmental awareness or working with older people in the community (adapted from Hirst et al. 2007).

CASE STUDY 8: WYTHENSHAW: THE UNITED ESTATES OF WYTHENSHAWE MANCHESTER

Street crime in parts of the estate seemed impervious to the range of regeneration initiatives coming from central government and Manchester city council. Local leaders came together to try their own approach and their own solutions. They converted a disused chapel as a base for various social enterprises – a gym and other sports facilities, hairdressing, second-hand clothes shop and street dance. Some of the most disruptive young people in the area were involved in the construction of the centre, which had the effect of 'vandal proofing' it, while the leaders showed that there were alternatives to anti-social behaviour as a way of making a mark on the neighbourhood. Crucially, the social enterprises raised sufficient income so that the project was not dependent on local authority grants.

Several factors were prominent in the success of this ground up initiative:

- the leaders live in the area and run local businesses, were confident in their standing within the community and their ability to command respect among local young people
- they adopted an entrepreneurial approach to possible solutions but had empathy with the socially excluded young people of the area
- they led by example and were prepared to be hard nosed when required
- faith was important to some of the leaders and their church was willing to take the risk of giving the group a lease on one of their buildings.

The project established a mentoring process through which ties were established with leaders and residents in other disadvantaged neighbourhoods and some of the insights the project passed on to other areas – Moss Side in Manchester, the Broxtowe estate in Nottingham and the Stubbin estate in Sheffield.

Family intervention projects

Family intervention projects (FIPs) began work in 2007 as part of central government's effort to develop an instrument for intensive support for families with multiple problems, specifically young people who engage in anti-social or criminal behaviour and are either homeless because of that behaviour or at risk of becoming so. FIPs are typically run either by local authorities or voluntary organisations and work with families in their own homes for between six and twelve months. They offer intensive engagement and services seven days a week, providing support for young people in alternative accommodation or family support in their own home. That support can provide counselling, training in parenting skills, anger management, workshops to build motivation and social skills, budgeting and benefit advice, and tenancy workshops.

While each of these elements is familiar, FIPs bring them together in a single blended service. Significantly a recent evaluation noted the effectiveness with marked improvements in all key areas: reduction in anti-social behaviour and improved outcomes for children and young people. That evaluation also noted that FIPs allow a creative social work ethos to flourish, free from bureaucratic procedures that standard social work service operates within. Their relative success is linked to the quality of the staff, small caseloads, a dedicated key worker who works intensively using a whole family approach and remaining engaged as long as necessary (White *et al.* 2008).

CHILDREN IN PUBLIC CARE AND CARE LEAVERS

Ensuring success in education for looked after young people

In general parents act as their child's best advocate from birth, knowing that certain choices, decisions and milestones will affect their children's life chances. In the main parents take their children's needs vigorously into account, pushing schools to respond to those needs, advising their child as he or she gets older, watching out for any special needs or health problems. Parents are particularly involved in their child's education: selecting schools, supporting – and if necessary enforcing – their child's attendance, helping to choose subject options, assisting and reminding on homework, getting in touch with teachers if there are difficulties and advising on work experience.

When a child enters public care, that is, 'looked after' by a local authority, the situation changes dramatically. The child, whether accommodated with the agreement of her or his parents or subject to a care order, rarely has an advocate equal to his or her parents or other family relations. Local authorities have a poor record when acting as the parent for children they look after. In the year 2006–8 nearly two-fifths of looked after children received no GCSE and a further fifth obtained fewer than five, that is, some 57 per cent of looked after young people in year 11 received fewer than five GCSEs – either because they did not sit exams or failed to pass them. This compared with the national average of 10 per cent of all year 11 children (DfCSF 2008). Nevertheless this does record modest improvement over the data in 1999–2000 when some 64 per cent of looked after young people received fewer than five GCSEs.

The relatively poor performance of local authorities at corporate parenting was recognised by Sonia Jackson who over the course of the 1990s revealed just how neglectful the social work record was in this respect: poor back-up of young people while studying for GCSEs or doing homework, living conditions that were not conducive to study (particularly in residential child care), little contact with schools, no interest or recognition of educational success (Jackson 1998). Jackson saw that organisational culture on corporate parenting had to change. She observed that 'residential care provided a positively anti-intellectual environment – no study facilities, reference books or understanding of the sustained effort and concentration required for serious academic work' (Jackson 1998: 52).

In the wake of such findings local authorities now have the legal obligation to bolster the educational attainment of young people in care. As corporate parents, local authorities are under a specific duty to promote the educational achievement of looked after children; and they must set annual targets on the attainment of looked after children in English and mathematics at Key Stage 2 and the attainment of looked after children at the end of Key Stage 4 (GCSE). In addition local authorities now:

- provide education allowances for looked after children with the express aim of insuring that looked after children reached the same sort of exam results comparable to national averages by providing additional, personalised support to those who appear not to be reaching expected standards of attainment
- have the power to place looked after children in any school in their area including the top-performing schools
- make the Choice Advice service on choosing schools available to social workers and foster carers
- create the presumption that looked after children should not move schools in years 10 or 11 (unless it is *clearly* in their best interests)
- introduce a dedicated budget of £500 per child for each social worker to spend on improving the educational experience of every looked after child
- ensure that all looked after children and care leavers have access to a personal adviser until aged 25.

For the great majority of looked after young people their parents should be as closely involved in their child's education as possible, including attending parents' evening, receiving reports and teacher feedback, and information on SATs results and progress through the Key Stages. All decisions and documentation should be shared with parents first, either directly from the school or through a small network of natural parents, foster carers or a key worker in a residential home, and social worker. It is important that schools and social services clarify who is to be contacted in the event of problems or to support the child's education, for example attending parent evenings.

Care leavers

Care leavers rank high among all groups of marginalised youth. Their under-achievement at school goes hand-in-hand with much higher rates of truancy and exclusions from school. A third of all looked after children are not in education, employment or training by age 19 (DfCSF 2008). Among homeless young people, young offenders and the prison population the proportion of those in care is extremely high: roughly some 30–40 per cent of each population.

In assisting the transition to adulthood the practitioner has to attempt to organise support in a number of domains including accommodation, life skills, education, career paths, social networks and relationships, identity and offending.

Accommodation may involve initial moves to transitional forms of housing such as hostels, lodgings or staying with friends which are often followed up by moves to independent tenancies in the public, voluntary or private sectors. Stein *et al.* (1997) found that over half of the care leavers studied had moved two or more times in their first two years out of care. About one-sixth made five or more moves while one-fifth became homeless at some stage. Levels of life skills were low – budgeting, negotiating with landlords or employers, practical skills such as self-care, and domestic skills such as cooking, laundry and cleaning.

Social networks, relationships and identity are another facet of leaving care that both the young person and practitioner have to come to grips with. As Biehal *et al.* (1995) have said, the point of leaving care is a time when young people are trying to make sense of their past – to trace missing parents, to find continuity in their lives and a sense of belonging. 'They needed a "story" of their lives that made sense, reduced their confusion about both how and why events had happened as they did and to provide a more secure platform for their futures in the adult world' (Stein 1997: 39). Even if family links had not been positive, retaining them was important and lent symbolic certainty to their lives. Those that did not have even this lacked self-esteem, and were less confident and assertive. Marsh and Peel (1999) noted particularly that awareness of who was in the young person's family was severely limited and that notions of partnership and efforts at family involvement with the care leaver were not really taken seriously.

The Children (Leaving Care) Act 2000 attempted to overcome some of these well-researched difficulties by imposing a number of duties on local authorities in relation to young people who had been looked after by them. Every eligible young person when they turned 16 is to have a clear 'pathway' plan mapping out a route to their independence for which local authorities must provide the personal and practical support. Local authorities are to assess and meet the needs of looked after young people aged 16 and 17 based on the Framework for the Assessment of Children in Need. The assessment should be based on extensive involvement of the young person and should look ahead at least to his or her 21st birthday. Health needs, future education, supportive family relationships and housing all form part of such a plan. Under the act the local authority is to remain in touch with all care leavers until they are 21 regardless of where they live.

ACTIVITY 5.5: HOW WELL ARE CARE LEAVERS SUPPORTED?

Anecdotal evidence has suggested that despite the duties in the Care Leavers Act 2000 local authorities have been very patchy in the degree to which they have moved from an old-style corporate parent to the more supportive style that oversees looked after children well into their twenties. Examine the practice in your area and answer these three questions:

1   Are young people being set up in accommodation on their own at age 16 or 17?
2   What are the procedures that a care leaver has to go through to attend university?
3   What is the form of contact maintained between the local authority and the care leaver until the age 25? Choose from: (a) regular and supportive (b) routine but regular or (c) distant or non-existent.

The impact of the Children (Leaving Care) Act 2000 has been varied. It transferred significant responsibility away from entitlements, small as they were, of the social security system to social services departments, giving them the power to pay personal allowances and housing costs of young people leaving care. These are discretionary powers and how they are exercised is different from individual to individual, the consequence of the social work assessment contained in the 'pathway plan' (Grover *et al*. 2004). But in general the baseline for establishing the financial need of the care leaver, for example for further or higher education or housing, is derived from peer cohorts of excluded young people who are not care leavers. Grover and colleagues conclude that it is therefore hardly surprising to find tensions and contradictions surrounding implementation of the act (*ibid*.).

KEY POINTS

❏   Young people in general face a prolonged and complex transition to adulthood but excluded youth, perhaps some 12 per cent or more of all young people, face this transition by having to negotiate a number of additional risks with far fewer resources behind them.

❏   Schools become critical institutions for combating exclusion and can often be the site where family oriented support programmes are delivered.

❏   Young people are widely associated with anti-social behaviour and this often presents the practitioner with dilemmas between different service orientations – those that offer support to families and those that attempt to reinforce informal social controls in neighbourhoods. Both are valid but both have their flaws.

KEY READING

Audit Commission, *Tired of Hanging Around?* (Audit Commission, 2008) reports the views of young people themselves on how they regard their own socialising in public.

Gerald Patterson, *Anti-social Boys* (Castalia Publishing, 1992) describes so well how harsh and erratic punishment at an early age can progress through a number of behaviour difficulties in and out of school, culminating in anti-social behaviour. It is the foundation of many parenting programmes and should be mandatory reading.

Monica Barry (ed.), *Youth Policy and Social Inclusion: Critical Debates with Young People* (Routledge, 2005) is a solid collection of essays on the interrelated themes of exclusion and inclusion.

CHAPTER 6

WORKING WITH SOCIALLY EXCLUDED ADULTS

OBJECTIVES

At the end of this chapter you should be able to:

- Understand the significance of outcomes in work with vulnerable adults.

- Develop a holistic approach to practice, working across service, neighbourhood and community systems.

- Maximise opportunities for user participation within mainstream social care practice.

- Reduce exclusion of different groups of adults.

Social workers working with adults may ponder what the concept of social exclusion adds to their work. Since the people they work with – those with disability, mental health problems or in old age – are already widely recognised as socially excluded they may wonder what further light the concept of social exclusion casts on their work. In fact a practice focused on exclusion highlights new approaches such as paying attention to social networks, engaging citizens in planning and maximising income. Such a practice, as with other user groups, also underscores the importance of preventive work and the vital role that neighbourhoods and communities play in securing outcomes.

In thinking about how the different elements of exclusion function in relation to adults we can discern four themes that shift in importance depending on which group of users we are working with. These are:

- Dominant ideas in the public mind about the lack of usefulness to society at large, especially in relation to the labour market.
- Exclusion from the labour market that results in low income through unemployment or part-time, low-waged work.
- Professional perception that specific groups of 'vulnerable' adults need to be protected and sheltered from responsibility because they are not equipped for it.
- Suspicion and harassment that stem from public anxiety about particular behaviours, or bigotry.

In working out a response in social work practice, however, it is important not to see any excluded group only as social victims who require the intervention of a strong professional agency to batter down exclusionary barriers but as having capabilities that can surmount a loss of opportunities and social connections.

Social exclusion affects adults in particular ways. It may result in exclusion from their own care planning through lack of influence and awareness of rights, or from low income whether through insufficient benefits or poor access to the labour market. Because of ill health or disability they may experience social isolation and loneliness through a combination of discrimination based on widespread social attitudes or the views of just a few individuals. Or they may be isolated simply through poorly performing or non-existent networks or other features of the environment such as poor housing or a menacing atmosphere in public places. Equally their exclusion may arise from the structural impact of inequality in health care for illness and disability or the lack of integrated services, for example in health and social care.

Since 1997 the proportion of pensioners[5] in low-income households (that is on less than 60 per cent of the UK median after housing costs have been deducted) has halved with a somewhat smaller fall for pensioner couples. This is largely because a greater number of pensioners now own their own homes. But if absolute income is looked at *before* deducting housing costs pensioners as a group and across the whole country are much more likely to be in low-income households than non-pensioners. And around 40 per cent of pensioner households entitled either to council tax benefit and/or pension credit are not claiming them, up from a third in the late 1990s. While some 15 per cent do not claim the housing benefit they are entitled to (Palmer *et al.* 2008: 86).

On another plane the proportion of older people feeling unsafe out alone after dark remains extremely high: women aged 60 or over are more than *four times* as likely to feel unsafe out at night than men, while those on lower incomes feel one-and-a-half more times unsafe than those on higher incomes. A third of adults between 65–74 have a limiting long-term illness or disability and within that group this is closely related to income: the lower the income the greater the chance of having a limiting illness.

Most tellingly the proportion of those aged 75 and over who receive home care

---

5   Terminology is rightly an important feature of describing any user group. I use 'pensioner' literally to refer to people of pensionable age and 'older people' and 'seniors' to refer more generally to people over 65.

from social services to live at home has declined dramatically since the mid 1990s, with some 50 per cent fewer of those 75 years or older getting no service to help them live independently at home (Palmer *et al*. 2008). This was in spite of two decades of social care practice developed by social service departments. The adult service systems that emerged after the passage of the National Health Service and Community Care Act 1990, were radical in that they separated the providers from the purchasers of those services, thus at a stroke setting up countervailing perspectives within the once monolithic local authority and health service. Yet the attitudes that accompanied this radical restructuring still relied upon the kind of calculations rooted in the scarcity of service associated with the old Poor Law. Like the National Assistance Act 1948 and the Chronically Sick and Disabled Persons Act 1970, the emphasis of the NHS and Community Care Act lay in public services providing a safety net to catch those who experienced the greatest difficulties or who had not been able to make provision for themselves. This led to narrow definitions of entitlement linked to a rigorous assessment of the needs and means of individuals who request services. Both ends of the assessment were deployed to fend off those deemed less in need or could afford to pay for their services.

Such a perspective contrasted with the kind of services that we have been discussing in previous chapters related to children and young people, services that are preventive and can deliver on universal outcomes related to universal standards of wellbeing. For example the focus on the 'safety net' type of service for older people has diverted the focus from considering how services, such as transport, supply of food, housing, education, leisure, can contribute to meeting the needs of this major age group of citizens.

FROM COMMUNITY CARE TO SOCIAL CARE

In the 1990s following implementation of the NHS and Community Care Act the 'care' supplied in the community became synonymous with care at home and in practice relied on informal care from families to look after those in need rather than placing individual need in the context of community networks and resources (Barr *et al*. 1997). Despite many articulate voices linking the strength of community care with building community capacity social workers had not yet linked these sufficiently. In his writings the late Gerald Smale (Smale *et al*. 1993; 2000), who was both prescient and ignored in his time by mainstream practice, urged bolstering carers through local neighbourhood work and strengthened social networks. Concepts such as negotiation and partnership, collaboration with community groups and the value of local knowledge all figure prominently in his thinking so that his work is still fresh and relevant today (Smale *et al*. 2000).

When social care practice relies on informal carers from within the family, or on low paid staff, women predominantly shoulder the main burden and responsibility for providing that care. The argument made by feminists is that caring is essentially a gendered activity and that community care policies rely on this fact but do not acknowledge it. To refer only to 'carers', without also specifying the fact that the preponderance of caring is carried out by women, hides the exploitation on which the policy is based and without which it could not succeed. Ungendered references to 'carers' suggest that who carries out caring tasks is not important and at the same time underwrites the assumption that women will take up these tasks as a matter of course.

This has the effect of perpetuating the general subordination of women in what dominant social convention considers to be an informal set of chores that carries little or no
value in the labour market. This exploitation, it can be argued, extends also to those
who carry out care tasks within the public services such as home carers, nurses and
residential care workers. Because caring carries so little public recognition or standing
those that perform it may themselves undervalue their work and lose self-esteem.

Thus the concepts of 'community care' and the now more ubiquitous 'social care'
mask the different roles assigned to men and women that need to be clarified before
building an inclusionary practice around them. If community care is little more than
another ideological device to extract unpaid, underpaid and low-prestige labour out of
women then it is an oppressive, exclusionary concept in its own right exacting a 'care
penalty' according to Nancy Folbre (Folbre 2001).

FUNDING FOR HEALTH AND SOCIAL CARE

Between 2002 and 2007 funding for social services rose by 2.7 per cent on average
while funding for the NHS rose at 7.2 per cent each year. Projected funding for 2010 for
the NHS is for a four per cent increase and for social services one per cent. By that year
the number of people over 85 will have increased by 7 per cent, with a proportionate
increase in disability. The burden on the social care system is such that an estimated £2.7
billion is required to allow social care to keep pace with projected demand.

Social care and empowerment

Inadequate resources combined with restrictive eligibility criteria have made inequalities
worse (McLeod and Bywaters 2000). The NHS and Community Care Act introduced the
concept of service user empowerment but left a legacy of disempowering practice largely
as a result of inherent contradictions of care management as policy. Tanner (1998) argued
that while care management increased the administrative and managerial responsibility
of practitioners at the same time it significantly diminished professional autonomy and
discretion to the detriment of users. Within this framework practice often proved counter-
productive and accelerated exclusion rather than diminished it. This legacy of the NHS
and Community Care Act was widely recognised early in its first term by the Labour
government which in a series of policy statements indicated its intention of reforming the
way social care and health care are provided. In the white paper *Our Health, Our Care,
Our Say* (DoH 2006), in the joint protocol *Putting People First* (DoH 2007) and in *Never
Too Late for Living* (Sillett 2008) various arms of government admitted that the earlier
legislation was too complex and did not respond to people's expectations. Together they
urged the development of local community-based support systems based on shared,
universal outcomes making it easier for adult users to live independently, recover quickly
from illness and to exercise maximum control over their own life.

It also recognised that while local authorities had improved the quality of their care on offer it was concentrated on fewer people with high level of needs, and excluded those who previously would have been supported. Higher charges, means testing and wide variations in eligibility criteria across the country, particularly for older people, undermined people's planning for old age. Social care for older people in particular is heavily dependent on privately funded and informal care, with only 25 per cent of care funded by local authorities.

Direct payments and 'personalisation' of services

The Community Care (Direct Payments) Act 1996 introduced the concept of direct payments to users in lieu of community care services, allowing people with a variety of disability and care needs to purchase their own support, particularly personal assistants. The act applies equally to people with physical disability, mental health problems or learning difficulties although the take-up is greatest among the first group. It is potentially an extremely radical, culture-changing innovation that should allow each user 'to be their own care manager', as Gerald Smale had long thought should be the case. Since 2002 in Scotland and 2004 in England and Wales direct payments have become mandatory for all those eligible for community care services who consented and are able to manage payments. The 2006 white paper *Our Health, Our Care, Our Say* extended the concept to include individualised budgets for disabled people; these merge funds from different sources including local authority social services, housing adaptations and equipment and individual living funds (Riddell 2006).

Direct payment schemes give disabled people the means to set up their own system of personal assistance with a level of personal oversight and control that is unlikely to be matched by agency provision. Direct payments are complex to implement and for them to work social workers need to develop trust in users' capacity to manage things independently and to ask for help when needed. To make any scheme workable disabled people need to be involved in all stages. Social workers are still gatekeepers so that most people become aware of the possibility of direct payments through their social worker. Moreover users need a social work assessment to determine whether or not they would be eligible for services – and hence for direct payment. As Smale *et al.* (1994: 6) long ago noted:

> Being a customer with money in your pocket is not an insurance against powerlessness. It is difficult for users to make real choices when their past experience of using social services is limited. There is always the tendency for people to want what they know rather than know what they want.

But the culture is changing and control is an increasing prize for disabled people. As one disabled person who employs a personal assistant has said:

> With social services home care I felt like they came in, 'did me' and then went off and 'did' someone else and I was beholden to them. With direct payments I'm the boss and the employee has a different approach to me as I'm paying them rather than someone else sending them to help a hopeless person. (Dawson 2000)

PASS, the personal assistance support scheme run by disabled people themselves, is able to assist individuals with the skills for selecting personal assistants and managing the relationship as an employer, as it is able to help disabled people find work.

But this sense of autonomy and control perhaps is coming at a price. Glendinning and Bell (2008) argue that those in need of social care may well be unwilling or unable to undertake the search for information for the service that would suit them best. Where needs are so specialised or in areas – certainly rural but others too – where few services are available in the first place undermines some of the principles on which personalisation is based. There is also concern on the differential impact of the personalisation agenda in a highly unequal society. Those that lack both the resources and the knowledge required to make a system of direct payments or individual budgets function smoothly will be the casualties in an arrangement that places more responsibility on individuals, families and carers and less on central or local authorities for optimising social care (Glendinning and Bell 2008).

ACTIVITY 6.1:   HOW DO YOU VIEW INDIVIDUAL BUDGETS AND 'PERSONALISATION' OF SERVICES?

While there is widespread consensus behind the concept of direct payments and individual budgets there are also questions about whether they are an appropriate way to arrange services simply because they are too complex to negotiate on one's own. Ideologically they can be difficult to categorise – do they empower users or are they a form of 'creeping privatisation' as Pearson (2006) maintains? As part of a growing trend toward 'personalisation' of services do they ignore wider issues of political power and social structure?

SOCIAL EXCLUSION OF OLDER PEOPLE

Old age is described by Erik Erikson as beginning at that point where a person has already reached the peak of their accomplishments, or if not is facing stagnation and self-absorption. The older person is in a transition to that final stage in which all prior stages are integrated with a sense of validity and appreciation, or if not falling into despair, regret and fear (Erikson 1969). Understanding how old age is socially constructed is an important first step in seeing the process whereby older people are excluded through ageism. The social conventions produce 'invisibility' which presumes a lack of sexual interest, an array of phyical weaknesses and the inability to work. Yet, as Bill Bytheway, reminds us 'old age' has no real scientific basis since there are no clearly identifiable set of physical changes that marks a person's entry into old age at a given point in time (Bytheway 1995). Physiologically the body changes and is less accomplished in different ways throughout life but often with compensating strengths developing at the same time. Despite this, older people are routinely barred from opportunities and services on grounds of age – often with tacit popular agreement particularly in relation to health service rationing – in a discriminatory way that would not be legally acceptable if based on race, gender or disability (*ibid.*).

Older people experience multiple forms of exclusion – through low income and social isolation, but also from basic services, civic participation, neighbourhood life (Scharf *et al.* 2005). Exclusionary forces gather pace as a person grows older: the older person may be out of the job market or have a precarious hold on it; friends die, children grow up, income falls off after retirement. While there is growing evidence that personal networks have a protective effect on health and wellbeing at all ages, as they erode with aging so that effect wears off (Sluzki 2000). The life course of the older individual affects network strength which thin out and become less responsive. Those who are over 85, unmarried or not in a partnership, have no children and are in poor health will often have weak networks (Keating *et al.* 2003).

Other trends also contribute to what might be called a 'new precariousness' for older people living in low-income neighbourhoods; one example is the social polarisation found on public housing estates, where pensioners feel intimidated by large groups of young people. Older people too experience the risks associated with the structural change in the labour market: ill-health and disability are less tolerated. Other factors in the new precariousness are the shrinking of social provision, the destruction of civility and the degradation of family ties through divorce and marital conflict that affect older people's support networks.

Elder abuse is also a particular feature of the social exclusion of older people with victims often socially isolated (Pritchard 2008). Those who suffer it want informed practical help, especially about leaving abusive situations, and need information on choice and availability of housing, entitlements to benefits, access to joint bank accounts held with the abuser; the concerns are for food and warmth, social contact and support. Frequently the abused older person's history of poverty and hardship in earlier life shapes their basic need simply to have enough food and live in a warm environment.

ACTIVITY 6.2: AGEISM IN THE NHS

Two-thirds of doctors working in the NHS thought that the NHS is institutionally ageist in January 2009, that older people are less likely to have their symptoms fully investigated and less likely to be referred on for essential treatment (BBC News 2009). Think back over work you have carried out either within a hospital setting, a primary care trust or in arranging post-hospital social care. Do your experiences confirm what the doctors are saying?

WHO IS OLD?

Mervyn Eastman from Better Government for Older People put it like this: 'The challenge is that we frequently – including older people themselves – think that older people are somebody else. In a sense, it is about how do we capture and articulate the fact that older people are like everybody else, simply older' (cited in Sillett 2008: 6).

THE WOODEN BOWL

In Iran they tell this story about old age:

Once there was a family living in peace and harmony: mother, father and a young boy of about six. Then the father's own aged father came to live with them. All was well for a time until the old man's eating habits grew sloppy and eventually declined to a point where he dribbled a lot and dropped his food so that he made a mess at the table and on the floor below his chair. He was unsightly and his mouth had to be wiped occasionally. The old man's son and daughter-in-law were repelled by this; they were convinced they had to do something lest the old man set a bad example for their young son. So they shaped a rough-hewn bowl from a lump of wood and gave him a spoon and made the old man eat with these utensils on a mat in a corner of the eating room. On the second night of this new arrangement, with the old man eating in his corner, the young boy suddenly jumped from his seat in the middle of the evening meal and ran outside. His parents heard sounds of woodworking, hammering and scraping. 'Whatever are you doing?' they called out to their son. 'Why I am making bowls for both of you when you are old', he replied. The old man rejoined the family at the dinner table that very night.

Outcomes for older people – those positive elements necessary for wellbeing that we all want for ourselves and our family – have been progressively clarified just as they have in relation to services for children and young people although their influence on service systems is still tenuous. While it is understandable that care of older people is the first concern of service providers it is striking to discover that the most important outcomes older people themselves seek, after personal comfort, are to do with participation in social networks and neighbourhood affairs. They believe strongly that their independence is based on them (Netten *et al.* 2006; Carrier 2005). The green paper on adult services, *Independence, Well-being and Choice* (Department of Health 2005) picked up on this research and laid out a wide range of outcomes to underpin older people's wellbeing:

- independence through choice and personal control
- equal opportunity to work
- engagement in social activities and social networks

- participation in community and neighbourhood affairs
- maintain personal dignity.

To develop services that deliver these outcomes as priorities means turning services upside-down: de-emphasising the current dominant focus on specialist and acute care while engaging seniors in their neighbourhoods, arranging learning and training, ceding control over housing and environment become central to practice. Collective responsibility for setting priorities to promote the wellbeing of older people is shared across community, agencies and older people themselves. Agencies are to focus on what needs to be achieved and what their contribution will be to this, rather than be preoccupied with internal organisation and partnership boundaries. As we have stressed in previous chapters the skill set of practitioners then changes as they become involved in capacity building and the capability of universal services enabling seniors to be supported in the community more safely and for longer. Those skills are overarching. Practitioners become facilitators, catalysts, and enablers in developing services in the community, co-ordinating and providing information, advice and other resources for accessing services when needed (ADSS 2003).

CASE STUDY 9: SURE START IN LATER LIFE

Sure Starts for older people make an explicit link between outcomes and neighbourhood in the way Sure Start galvanised local communities to reshape children's services (Social Exclusion Unit [SEU] 2006). It commits government policy to move beyond the basic standards of maintaining health and income to focus on the right of older people to participate in their communities and to engage throughout their lives in meaningful roles and relationships. Sure Start for older people says very clearly that this can only be done by building 'inclusive communities that meet local needs where the contribution of older people is key to their success' (SEU 2006: 8).

Sure Start in later life means providing a single gateway to services and opportunities to be engaged in the locality. But the extent of improved participation and improved wellbeing relies as much on what the neighbourhood and community have to offer as on the individual qualities of the older person. Individuals, families and communities (neighbours, general practitioners, pharmacists, shopkeepers) need to consider the implications of how this reconfigures and makes more explicit the role of neighbourhoods and local people in maintaining a system of connections available for older people.

Self-advocacy

In common with other user groups, older people have developed a strong self-advocacy movement – pressing a political agenda, educating the public and arguing for human rights. As with all self-advocacy movements a key step forward has been to throw off the passive, medicalised and individualised view of old age as constructed around the social conventions of 'inevitable decline' and 'failing powers'. The introduction of the Human Rights Act into UK law in 2000 and awareness of the powerful political activism of self-advocacy groups in the US staffed by older people have offered further impetus to the movement already under way.

CASE STUDY 10: JOINT PUBLIC AFFAIRS COMMITTEE (JPAC) FOR OLDER ADULTS

JPAC's Institute for Senior Action in New York City integrates education on effective advocacy and critical ageing policy issues with practical grassroots application. Its aim is to hone the skills of long-time community activists as well as provide a way for recent retirees to become more involved in social action. It explicitly addresses the capacity for 'generativity' which Erik Erikson noted as marking the last of the eight stages of life – old age (Erikson 1969). JPAC and its affiliated Institute for Senior Action run a comprehensive leadership training course which has become a powerful tool for introducing and engaging recent retirees into advocacy activism. Their curriculum serves as an excellent model for all advocacy and community development programmes interested in strengthening local leadership. The curriculum includes:

- the budget and legislative process at national, regional and municipal level
- voter registration and outreach
- policies, programmes and entitlements for seniors
- organising across the generations and within a multi-cultural community
- fundamentals of fundraising
- techniques of social action
- volunteerism and mentoring
- running an effective meeting
- working with the media
- writing skills and techniques
- conflict resolution
- public speaking with confidence.

(adapted from JPAC 2008)

Social isolation, loneliness and the importance of social connections

Personal social networks may be stable but the fabric of relationships generally constituted by family members, friends, acquaintances, associates from work and relations that grow out of our participation in formal and informal organisations – social, religious, political, neighbourhood – are ever-evolving. These networks have been described as a 'social cocoon' which constitute 'a key repository of our identity, our history and our sense of fulfillment and satisfaction with life' (Sluzki 2000: 271).

Several of the outcomes discussed above emphasise that important goals for older people are tied to them remaining engaged in their locality. And in this social networks play an important part in this stage of life. A person's social network tracks the individual life cycle to a degree with some weakening of social bonds from the death or movement of members, loss of some social roles and tasks often related to retirement. A decrease in the older person's capacity to undertake the social tasks required to maintain network links and a reduction in the opportunities for making new friends or new social ties also affect network ties. On the other hand this trend can be offset by intensification of select friendships, the expansion of social tasks through volunteer work or by re-activating family tasks (Wenger 1997).

Demographic and social changes have weakened the capacity of support networks that practitioners have, perhaps more than they recognise, come to rely on. More women working (and fewer seeing it as their job alone to care for an older person), fewer children, higher rates of divorce and greater geographical mobility have all made family networks more fragile (Keating *et al.* 2003). Not surprisingly, unmarried older people will have invested more in non-family supportive relationships and so may still have robust networks. For those over 85 the loss of same-generation relatives and friends and the tendency to put energy into only the closest relationships (Keating *et al.* 2003) can undermine what a wider, more dispersed support network is capable of achieving.

The difference between support networks and care networks

Networks of both family and friends have the widest capacity to perform tasks and give substantial amounts of support. This may include emotional support tasks such as providing social interaction, reassurance, validation, cheering up and monitoring as well as material support such as household jobs like preparing meals, cleaning, shopping for food, providing transport, bill paying and banking money. The size of a social network, however, is not always a reliable predictor of support since any network may contain ties that have lost their friendship roles or have become impersonal. Support is more likely from those with continuing contact who form a smaller group (or 'subset') within the larger network. Such a subset might include immediate family, relatives or particular neighbours. But assumptions that older people who apparently have sufficient social ties will have the support they need are not always accurate. Support networks (with on average five to ten people) are smaller than the personal social networks (on average twelve to thirteen) from which they come and are usually found among long-standing kinship and friendship ties with high expectations to provide reciprocal support (van Tilburg 1998).

In post-hospital care social networks, to the extent that they are available, obviously become extremely important. McLeod and colleagues (2008) examined older service users' feedback and experiences in the wake of hospital discharge and confirmed the health benefits of practitioners facilitating access to social networks. By combining sensitive interpersonal interaction, advocacy and 'educational' assistance, social care workers supported older service users' re-engagement in a variety of networks. These included:

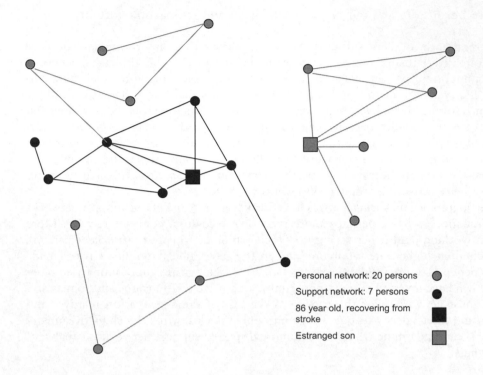

Personal network: 20 persons
Support network: 7 persons
86 year old, recovering from stroke
Estranged son

FIGURE 6.1   Support and personal networks compared for an 86-year-old woman recovering from a stroke

- friendship, recreational and family groups
- health care treatment programmes
- local contacts and organisations.

Through such networks, material, interpersonal and health care resources are obtained which help sustain physical health and psychological wellbeing. Also critical is the process of such social care, which includes ensuring that reflected service users' priorities are included in any plan, befriending and challenging the short time frame for intermediate care. Social support has been convincingly related to improved health outcomes – lowering blood pressure, maintaining cognitive functioning and greater psychological resilience (McLeod *et al.* 2008).

PEOPLE WITH DISABILITY

People with disability articulated the experience of exclusion long before it became a concept in social policy. Their discussion and practitioners' responses contribute extensively to our current understanding of exclusion as a process that occurs across a whole range of activities from the labour market, to shopping mobility, to simple

CASE STUDY 11: SAFE TRANSITIONS

McLeod and her colleagues examined the prerequisites for the safe transition – the essential preliminary to social re-engagement – of an older person from hospital to back home. These included assistance with practical home care and personal care; advocacy to assist access to material and social resources; educational assistance to acquire new skills or old skills that had been lost; assistance to tackle psychological barriers to re-engage social networks; access to health care organisations. But more than all of these was the process: receiving friendship and befriending from practitioners or volunteers (McLeod *et al.* 2008).

access to buildings and across city streets. Generally, social work in the past based its practice towards people with disability on the basis of 'individual pathology' and meeting individual needs; as we have seen, disability in the Children Act 1989 automatically renders a child 'in need'. Disability was defined as a set of deficits and needs, and practitioners approached disabled people and their families holding attitudes that linked disability with dependency and care. For decades services were segregated through special schools, adult training centres, residential establishments and long-stay hospitals. Separate leisure facilities are still common with clubs and special holidays still undertaken in groups.

This legacy of segregation underpinned a depth of discriminatory attitudes in society at large based on a toxic mix of distaste, distance, pity and condescension. Disabled people felt the full force of multi-layered exclusion: low income through inadequate benefits, exclusion from the labour market, exclusion from cultural and intellectual activity and disrupted social networks. They also faced a variety of threats to their very existence. One threat came from legal judgements that a potentially disabled foetus can rightfully be aborted while others feared that court-sanctioned euthanasia of those in 'vegetative state' was the start of a slippery slope that could extend to other disabling conditions. The latter raised within disabled groups the explicit memory of the National Socialist programme in Germany in the 1930s that undertook the first mass euthanasia of disabled people (Burleigh 1994).

Largely through persistent advocacy and argument, dedicated activity and civic protest, disabled people have shaped and communicated a positive idea of disability. 'The social model', as it is generally called, focuses on how social attitudes have excluded people with impairments. It is society and not the disabled person that has failed to adjust. In this view disabled people do not need a mobility allowance but a transport system that eliminates the barriers to people with impaired mobility. The way homes are constructed do not cater for the full range of physical capabilities; the world of work is completely geared to maximising profit from the able bodied (Oliver and Sapey 2006).

Others are now arguing that the social model of disability should be the basis for a 'mutual model', which could be used as a tool for promoting greater understanding and inclusion by focusing more on the common ground between disabled and non-disabled people. In this perspective impairment and related 'disability' are present throughout society with large additional numbers of people, including carers, family, friends and colleagues also involved. In this view disability in some form is not the 'fate' of a restricted minority but a development faced by many millions at some point in their lives, particularly as they grow older (Christie 1999). From this flow an agenda for 'mutualism' emerges – re-designing workplaces, services and infrastructures – that has the potential for including the, currently, non-disabled, but also addresses disabling barriers in workplaces and other environments.

THE SOCIAL MODEL EXPLAINED

In our view, it is society which disables physically impaired people. Disability is something imposed on top of our impairments by the way we are unnecessarily isolated and excluded from full participation in society. To understand this it is necessary to grasp the distinction between the physical impairment and the social situation, called 'disability', of people with such an impairment. Disability [is] the disadvantage or restriction of activity caused by a contemporary social organisation which takes no or little account of people who have physical impairments and thus excludes them from the mainstream of social activities.

(from a statement by the Union of Physically Impaired Against Segregation 1976, quoted in Oliver and Sapey 2006: 30)

Income, benefits and work

The employment rate of people with disability is just under 50 per cent, improving by a full 10 per cent over the decade 1998–2008. Nevertheless this is a far lower percentage than the national average and is *by far* the lowest of all the major groups of disadvantaged adults. Disabled people consistently report that they would like to work but regardless of qualification held – whether degree, A level, GCSEs or no qualification – the proportion of people with a disability who want to work but remain without work is much greater than those without a disability (Palmer *et al*. 2008: 71).

In the government's view work is the most important means for overcoming social exclusion and it has made regular programmatic efforts to raise levels of employment among disabled people. Pathway to Work projects are the most familiar of the string of programmes which offer individual support for disabled people as they move towards work. The introduction of employment and support allowance (ESA) in 2008 was more radical. ESA replaced both incapacity benefit and income support paid on grounds of incapacity and introduced new ways of assessing incapacity to work that place more emphasis on identifying an individual's positive capacities rather than incapacity and no longer rests on the strict divide between those who are and those who are not capable of work. This work capability assessment identifies whether a person has a 'limited capability for work' and if found to be so he or she is entitled to ESA. A second part to the assessment then determines whether claimants have a 'limited capability for work related activity' which determines whether they are placed in the 'support group' or the 'work-related activity group'. Those in the latter group undertake a third part of the assessment which looks at barriers to work and what support the person needs to move into work. They must also meet certain conditions including attending six work-focused interviews. Failure to meet these conditions can lead to the ESA payment being 'sanctioned' (DWP 2009).

The new suite of work-oriented benefits can present uncomfortable questions for a practitioner working with people with long-term health conditions or disability. It is quite likely that the person wants to work but faces difficulties arising from discriminatory attitudes by employers or a loss of skills and confidence after a lengthy time out of the labour market. On the other hand the benefits systems now based on conditionality may apply time limits and tasks that are difficult to meet. Moreover to deliver this back to work support government has stated that it will call on a range of public, private and voluntary sector providers. Helping those in the transition from benefit to work, then, depends on effective joint working with local employment services to provide integrated support. For the social worker full exploration with the user of the consequences of such a transition becomes an overriding objective.

The incapacitated or disabled person and social worker jointly should consider how and in what ways their capacity for work can be maximised. This might include looking at how training centres might be used to enhance particular skills or how the direct-payment scheme could be invoked to allow users to purchase their own training or equipment requirements in preparation for employment. Or it could include using a 'permitted work opportunity' whereby an ESA claimant may be permitted limited opportunity to undertake work while still receiving ESA – especially if this would facilitate later take up of more sustained work. A range of other partners might assist such as local user and advocacy groups, local rehabilitation providers, supported employment agencies, or local education authorities. Other service departments such as housing, transport and economic regeneration can also play a useful role. But of course when engaging multiple systems in this way it is essential to remember practice is participant centred and aims at creating confidence and building capacity and skills.

People with learning disability

As with disability campaigns advocacy organisations have made concerted efforts to promote greater participation of learning disabled people in community life and employment. This process began long before the phrase 'social exclusion' took root in the UK but the objectives are the same. The concepts of 'normalisation' and 'social role valorisation' (Wolfensberger 1975) opened up the link between local communities and people with learning difficulties as they learn specific sets of social skills. The de-institutionalisation that followed – the closure of the long-stay hospitals for the 'mentally handicapped' and the old adult training centres where basic, repetitive 'employment' was available in a highly institutional atmosphere – was gradually transformed into a wider variety of education centres and concerted efforts to improve special needs education in mainstream schools.

There have recently been several important developments in both personal planning and in the kinds of services available to break down this enforced separatism of people with learning difficulties:

- introduction of person-centred planning processes
- adult family placements
- supported employment.

Person-centred planning

There is a growing recognition that people with learning difficulties need a greater range of opportunities to work and pursue interests and leisure activities that are community based and expand their friendship networks. One way of doing this has been through the introduction of a 'person-centred' planning process which has both enabled people to realise more of their aims and goals and developed an effective form of participatory engagement.

The concept of person-centred planning grew out of the UK-wide Changing Days Project which was set up to explore ways of promoting user involvement in choosing and arranging day-to-day activities (including work). Each person with learning difficulties has their own 'planning circle', made up of people he or she has chosen: circle members care about the person and are committed to improving their life by helping them to work out what they want to achieve. Importantly the circles draw on people from outside the service itself thus acting as a change agent for the service culture (Cole *et al.* 2000).

The planning circle focuses only on the interests and personal goals of the user. Because of this overriding individual focus, independent facilitators – rather than service-based personnel – are more effective in establishing and nurturing the circles. Independent facilitators are able to hold more firmly to the principle that the person with learning difficulties is the driving force in the planning process and can negotiate more effectively any possible conflicts with the person's care establishment than if the facilitator were a member of staff.

Within circle discussions it may become clear that many users want to find part-time work. Because most have not worked before, intensive long-term support is required to realise this objective, usually in the form of access to supported employment (see below). Leisure or educational objectives are perhaps easier to pursue although they have implications for carers and for those with whom users are living, such as residential home staff or placement families. Planning circles can lead to more involvement in the community and established friendships with local people. This takes time, however, and requires deliberate action, persistence and creative thinking from within the planning circle itself (Cole *et al.* 2000).

Adult family placement

In adult placements a vulnerable adult goes either to live or to stay with a family not their own. ('Family' here is used in the widest possible sense and may involve any number of carers in a settled relationship.) The family – often referred to as 'carers'

– are themselves usually recruited and supported by some form of adult placement scheme. The general expectation is that the vulnerable person lives as part of the family and the carers are paid a fee in return for providing appropriate support. Such placements are quite distinct from board and lodging arrangements or small group homes. Through them a range of exclusionary barriers can be addressed and overcome, particularly the isolating effects of institutional or semi-institutional living.

Robinson and Simons (1996) outlined the common concerns that have evolved among users and which need to be explicitly addressed in any arrangement. In particular any 'family rules' or norms with which the user is unfamiliar need to be explained prior to placement and, if they are deemed inappropriate for adults on placement, to be acknowledged as such by the carers. The adult on placement should have accommodation and facilities that allow for privacy. Personal keys, access to transport, reasonable levels of weekly allowance and holidays are all of great practical significance and need to be agreed in advance. Having a personal key, for example, means that the person with learning difficulties has some opportunity to make informed decisions on their own about risk and the freedom to act on those decisions (*ibid.*).

Supported employment

People with learning difficulties have regularly voiced their aspiration to have a real job, yet for decades the daily routine for most were days spent in day centres, training centres or sheltered workshops, segregated from their non-disabled peers and earning negligible wages. The notion of supported employment runs counter to this long-standing practice: a person with learning difficulties is helped by a supported employment agency to find a job, internship or work experience that matches their skills and interests. Social workers and care managers should look closely at this option with their service users and be more energetic in stimulating the provision of supported employment opportunities where none exist.

Supported employment agencies offer a variety of objectives:

- Helping people identify their skills and preferences through the development of a vocational profile.
- Job development to find the person's preferred job through contact with employers.
- Job analysis to find out more about the workplace, co-workers and the support needed in that environment.
- Job support to ensure that both employee and employer receive 'just enough' creative assistance, information and back-up so as not to undermine independence and growth of skills.
- Career support to help people think in the longer term about progression.

(O'Bryan *et al.* 2000)

But there are barriers to supported employment opportunities: access remains difficult for many, funding is precarious and fragmented and the benefit system continues to cause difficulties through its lack of familiarity with the concept. Practitioners can assist in overcoming such barriers by ensuring that strengths of supported employment

CASE STUDY 12: RICHARD

Richard is in his fifties and lives in a small, staffed hostel with five other people who have learning difficulties. He has recently been introduced to a job as a storeman – cleaning, loading and stacking – through supported employment after spending many years attending an adult training centre for five days a week. Following a recent change in the policy of his social services department he no longer earns anything for his attendance at the centre. Richard's IQ is 51. He can write his name and read a few single words while his numeracy enables him to count up to ten. Richard is able to look after himself in all areas of his life, only requiring help to budget and to deal with his benefits and medical appointments. He can cook, launder his clothes and shop independently. When he was at the training centre he was known as a hard and dependable worker who completed his tasks thoroughly. Now he has left his training centre altogether and is working 39 hours a week as a storeman earning above the minimum wage. By certain identifiable scales his support needs might be thought greater than others with learning disabilities, and his measured IQ is certainly lower than many of his peers in the training centre. But he fitted into his new job well, has high levels of interaction with other employees and regards himself as quite happy.

(adapted from Bass and Drewett 1997)

are fully understood by other professionals and would-be service partners, including personal advisers, and by identifying supported employment as a key component of better services, especially for young disabled people. Local authorities should include supported employment objectives in all community care plans as a core component, and should ensure that the Connexions service offers job tryout, and assistance with transport. Using direct payments for in work support, to increase a person's productivity, is a further promising step forward (O'Bryan *et al.* 2000).

The key to effective employment is in the support. Once a person is matched to a job, the supported employment agency provides a staff member, known as job trainer or job coach, to accompany the new employee to their new place of work. The job coach helps the employee to learn how to carry out the various responsibilities of the job. As those responsibilities are mastered the job coach withdraws but continues to keep in touch and to be available if needed. The principle of supported employment works for several groups of would-be jobseekers – those with mental health problems, physical disabilities, sensory impairments and brain injury (Bass and Drewett 1997).

There are generally three stages in the supported employment process:

- Vocational profiling that determines the jobseeker's skills, interest and personality.

- Job development which secures a job that matches the profile and meets an employer's need.
- Job analysis which examines in detail the tasks required in the job and the type of social behaviour valued by the workplace culture (*ibid.*).

For practitioners the importance of supported employment as a means for overcoming the social exclusion experienced by people with learning difficulties cannot be emphasised too strongly. Powerful research has established that the levels of engagement (defined as taking part in purposeful activity) in the kinds of activities that users find interesting are raised very significantly above what users had experienced in their previous training centres (*ibid.*).

KEY POINTS

❏ Older people, people with disability and people with learning disability face substantial discrimination and are too often left to cope with exclusion without resources.

❏ The development of universal outcomes for older people, based around social integration in neighbourhoods, provides a much needed orientation for services and brings them more in line with children's services. They are however still not widely adopted in practice.

❏ There are specific ways of breaking down the exclusion of particular user groups such as older people, and people with learning difficulties or disability. These include supporting self-advocacy, links with supported employment, promoting networks to overcome loneliness and family placements for adults.

❏ Government has introduced new conditions requiring adults to train for work and search for work in order to receive some benefit. This can present dilemmas both for individual users and practitioners.

KEY READING

Eileen McLeod and Paul Bywaters, *Social Work, Health and Equality* (Routledge, 2000). Social workers have to learn to deliver their services for adults in close relationship with health services; this book provides an excellent grounding for this with a strong emphasis on overcoming exclusion and inequality.

M. Oliver and B. Sapey, *Social Work with Disabled People*, 3rd edn (Palgrave Macmillan, 2006). This is an authoritative exploration of the 'social model' of disability, now in a new edition.

CHAPTER 7

WORKING WITH DISADVANTAGED NEIGHBOURHOODS

OBJECTIVES

At the end of the chapter you should:

■ Understand how specific neighbourhoods become excluded from the prosperity and opportunity found elsewhere in the town or region of which they are a part.

■ Know certain techniques for building up community strengths or 'capacity building' in support of local citizens and organisations determined to shape their own future.

■ Understand the importance of maximising resident participation in any community development project and how to audit levels of participation.

■ Be familiar with approaches and strategies that help local services play a key role in reviving such areas, such as creating partnerships and neighbourhood teams.

Social exclusion has a spatial or geographical dimension. In short 'place' matters. This chapter explores the approaches and techniques of working with excluded neighbourhoods, helping to build the structures and capacities on the ground so that local residents can more actively shape and contribute to the renewal of their own localities.

NEIGHBOURHOOD EFFECTS

In disadvantaged neighbourhoods various components of exclusion reinforce each other so that everyone in that particular area is affected. Services have been withdrawn, fear of crime is high, levels of political participation low. Employers and commercial outlets have left the area taking jobs with them. Without the resources from effective services, wages from steady employment, and support networks based on reasonable levels of trust, neighbourhood stresses mount on children, parents and vulnerable adults alike. When an entire neighbourhood is excluded, such as a social housing estate, the most damaging long-term impact arises from what sociologists call 'neighbourhood effects' – the decline in the social fabric and loss of control over public space that affects the quality of life of all residents in a particular area regardless of individual levels of aspiration or motivation.

Many of these effects on individual behaviour profoundly impact on social work. For example child and adolescent outcomes such as infant mortality and low birth weight have been tied to neighbourhood disadvantage; so have rates of teenage pregnancy and school exclusion, while child abuse and neglect and anti-social behaviour by young people have all been linked to living in neighbourhoods with particular characteristics (Brooks-Gunn et al. 1997); so has accidental injury to children and the suicide of young people (Almgren in Sampson et al. 2002).

A link between the prevalence of crime within neighbourhoods and the 'efficacy' of neighbourhoods, that is the effectiveness within which social norms are projected and protected in public spaces is also well established (Sampson et al. 2002).

Where ethnic minorities are concentrated in relatively deprived urban areas employment prospects are affected with, for example, higher rates of unemployment and lower rates of self-employment than ethnically balanced areas (Clark and Drinkwater 2002). A profound negative effect on the emotional stability of pre-school children exposed to neighbourhood violence has been established (Farver and Natera 2000). Neighbourhoods also impact on a range of health outcomes, whether low birth weight, health protective behaviours, levels of adult mortality, cardiovascular risk factors and many others (Diez-Roux 2001; Acheson 1998; Browning and Cagney 2002).

ACTIVITY 7.1: WHAT IS A NEIGHBOURHOOD?

If neighbourhoods are to be regarded as a target for intervention it is important to reach some understanding of what a 'neighbourhood' is. Write a list of what you consider to be the characteristics of a neighbourhood – not what an ideal neighbourhood should be, but as it is. It may help for you to consider first the areas in which you work, or live, or were brought up. In your understanding of what defines a neighbourhood which of the following is the most important: physical boundaries such as roads, cultural or ethnic make-up, social networks and local associations, income levels or housing tenure?

The neighbourhood as the focus for combating exclusion is not the rosy world of mutual help evoked in memoirs of working-class districts (Roberts 1973; Woodruff 2002) and mining communities or in the idyllic pictures of suburban living in the 1950s. Today when we talk of neighbourhood we may mean nothing more than an area with some sense of physical boundary or other defining limits. In tackling exclusion neighbourhoods become the focus, not because of any belief in a false consensus but because local areas are sites where multiple strands of exclusion come together. In fact practitioners will want to ensure that they uncover any false consensus and recognise local diversity whether in culture, ethnicity, gender or income levels.

NEIGHBOURHOOD – A DEFINITION

A neighbourhood is a geographic zone or area which is continuous and surrounds some other point, usually a person's home, and is smaller in size than some other recognised spatial entity, for example a 'locality', 'district' or city. Neighbourhoods can be defined by individuals, groups of individuals or organisations who live and work there and they may be characterised by a single function, social class or ethnic group or alternatively by its diversity, mixed tenure housing and wide variations in occupations and professions. Neighbourhoods do not have precise borders but are judgements about who and what to include in a fluid, ever-changing social unit (adapted from Maclennan 2000: 11).

The most disadvantaged neighbourhoods in Britain are generally found in inner-city social housing flats such as high rises, the decaying owner-occupied or privately rented terraced housing of older cities and the peripheral housing estates that ring many of Britain's urban areas. Even prosperous towns have large council-owned estates which over a period of time have experienced intense deprivation. The overall impact of disadvantage is that residents do not see themselves as being in control; what they want is to have influence over regular services rather than special projects. Yet neighbourhoods do matter to their residents, and it is wrong to simply assume that disadvantaged areas totally lack social cohesion or are empty of support networks and people with skills and talent.

Neighbourhoods in decline

What cuts a neighbourhood off from the economic, social and political activity of the city or region within which it is located? Physical layout and the nature of the housing have something to do with it. The mass estates built for thousands of citizens after the Second World War were constructed around road layout and housing design that made looking after property difficult over the long term. From the mid 1960s, as the British housing market was dominated by owner occupation, only those on relatively low income began to be concentrated on such estates. In the 1980s the collapse of industrial production in particular areas of the country – the northeast, the northwest, south Wales for example – combined with the right to buy conferred on sitting tenants proved to accelerate the movement of those on low income to these estates.

Whether run by the local authority or, increasingly, by an independent housing trust or housing association, social housing has today become an under-resourced, residual service for those individuals and families who could not find housing in other parts of the housing system nor had the resources to prevent their being assigned to the most stigmatised neighbourhoods. As a result low-income households, who often need substantial supports, are channelled towards specific areas within a local authority area. For example, lone mothers may be housed near one another; this is not a coincidence but deliberate housing allocation policy by the local authorities. The consequence is greater turnover within housing as the council estates provide for an increased proportion of excluded people and to cater more exclusively for this group.

But poor housing is not the only factor in the social exclusion of entire neighbour-hoods. As a result of the concentration of poor people living together the social fabric of the estate – that is the way people relate to each other and the strength of local organisations such as churches or mosques – is also changed. In *Estates On the Edge*, Anne Power (1997) provides a good overview of how a range of negative pressures build up within large housing estates.

Figure 7.1 simplifies what is an exclusionary process that affects many social housing estates:

- larger economic pressures such as the demands of the labour market for highly skilled people combines with
- local conditions such as the layout and structure of individual estates (for example with back alley access to individual houses which facilitates burglary, and no on site warden or manager) and
- disrupted social fabric as excluded, low income families take up shorter-term tenancies. These factors result in loss of confidence accumulating, property being abandoned and declining in value, levels of local activity and energy being run down, services being withdrawn, loss of authority and collapsing viability (Power 1997; Power and Mumford 1999: 81).

Social capital

Getting an idea of the extent of social cohesion or what is now referred to as 'social capital' for an entire neighbourhood is difficult. Social capital is the accumulated social networks and connections in a given neighbourhood which includes things like the level of activism in civic organisations, the degree of political involvement and the vitality of local institutions such as churches or mosques. A number of indicators have been developed that show the extent of social capital in a given area. One such indicator is the proportion of individuals who are not involved in any civic organisation – whether political party, church, mosque or temple, trade union, tenants' association, club or social group. Another is data on community safety, say the total number of burglaries, access to insurance against crime, individuals expressing dissatisfaction with their neighbourhood (Putnam 2001). Also included in an audit of social capital are new organisations associated with environmental activism, social enterprises, credit unions and other participatory initiatives.

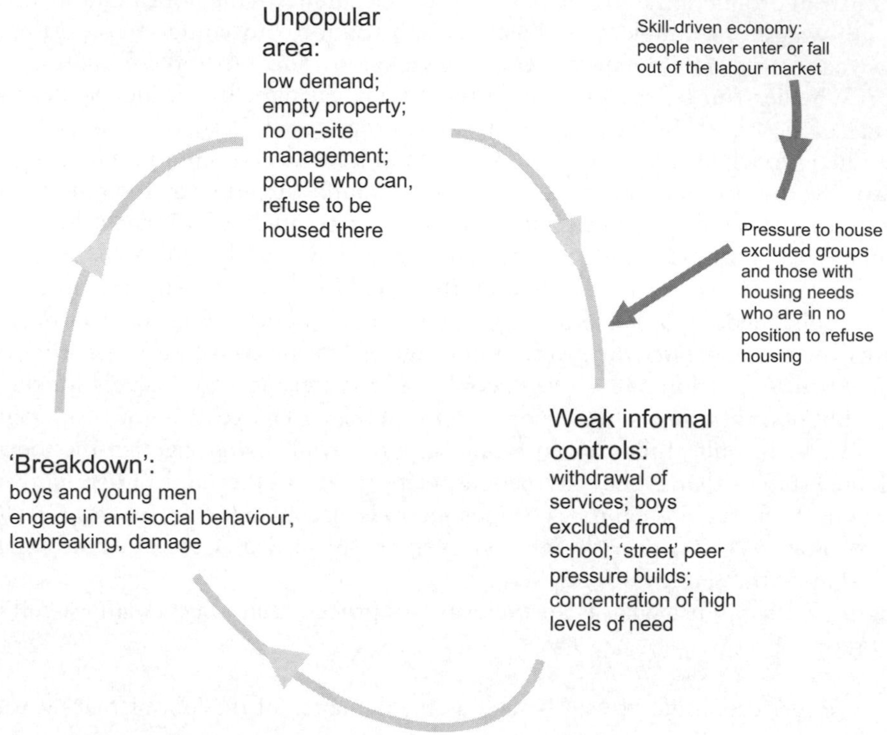

Unpopular area:

low demand;
empty property;
no on-site
management;
people who can,
refuse to be
housed there

Skill-driven economy:
people never enter or fall
out of the labour market

Pressure to house
excluded groups
and those with
housing needs
who are in no
position to refuse
housing

Weak informal controls:
withdrawal of
services; boys
excluded from
school; 'street' peer
pressure builds;
concentration of high
levels of need

'Breakdown':
boys and young men
engage in anti-social behaviour,
lawbreaking, damage

FIGURE 7.1 Cycle of disadvantage in excluded neighbourhoods
Source: adapted from Anne Power 1997

CAPACITY BUILDING IN NEIGHBOURHOODS

Initiatives for tackling the social exclusion of neighbourhoods have to address both the physical fabric and the social fabric of a local area. The *National Strategy for Neighbourhood Renewal* published by the Social Exclusion Unit in 2000 outlined a broad range of approaches and measures to restructure the social capital of many of Britain's most deprived estates. This has been followed by regular appeals from government for all services to pursue community development as part of their practice (DfCSF 2006).

Looking closely at such initiatives you will see how the many threads of social exclusion, discussed in earlier chapters, are being tackled simultaneously. The only way to lift a neighbourhood out of exclusion is to address community safety, educational attainment, local economic development and health inequalities at the same time. For good reason in the US such strategies are called 'comprehensive community initiatives' (Kubisch and Stone 2001).

Many of the approaches discussed in earlier chapters can be integrated into a broader plan for community development. For example, practitioners may contribute to a community safety plan by working with young offenders, or work closely with a children's centre to promote parents' ability to stimulate development in their young children. One helpful distinction is that between community-based services and community level services. *Community-based* services are services made accessible by locating their delivery in a particular locality – for example a benefits office for handling council tax benefit, a parent's support group in the youth centre on an estate or a young carers group meeting locally. *Community level* services aim to impact on the entire neighbourhood, for example reducing the level of truancy in a given area or reducing the rate of anti-social behaviour. The Sure Start local programmes, established in over 500 of the most disadvantaged neighbourhoods in Britain in the early 2000s sought to do both at once: offer particular services to individual parents in the locality and to educate *and* improve approaches to parenting of under fives across the entire area.

The common thread that runs through all neighbourhood work is 'community building' or as it is now more frequently called, 'capacity building'. Capacity building means helping a local area develop and strengthen its own organisations, increasing levels of resident participation and engagement, developing local leaders – all with the purpose of strengthening the neighbourhood to take control of its own affairs. Capacity enables local residents and organisations to engage in consultation, planning and implementation of regeneration objectives. It includes training, personal development, mentoring and peer support, based on the principles of empowerment and equality provided they ultimately benefit the neighbourhood (Skinner 2005). If capacity building can be reduced to one phrase it would be 'learning to acquire and to use power and influence to secure certain democratically determined objectives'.

Examples of capacity building initiatives include:

- Development of community vision and action plans.
- Negotiating a written service agreement between the locality and the agencies involved.
- Ensuring community representatives chair and take up a majority of places on partnership boards and other forums.
- Resident-led consultation including street meetings, door-to-door surveys and local planning events.
- Resourcing and supporting resident involvement in developing new local organisations, such as credit unions, to the point where they manage the project and assets.

Learning needs of local citizens

The kinds of skills and knowledge local citizens need include:

- Institutional knowledge, which provides local citizens with an understanding of how services and political machinery work, together with the opportunities and constraints.
- Literacy and numeracy skills that provide the platform for more significant roles in decision making and oversight of projects.
- Negotiating skills that enable dialogue with other partners.
- Confidence building, particularly for those in groups unable to engage in earlier participatory initiatives through cultural pressures.
- Conflict and dispute resolution skills in order to manage the dynamics of community organisations (Plummer 2000).

It is important in organisational contexts where certain groups dominate the decision-making processes that other voices be given space to participate in the early stages of capacity building. This can be achieved through the development of smaller focus groups with particular goals such as literacy or vocational training which can then feed into the broader community groups when some capacity is built.

CASE STUDY 13: THE CITIZENS ORGANISING FOUNDATION

The Citizen Organising Foundation (COF) is a network of broad-base organisations which runs its own training programme for local activists and leaders. In a week-long series of seminars, discussions and role plays trainees are exposed to the practicalities of mounting a local 'action': from highlighting local issues to identifying and confronting those with the power of redress. The training coincides with a chance to watch a real action in progress: for instance an 'accountability session' when citizens call on their local officials or councillors to agree to particular policy pledges. This provides an opportunity to assess the application of the principles and techniques they have learned in the workshop. But the purpose of the COF training* is also to teach the wider obligations and responsibilities of civic action. Their curriculum has several key learning points:

1   Knowing how to clarify the difference between public and private roles for an individual, and how to conduct yourself and meet your responsibilities with regard to the former, not mixing or confusing the two.
2   Learning to respond to public officials by developing the skills needed to hold your ground in a meeting or negotiating session.
3   The nature of power – that power is both unilateral (that is directive, compelling and coercive) and relational (built up through association, building consensus and finding common interests and motivations among diverse groups of individuals and organisations).
4   The skills and conduct for successful 'relational organising' which is built on listening and engagement with residents in small formats such as one-to-one sessions or small house meetings.
5   Applying pressure: how to build countervailing power locally to help in the bargaining with city officials and politicians.
6   The nature and conduct of negotiation – learning to balance conciliation with the application of pressure. (COF 2008; Chambers 2004)

---

*   President Barack Obama undertook very similar training in the 1980s. His curriculum was devised by the Industrial Areas Foundation in the US, to which the COF is closely related in approach.

CASE STUDY 14: CAPACITY BUILDING – ROYDS COMMUNITY ASSOCIATION

The Royds Community Association is a prominent example of local citizens developing immense capacity and strategic range within what started out as a small organisation. It was set up in 1993 to regenerate three local authority housing estates in south-west Bradford. Its aim was to build self-sustaining communities with residents centrally involved both in identifying their future needs and in achieving them. The original group included several residents, a person from the private sector and a local authority housing officer. They spent three years doing their research and preparing plans and proposals before a major bid for urban regeneration funding was made. Now the Royds Board has 22 directors, including 12 elected locally. Most of its committees and groups are chaired by local people and assets are controlled by residents.

As an indication of how its prowess is viewed the Association is deemed the accountable body for central government monies rather than, as is much more usual, the local authority. Its objectives include major social, economic and physical development. To be sustainable the Association offers extensive capacity-building training and support for local residents allowing the various communities to be involved in its affairs. The association has grown to be a major element in Bradford city council's engagement strategies. Building local capacity and holistic services around housing provision is a community development model that has gained recent credibility. Its activities have continually expanded and now include advice services, a youth action programme, an environmental warden scheme that educates community and youth groups on ecology and neighbourhood clean-up (Royds Community Association 2008).

Credit unions and financial exclusion

Exclusion from access to financial services in deprived neighbourhoods, especially in inner-city areas and peripheral housing estates, is well documented. Local citizens in low income neighbourhoods are vulnerable to expensive forms of credit such as catalogues, hire purchase, local money lenders, store cards and bank or building society overdrafts. Within this context people on excluded housing estates and a low income who are forced to borrow to make ends meet are subject to predatory lending practices and outright intimidation from loan sharks.

Credit unions are one tool for repairing the effects of financial exclusion, particularly for those living on benefits and those with poor credit records, and are now being promoted vigorously by both central and local government. Essentially they are self-help, financial cooperatives owned and controlled by their members. Members are brought together around a 'common bond'[6] – either living in the same area or

6   Government has redrafted the rules for credit unions with effect from 2009 doing away with the notion of a common bond and allowing more diverse groups to come together to form a union.

for members of the same organisation, for example a church. A credit union encourages members to save regularly, thereby creating funds that can be used to provide other members with low-interest loans. When members have been saving for a certain period of time (usually for a minimum of 12 weeks) they can apply for a loan from the pool. Interest on the loan is traditionally charged at only 1 per cent per month on the monthly reducing balance. Until recently however they have not been allowed to pay interest on savers' accounts; this restriction is to be dropped in 2009 allowing unions to compete directly with banks.

CASE STUDY 15: NEW HORIZONS SAVING AND LOAN SCHEME

This credit union is a joint venture between a housing association, Cambridge Housing Society, and Cambridge Building Society. It began work in 1997 among tenants from four residential homes, supported housing projects for teenage parents and adults with learning difficulties together with sheltered housing and a nursery. From the start it adopted an explicit anti-poverty strategy when it discovered that some tenants had been approached by loan sharks looking for interest rates of up to 300 per cent.

At the outset the development worker faced certain obstacles: tenants were dispersed over a large area, there was little tradition of tenant involvement in managing their affairs and numbers were small. Nevertheless the credit union was established after careful research and links with a building society in the city.

What is distinctive about this particular credit union is the repeated survey research it undertakes and its willingness to adjust practice and renegotiate procedures very quickly. In ten years, and now expanded to cover two additional housing associations, it has provided some £80,000 of small loans and has enabled 300 people to open saving accounts with Cambridge Building Society. With this capital members have borrowed money to set up small businesses, buy major household items, computers, go on holiday or spread the cost of their wedding (Randall *et al.* 2005; Let's Talk Money 2007).

Helping a small group set up a credit union is a good example of a neighbourhood-level intervention in which you can assist. A credit union may begin as an informal group of savers with only a handful of members, but the idea can come from anywhere, including yourself in house meetings or working with tenants' groups or clusters of service users. Some guidelines and characteristics are listed below:

- Any credit union needs to define its network and location boundaries. This requires some thought and local knowledge. For most credit unions choosing an agreed area can take six months.
- Raising money and training requires a number of volunteers. The work of most credit unions is carried out by volunteers and calls for considerable levels of skill, particularly in managing organisations and working in teams. While permanent staff are a great resource, often credit unions' backbone are their volunteers.

- Start-up grants are provided but are usually inadequate for the purposes – insurance, registration fees, printing and equipment.
- Finding low-cost office accommodation is often beyond reach so that all materials, books and equipment have to be taken home by volunteers after each session.
- Ideally, permanent secure accommodation is required for an office but also to enable confidential discussion among members.
- Election of a board of directors and constituting a local development committee to take responsibility is a necessity. An elected board of directors and various committees govern day-to-day operation and strategic policy. These are usually made-up from the volunteer work-force; local committees need to comprise of at least six people from the community.

GETTING STARTED IN THE NEIGHBOURHOOD

Practitioners and their agencies have a large role to play in capacity building. There are several steps to take to engage effectively with a specific neighbourhood:

- Think through your role, your agency's role and its relationship with other prospective partners.
- Get to know the neighbourhood.
- Develop goals, objectives and plans in collaboration with a broad section of stakeholders in the neighbourhood.

Thinking through your role

Before beginning any concerted neighbourhood work you will want to resist the temptation to undertake some form of immediate engagement and think through what your objectives are in the work ahead. That temptation is to begin immediately – by making all kinds of contacts and carving a path of your own strewn with suggestions for residents to chew over – and is especially strong if you are new to the work or new to a neighbourhood. It is unlikely however that as part of a larger effort to tackle social exclusion on an estate that you will be given a broad, open-ended brief to do 'community work' without some broad objectives already in place. Such initiatives are always complex projects and often tied into larger neighbourhood renewal or regeneration programmes. These extend over long periods of time so you, your team and your agency will want to discuss what its contribution as part of a long-term strategy will be and how it will be able to sustain the effort. You will need to think through in advance what is possible within your existing role and responsibility and also how those roles and responsibilities might be altered to incorporate explicitly some form of neighbourhood involvement. Are you and your agency really willing to work in partnership and perhaps to let others receive credit for a well-handled project? Will your agency provide funding to local residents' groups even though it means diverting funding from elsewhere? Are you able to merge activities with other service agencies who may be identified as a 'lead body'? How far do you think resident participation and control should go? Are you willing to set aside notions of professional expertise and control to allow residents and their organisations to develop their own projects and approaches although they may diverge from your notion of what ought to happen?

For any particular project a broad brief may already have been formulated by your agency, or by a local partnership board. But the basis of your entry into the neighbourhood still requires explanation and negotiation. You will need to know where you fit within the broad outlines of the project or emerging regeneration plan. Explaining what you see as your role and how it fits with the aspirations of local people will be a distinct challenge. The local priest, Bangladeshi youth leader, activist nun, tough-minded pensioner who heads the local tenants' association, the local councillor, the manager of the local women's centre, the committee raising funds for a mosque will all have influence and all will want to know what you are about.

Getting to know the neighbourhood

It is essential to become familiar with the area. Talking to as many persons and the leaders of local organisations as you can provides the best way of building up a picture of who holds influence and what the effective networks are. This is often described as 'tacit' knowledge – the experiences and understanding of those who have lived in the locality for a long period of time or who have themselves large social networks along which knowledge – of events, people, institutions – pass.

Gathering data

Certain elements of a neighbourhood's exclusion are easier to identify than others. Some, such as poor housing stock or level of unemployment can be tracked quantitatively and shows up in data provided by the local authority or the Office of National Statistics (ONS) – for example on the proportion of households where the head of household is not in work, the proportion of households that are overcrowded or the number of households living in temporary accommodation. There is also the hard data to collect and this task is now much easier than even ten years ago.

ACTIVITY 7.2: CAPTURING RELEVANT DATA

Data on many aspects of community and neighbourhood life is readily available from the ONS. Go to www.statistics.gov.uk, click on 'Neighbourhood' and enter the name of the area, city, neighbourhood or specific streets you are interested in. The full range of data to do with socio-economic status of the area becomes available. Data that previously would have taken months to accumulate is now only a couple of mouse clicks away. Search for data on the neighbourhood or area where you are regularly involved and see whether it confirms your own estimates as to (i) how many adults have a work limiting liability; (ii) how many people are living on benefits; and (iii) the type and number of crimes committed.

Highly local data, focused on only a few streets, is also available. These so-called 'super output areas' (SOAs) bring together a high volume of information provided for small target areas. It may be possible to define your neighbourhood or district precisely by adding together several output areas. SOA data provides multiple data sets on key areas of neighbourhood life, which includes numbers of households with limiting long-term illness and dependent children, number of lone-parent households with dependent children, breakdown of ethnicity, economic activity and gender. To access this information from the Office of National Statistics website practitioners need only a postcode or the name of an area they wish to explore.

Accumulating vital accurate information is useful in subsequent negotiations with other stakeholders, for project proposals and funding applications. It is surprising how fast you can build up your familiarity with the networks in the neighbourhood. Soon you should be able to put together, for example, a rough neighbourhood network map and a list of local organisations with the names of individuals prominent within them.

Community profiling

You may want to gather much more detailed information because you do not want to be caught out using hearsay or surmise in a crucial meeting with prospective funders or in a neighbourhood forum. You will find that gathering and making sense of local facts and figures will strengthen your arguments and make your objectives more useful to local residents, organisations, service managers and funders.

This level of research has to be carefully planned and before you rush into it there are a number of points which you and your team or group should consider. It can:

- be time-consuming to plan and carry out
- absorb a group's attention and divert time and energy from other main tasks
- produce poor-quality information which you find in the end is unusable
- raise expectations that the findings on their own will lead to change.

If you do require more sophisticated information it may be possible to draw on the research skills of a local college or university who would be eager to join a collaborative effort. If you decide to go ahead ask yourself and your team two key questions:

1   What do we want to find out? The more amorphous or general your objectives the greater the chance of not meeting them. Be clear and opt for specified areas of inquiry: for example, finding out the extent of closure of bank branches (leading to financial exclusion) is an easier task than say the extent of 'dumping' of lone parents into run-down housing.
2   How do you intend to use the information? Will you use the information to:
    - Lobby within your own or other service organisations to improve the level of provision?
    - Present to the media or use at a public meeting in order to raise public awareness or support?
    - Develop better relations with neighbourhood residents and activists who

want to move on some issues? (see Henderson and Thomas 2001; Hawtin *et al*. 1994)

Answer such questions as clearly as you can and you will save yourself a lot of wasted effort. What you intend to do with the information is crucial to the form in which you gather it. In drawing up your research plans there are a few rules to remember:

- Try to keep it simple – a lengthy questionnaire will put residents off. It must be easily understood by all who come in contact with it.
- Make sure that information you want can be easily obtained.
- Collect all relevant information, especially that which might run counter to what you expect or want to get out of it.
- Make sure your research methods are sound so that they cannot be easily dismissed. The point is that sooner or later, if the research has any value at all, you will want to use it in negotiations, in advocacy, or to apply pressure whether inside or outside your agency. The information has to be reliable; you can be sure that those with whom you are negotiating will have their own research and will pick up anything that does not support your case. (Hawtin *et al*. 1994)

Social networks

Neighbourhoods have their own system of networks with various capacities, strengths and weaknesses and practitioners should know what these are. 'Informal networks consist of a variety of personal and associational relationships which connect individuals and families in informal but often effective ways' (Gilchrist 1997). They change and expand or contract as they encounter other networks.

Learning to map networks for a neighbourhood is as important in relation to a neighbourhood as for a family or individual. These may be built around formal associations or institutions – a mosque, luncheon club, temple or school – or they may be freestanding. Age, gender and social status are all prime determinants for shaping networks in a neighbourhood.

ENSURING PARTICIPATION

High levels of participation in neighbourhood-based services or projects are essential for several reasons:

- Residents are the major stakeholders of any efforts: there are likely to be already active groups with concerns, knowledge and capacities to undertake sustained effort. They experience local problems at first hand and as a whole and not from the point of view of an agency's set tasks. They know the networks and can reach people that agencies cannot (Taylor 2003).
- If residents feel they own regeneration initiatives they are much more likely to be effective. Youth centres are more likely to be used if local young people have had

a hand in setting them up. After-school clubs will have greater support if parents have been involved. A jobs training programme will have greater take-up among long-term unemployed if prospective trainees have been brought in alongside employers in setting up the scheme.

- But the most powerful reason has to do with capacity building: unless the area itself is able to ultimately generate the knowledge and skills for residents to run a project themselves, the project will not succeed because it will not last. This is the lesson that 30 years of neighbourhood initiatives has taught us (Burns *et al.* 2004). Deprived neighbourhoods often need a multi-pronged approach to participation. It may be that to engage a seriously demoralised neighbourhood, structured consultation lasting several weeks may be necessary to inform properly and motivate local residents and organisations while other neighbourhoods may be ready to engage in higher levels of participation immediately.

Developing a vision together

'Vision' essentially means the long-term outcomes that local people want to see occur in their neighbourhood – the world as it could be. A vision looks ahead to the specific desired changes to the quality of personal and community life. Vision will have a strongly aspirational, even utopian element to it because it is based partly on what people hope will happen. Because of this factor it has a powerful, motivating role. Vision is important because:

- It sets a clear framework in which activities can be planned and evaluated.
- It provides a sense of directions and helps bring people, practitioners and local organisations together.
- It inspires people to be creative and dynamic.

(Barr and Hashagen 2000: 29)

The process of defining a vision can be illuminating. It can expose and then address conflicts among the various stakeholders in a project, identify changes in priorities, stimulate all sides to think and debate in public and to examine whether local residents are actually going to be empowered or not (*ibid.*).

ENGAGING COMMUNITIES

Maintaining high levels of participation by local people throughout the duration of any initiative is difficult. The often technical nature of developing holistic projects to counter social exclusion of a neighbourhood means that local residents face formidable obstacles to their ongoing participation. These include the inevitable influence that professional expertise retains – not just from education or social services but architects, planners and 'experts' from leisure and transport. Paradoxically then, participation strategies often reinforce professional authority. Other barriers will be particular to the locality.

ACTIVITY 7.3   MAPPING LOCAL BARRIERS TO PARTICIPATION

A thorough audit of participation in any initiative or project will reveal not only a great deal about the project with which you are involved but will also tell you a lot about how to maximise participation in other projects. Burns and colleagues have put together a handbook for assessing the degree and effectiveness of participation that is applicable to virtually all projects. There are several main tools for carrying out an audit of participation:

- Baseline mapping exercises.
- Checklists of activities or approaches that contribute to effective community involvement.
- Questions that need to be asked if community involvement is to be effective.
- Scales to help practitioners and stakeholders to think through the quality and extent of the participation activities they are planning.
- A 'decision trail' to track whether particular matters raised by local residents got into the decision-making arena, how these matters were decided upon and by whom, and finally whether or not they were actually implemented.

(Burns *et al.* 2004)

'Planning for Real'

Developing strategies for involving and maintaining high levels of involvement is essential. There are techniques for overcoming this gap and in fact exploiting the differences in perspective and types of expertise. One such is called 'Planning for Real' developed by the Neighbourhood Initiatives Foundation (NIF) and used across the country in a variety of situations.

Its focus is the mutual construction of a 3D model of the locality which provides an initial informal opportunity to involve local people whether school children (especially those aged 7–11), adults or members of a tenants' association. All participants learn something of the history and physical, economic and social development of the area. The pack provided by NIF is on a scale of 1:250; sufficient to allow residents to recognise their own front doors and other landmarks easily. Once the model of the locality is constructed it takes centre stage, giving a bird's-eye view of the neighbourhood. It becomes the common ground and focus for everyone – whether resident or outside expert – to mill around and ponder the future. Its physical centrality has the effect of diminishing confrontation and expression of conflict. Through colour-coded cards participants make suggestions as to what they think ought to happen and they place those cards at the location on the model most associated with that problem. Each card colour represents a different issue area – yellow cards for housing, green cards for the environment, orange cards for crime and safety and so forth. Cards are placed anonymously and no one has to argue for or defend their idea at that point. The only rule is that no one is allowed to move or remove someone else's suggestion cards from the model (NIF 2008).

Soon the model is covered with a range of suggestions. By the end of the event it will be clear to everyone present from the predominance of a particular colour or the accumulation of cards in a particular spot that that is *what* matters most to people and *where* it matters.

This is only the beginning of the 'Planning for Real' process. Small working groups then focus on particular topics such as care services, education or public safety. They collate all the suggestions within their topic, giving each one a priority rating ('now', 'soon' or 'later') with a note as to its location. In this process local knowledge plays an important role, for example in identifying who in the area holds local skills through a survey. This is undertaken by local people starting small – their street or block of flats, perhaps practising on each other first and then moving from house to house. Gradually an action plan for the area emerges: one based on consensus, which is one of the 'Planning for Real' objectives.

ACTIVITY 7.4: WHERE IN THE PROCESS ARE COMMUNITIES INVOLVED? A CHECKLIST

Burns *et al.* (2004) have developed their own ratings scale on which to chart how much influence communities have over particular neighbourhood projects: 9 = lip service – participation amounts to nothing; 8 = consultation around pre-arranged options; 7 = provision of high-quality information; 6 = genuine consultation; 5 = community has formal advisory role; 4 = limited delegation of control over decision making; 3 = substantial delegation of control to community; 2 = community control over all activities within agreed conditions; 1 = community ownership of all assets.

In your team choose a major 'partnership' project in which community participation is emphasised. Using the scale above note the extent of participation in each of the following functions.

- Policy making.
- Strategic planning including budget decisions.
- Commissioning or deciding who gets funded.
- Budgetary control – who has day-to-day responsibility as well as overall accountability.
- Managing staff – including appointment, appraisal and training.
- Identifying objectives and performance indicators.
- Planning individual projects.
- Managing individual projects.

(Burns *et al.* 2004)]

Strengthening neighbourhood leaders

The role of leaders and leadership is crucial to the success of area-based initiatives to overcome social exclusion. One of the major ways of talking to 'the people' is through their leaders. Saul Alinsky, one of the chief architects of community organising in twentieth-century America, argued that you talk to people through their leaders; if you do not know the leaders you are in the same position 'as a person trying to telephone another party without knowing the telephone number. ... Talking with these natural leaders is talking with the people' (Alinsky 1971).

Tensions can arise between a first generation of community leaders, often recruited at speed to legitimise a project bid (and given responsibility but not much power) and a second generation which emerges after a period of local capacity building. Leaders may occupy formal positions – such as the manager of a Bangladeshi resource centre – or they may be informal, such as a member of a youth club among peers, or among a group of Asian women organising their own IT training.

Think of leaders in terms of their constituencies, organisations and the number of people over whom they have influence. Individual capacity is not the only criterion for leadership; others are the social networks and strength of connections that potential leaders have. It might help to think of different kinds of leader:

- Primary leaders are individuals with a large following who have broad vision and a willingness to work hard on themselves to develop leadership skills.
- Secondary leaders have an institutional base of support and an appetite for power but are less broadly focused on the common good.
- Tertiary leaders are issue-specific and task-oriented. All levels of leaders are required for a broad-based organisation to become powerful.

(Jameson 2001)

Decide carefully who you think might be an influential leader given time and preparation. Henderson and Thomas (2001) describe someone who can:

- demonstrate real commitment to the purpose of the organisation or project
- feel confident about taking a leadership role
- show awareness of the need to hold the trust and support of local people or organisation members
- be committed to democratic forms of organisation and to including others.

Leaders need support and training. They have a tough job and often give up large amounts of time and energy for no pay and often little or no power. Expectations of them from the neighbourhood and agency personnel can be huge, however, with blame, accusation and cynicism quickly expressed should they stumble. They need training in civic involvement.

FAITH-BASED WORK IN THE NEIGHBOURHOOD

Faith communities of all kinds – Islamic, Jewish, Sikh, Catholic, Evangelical Protestant, for example – have played an important, if at times ambiguous, role in underpinning the social capital of a neighbourhood. Social work's discomfort in working with such movements and institutions resulted in it keeping its distance from institutions which have strong roots in local communities and a long record of service provision, some of it quite innovatory. This distance arose partly because of social work's secularist orientation and, more recently, a deeper appreciation of how many religious institutions confine the role of women and harbour hostility to gays and lesbians. Against the perceived negatives of a faith-based project must weigh the evident dedication of religious groups to providing some voice, often in the poorest neighbourhoods, and links with some of the most excluded and unwanted individuals. At a time when other institutions no longer maintain a neighbourhood presence churches, mosques, temples and synagogues have maintained their involvement, and they will be there long after the partnership pilot schemes, pilots and projects have all gone. The tenets of faith provide an incredible source of energy – bearing witness, working with the poor and engaging in prophetic action. Other faith-based movements have resulted in huge social and political change in the past: Catholic social doctrine, liberation theology, church action on poverty, Jewish and Islamic dedication to service. Newer ranks to such movements include black majority churches and Pentecostal and independent evangelical institutions. 'Civic life', 'third-way politics' and 'community capacity' do not excite, motivate or agitate people in the same way.

ACTIVITY 7.5:   THE DIFFERENCE BETWEEN A FAITH-BASED PROJECT AND A SECULAR PROJECT – CHRISTIAN VALUES IN YOUTH WORK

A youth club operates from a church basement in the midst of a multi-faith community. The youth worker recognises that the project may cause some tensions. From the church perspective there are a number of boundaries that should not be crossed, for example the youth worker should have a Christian background. Deeply held moral convictions by leading members of the congregation mean that there is often unease about homosexuality. In general the church's standards and the personal moral standards of the youth worker do not match those of local young people. Yet the project is open seven days a week until 11 p.m. and has a full complement of volunteers, some of whom are drawn from outside the church. During its opening hours there is always an adult for young people to talk to if they so wish. What do you think are the main differences between faith-based and secular projects? Would you be willing to enter into a partnership with such a youth project?

FAITH, VALUES AND COMMUNITY WORK
IN AN ISLAMIC CENTRE

The need for a mosque in the area led to the creation of the Centre on the Medina model of combining faith and community work. The model includes a community meeting place, a centre for learning and a place of refuge for those in need. This model provides a natural blueprint for the relationship between faith and community work. The provision of the Centre will therefore be geared to helping people appreciate their own culture and identity and then encouraging work and community life with others. The practical outworking of this is that the Centre will have a community relations forum built into it to begin a dialogue and application on community relations issues. They will also partner with other (non-Muslim) agencies to deliver 'non-spiritual' services that are part of the Centre. The services will be open to all but some will still retain an Islamic value base. The services will also seek to learn from the best practice of different and secular agencies. It will seek to be pluralistic and broad-minded in terms of theology, philosophy and practice. A significant aim will be to educate people and build up identity while counteracting the attitude of superiority and feeling that one group is better than another and will be honest about the positive and negative aspects of Islamic culture. (Shaftesbury Society 2000)

It is also important to recognise that changes in how doctrine is understood are under way, while at the same time there is a growing understanding of the commonly accepted broader principles and practice of community development toward inclusiveness. Faith institutions are increasingly aware of their shortcomings and recognise that they cannot 'do' community development on their own but must work with partners.

ACTIVITY 7.6: WHAT IS YOUR RESPONSE?

Aisa is a community-support worker for an early years project. Her parents came from Bangladesh some 12 years ago. They and Aisa are devout Muslims. Four members of the project are developing a model for 'women-centred practice'. Aisa notices that she has certain disagreements with some aspects of that model but keeps these to herself. At one meeting two of these colleagues begin talking about 'the mosque' in ways that Aisa regards as disrespectful and condescending; in particular, they underscore several times how men run the affairs of the mosque and are quite oppressive.

What should Aisa say at this point? Should she discuss the tone of the meeting with her parents? To whom should she turn for support? Should she begin to think about modifying her devotion?

This exercise requires research and some deep thinking. Work in a small group of three: outline the matters which you think collectively you need to have greater knowledge about and arrive at your answers by consensus.

KEY POINTS

❏   Neighbourhoods are important arenas for tackling social exclusion not because they are naturally endowed with mystical strengths but because exclusion has a spatial dimension.

❏   'Capacity building' requires the patient building up of human and social capital within the neighbourhood, including investing in local people and local leaders. Credit unions are a growing resource for communities experiencing financial exclusion.

❏   Gathering data is critical so that, regardless of the forum in which policy or practice is discussed there is hard information to hand about the extent of exclusion in a particular neighbourhood.

❏   Opening up channels for local participation is essential; initiatives are fruitless without it. Maximising that participation and learning to audit the extent of local involvement in your project are critical tools to use.

❏   Faith-based community development has been long ignored by social work; some more positive understanding at least is required as it is one form in which 'capacity' still survives in poor urban neighbourhoods.

KEY READING

D. Burns, F. Heywood, M. Taylor, P. Wilde and M. Wilson, *Making Community Participation Meaningful: A Handbook for Development and Assessment* (Policy Press, 2004) is an indispensable manual for checking the level of participation by local residents in community projects.

John Pierson, *Going Local: Working in Communities and Neighbourhoods* (Routledge, 2008) develops community practice for social workers in some detail.

Steve Skinner's *Assessing Community Strengths: A Resource Book on Capacity Building* (Community Development Foundation, 2005) is in manual format and full of practical advice on local capacity building.

CHAPTER 8

SOCIAL WORK AND SOCIAL EXCLUSION IN RURAL AREAS

OBJECTIVES

By the end of this chapter you should:

■ Be familiar with different definitions and categories of what is 'rural' and how it contrasts with 'urban'.

■ Recognise the extent of social exclusion in rural and small-town Britain.

■ Understand the particular constraints of organising service systems for dispersed populations in rural areas.

■ Be able to develop service approaches that overcome barriers to inclusion specific to rural areas.

In the early 1900s Britain became an urban nation when, for the first time in global history, more people began living in cities than in the countryside. This was the result of the huge population shifts from the countryside generated by the industrial revolution that had begun in the late eighteenth century. (Population experts think that a majority of the global population for the first time live in cities in 2007.) This chapter discusses the changes that have taken place within the countryside in recent years and how these changes have inhibited recognition of exclusion in the countryside.

Many of the approaches to tackling exclusion in the countryside are the same as outlined in earlier chapters. The aim of this chapter is to alert readers to the distinctive constraints that beset the delivery of services – time, distance, and dispersed populations – and looks at ways that these can be overcome.

Historically, the countryside had been a place of extreme physical exclusion – expulsion, incarceration, loss of rights. Enclosures of common land in England and clearances of crofters in Scottish highlands together with strict anti-poaching laws[7] deprived local populations of resources for raising livestock and grain that once were open to all. Famine combined with rapid industrialisation and the effects of the new Poor Law in the nineteenth century caused widespread forced migration from all parts of the British Isles but particularly from Ireland.

This was exclusion on an epic scale and took place against a backdrop of peasants dependent on common land for survival and indentured farm labourers living in tied cottages while working for chronically low wages. They made a subsistence living only by working their small personal plots of land. Once these were taken away they were often reduced to absolute poverty. Attempts by farm labourers to protest the rise in the price of bread, a key staple for energy, or to forestall wage cuts through unionisation were repressed throughout much of the nineteenth century. The local magistracy representing the established church and landed interests rigorously upheld strict social and legal codes based on the hierarchy of the established order. Anyone who opposed this order was deemed alien to morality and undermining propriety and possession of property.

URBAN AND RURAL CONTRASTS

Contrasts between rural and urban life remained a source of investigation and social thought even as the number of people living in the countryside declined. Given the extent of the social problems that emerged from cities – whether poor sanitation, overcrowded and poorly built housing, unemployment and mass poverty – commentary contrasting urban problems with the timeless nature of rural life became a dominant theme. Ferdinand Tönnies a German sociologist over a hundred years ago captured some of these differences in terms that were dominant in British and American social science and have proved remarkably durable. He argued that in a rural 'community' (*gemeinschaft*) social order is based on multiple social ties. People know each other across different roles – as parents, neighbours, employees, friends or kin. In contrast, urban residents live in 'association' (*gesellchaft*) and know each other only in single, specialised roles either as neighbours or employees, but not both. *Gesellschaft* relations, Tönnies thought, are more calculating and contractual (Tönnies 2001).

Such thinking about rural communities was and remains influential and some generalisations built on it still abound. The countryside is said to be a place of face-to-face communities where the boundary between private and public life is blurred and where individuals live under close scrutiny. 'Village hall' politics is dominated by closed networks that have been in place for years, underpinned by a social structure shaped in an era of landed and agricultural interests where hunting and field sports were

---

7   In the eighteenth century the so-called 'Black Act' rendered many offences against property subject to hanging and Britain for a time had the greatest number of capital crimes in Europe (see Thompson 1977).

prominent and notions of economic growth powerfully influenced by farming practices. Recent stereotypes have also emerged – for example the countryside as lacking
diversity in its ethnic and cultural make-up, or its public services lagging behind in
innovation and outlook.

CHANGING NATURE OF THE COUNTRYSIDE

The countryside is experiencing accelerating change. The boom in productivity in agriculture brought with it a decline in the number of agricultural workers required for
agricultural production – employment in agriculture has declined by some 30 per cent
from the mid 1980s – and at the same time has brought about greater diversity in land
use. The trend of the population at large to view the countryside either as a place for
recreation or as a place of residence from which to commute to work has introduced
new elements into a social mix that had been long dominated by farming.

Along side this the availability of land and premises for industrial parks and small
businesses has further diversified the rural economy. Rural employees are now more
likely to find work in manufacturing (25 per cent), tourism (9 per cent) or retailing (7
per cent), than in agriculture (6 per cent) (DEFRA 2003). Around 73 per cent of jobs in
rural Britain are now in services, compared with 60 per cent in 1981. Rural areas have
thus shared in the general shift to a service-based economy in which the information
and knowledge-based industries play an increasing role (Shucksmith 2000).

Migration *into* rural areas is now significant with some 60,000 people migrating
per year between 1991 and 2002. But this masks other dramatic changes in rural demo-
graphics. The rural population is aging with the number of people aged 65 or over
increasing by some 12 per cent (161,000) in the same ten year period while the number
of people aged 16–29 decreased by 237,000 or 18 per cent. The rates of net loss of
16–19 and 20–24 year olds are especially high for smaller villages and hamlets (*ibid*).

As a consequence the rural economy is diversifying with some of the hallmarks
of growing affluence. On the whole unemployment tends to be lower, car ownership
higher, and housing conditions better than in urban areas. Specific constraints, however,
contribute to extensive social exclusion in the countryside:

- public transportation is limited (75 per cent of rural parishes have no daily bus
  service);
- 40 per cent have no shop or post office (70 per cent have no general store);
- 80 per cent have no general practitioners;
- 50 per cent have no school;
- shortage of affordable housing.

In general it is difficult for young people to find entry-level housing. Rural-based
industrial estates draw their employees not from the locality but from towns and more
distant commuter belts.

Changes in the rural economy and social make up means that it is not uniform in
social characteristics. Greater differences exist among rural areas than between rural
and urban areas. Life in small mining villages, towns of the former textile industry,
small fishing villages now unable to find sufficient fish, hamlets of tied cottages of

farm labourers, small council housing estates of rural district councils constructed 70 or 80 years ago have greater differences than similarities. Nor do those who live there have much in common with those who own second homes, or work 30 miles away in a large city, or who have moved to a village location to get away from urbanised lifestyles. This newly arrived population may in fact hold traditional ideas of what the countryside should look like and be as vociferous as any in opposing changes in land use or approving low cost housing schemes introducing yet another element of social polarisation (Pugh 2003: 72).

EXCLUSION AND DISADVANTAGE IN THE COUNTRYSIDE

Policies to tackle social exclusion, from 1997 on, developed at first within the context of extreme urban disadvantage. Area-based projects such as the New Deal for Communities, Health Action Zones, Sure Start local programmes, community safety and crime reduction partnerships, community cohesion, and neighbourhood renewal were generated by policy action teams essentially responding to the obvious concentration of exclusion in Britain's cities. Factors such as cost effectiveness of programmes, targeting large numbers of the excluded and the hope of delivering on quick, measurable outcomes persuaded government to begin there, and for a time ignore rural areas.

The face of exclusion in rural areas

Disadvantage in rural areas is dispersed in relation to the relative sparseness or remoteness of the population. Unlike major urban centres where those with similar income levels tend to cluster, people facing very different material circumstances live in close proximity. Families on low income may be living next door to owners of a second home, social housing may exist across the street from large owner occupied houses, those who have to take the bus may live near but are distinct from those who have multiple car ownership. As a consequence social exclusion in sparse rural areas can feel like an individual, private matter. In less sparse areas it may form identifiable 'pockets'; some of these fall within the top fifth of the most deprived areas in Britain but are still too small an area to fall within neighbourhood renewal schemes.

Shucksmith has highlighted this distinctive aspect to rural exclusion.

> It is apparent that most poverty and exclusion in rural areas are not concentrated in deprived areas, where area-based regeneration strategies can address their needs in a straightforward way; instead poverty and affluence exist side-by-side in rural areas, making it harder to engage with rural communities using traditional community development approaches. (Shucksmith 2000: 39)

As a phenomenon then social exclusion in the countryside is more difficult to identify. In urban areas exclusion can be collectively experienced by people living in proximity – are more visibly 'people in the same boat' – in a way that it is not in rural areas. As Shucksmith (2003: 39) puts it in rural areas, 'Neighbours often do not share the same experiences and poor rural households have little or no means to join forces in order to campaign for a better future.' Nor are rural communities autonomous, free standing units; their degree of integration into the global economy, stability of the economy and proximity to metropolitan areas all impact on a community's capacity to resolve social problems (Reimer 2006).

There is growing recognition that the countryside has its own patterns of disadvantage, inequality and exclusion that require action as part of a wider strategy for the countryside. A succession of government policy statements from 2000 on urged bringing services closer to local people, through improved accessibility and co-ordination, devolution and decentralisation. The creation of the Countryside Agency[8] in 1999 aimed to improve rural environments and began to reformulate conceptions of rural exclusion in its landmark report Pockets of Deprivation: Rural Initiative (Countryside Agency 2003).

In the wake of this report government pledged a rural dimension in reporting its annual appraisal of progress on tackling exclusion, *Opportunity for All*, and to introduce into its indices of multiple deprivation criteria more applicable to rural settings. Devolution of governmental power in 1998 to the three more rural countries of Britain – Wales, Scotland, and Northern Ireland – also encouraged greater attention to rural affairs on the part of central government. (In terms of land area Scotland is 95 per cent rural and one of the major political parties, the Scottish National Party, has major strength in the countryside ensuring greater visibility in policy development in that country.) Funded research began to inquire into the extent of social exclusion in rural areas – in Scotland, in Northern Ireland and in the upland farming areas of Wales and England where centuries of viable small farming households were suddenly in jeopardy. More specific investigations were also begun looking at the consequences of pit closures on mining villages, the experience of those with HIV and the pressures on lone parents in rural areas (see for example Hughes n.d., and Bennett *et al.* 2000).

The fragmentation of rural services: 'no one is in charge'

From the late 1980s on government has sought to remove itself from providing services and instead to lay responsibility for that provision across partnerships involving both public and community voluntary organisations. This re-orientation has had a profound impact on rural life. Direct services from local authorities once had guaranteed the delivery of uneconomic services to more remote areas. Now local authorities no longer lead in service development or co-ordinate provision in the way that they once did, and instead we find a whole host of agencies involved in rural governance, drawn from the public, private and voluntary sectors. The countryside has been peculiarly vulnerable to the changes in those services. First, the concepts of new public management and the separation of service providers from purchasers, targeting resources at identifiable groups of users most in need and performance measurement all have built into them a bias tilting services toward dense urban settings and leaving rural areas without cover.

8   In 2008 different parts of the Countryside Agency merged into Natural England and the Commission for Rural Communities.

Fire, ambulance, police, and hospitals have been consolidated within wide geographical areas, and are no longer located in identifiable geographical communities. This consolidation has especially affected emergency and out of hours services leaving rural populations feeling more insecure.

Second, creating competitive markets for services has often meant the thinning or withdrawal of all service provision in rural areas. For highly populated urban environments the resulting gaps in services were more easily filled by the voluntary or private sector (to a certain extent). For dispersed rural environments, however, this requires staffing day centres and youth centres, for example, either on a completely voluntary basis or around a part-time salaried post that itself has to rely on a staff of volunteers. And if they are to survive it leaves small, fledgling voluntary and local community organisations applying for grants, stretching their resources in time and knowledge even further.

Third, successive reorganisation of political jurisdictions often means that sustaining existing services, for example youth services or parent support initiatives in rural areas is put on hold or overlooked. The total effect of these three factors has led Shucksmith (2002) to call it a 'nobody-in-charge-world'.

CASE STUDY 16: OUT OF HOURS HEALTH

For decades residents of a small town in a well-off shire county were able to contact a general practitioner from their local practice out of hours – 6pm in the evening to 8am the following morning – by ringing the local surgery and getting the number of the GP on call for that night. About a decade ago that service was replaced by a pool of out of hours GPs not connected with the local practice but available for consultation in the event of an emergency at a local cottage hospital some five miles away. A year ago that service in turn was abruptly suspended and replaced with a telephone consultation with a GP. There is still the possibility of a consultation in the direst emergency but the distance to drive for that is some 25 miles.

ACTIVITY 8.1   WHAT ARE THE BARRIERS?

Assume that parents suspect one of their twin daughters of 10 may have contracted measles, despite having been vaccinated; she has awoken in the middle of the night, is hot and has a red rash on her stomach. Assume further that they live in the area described in the case study above. List the factors that they would need to have in place to make the 25 mile trip for a consultation at 3 a.m.

CASE STUDY 17: HOW TO STAFF A RURAL YOUTH CENTRE

A rural youth centre runs two-hour sessions three evenings a week. The largest of these has some 35 young people between the ages of 10 and 13 attend. It is staffed entirely by volunteers, with all three sessions relying on the same small core of people. By any stretch this core is overworked: when you add in the duties for getting the centre ready for young people and cleaning up afterwards, together with all the paper work expected by the county council relating to the five outcomes of *Every Child Matters*, the never ending filing applications for new grants and completing evaluation forms for funders of grants already made, this core of personnel is putting in a very substantial working week – all unpaid. Ancillary duties such as opening the centre up for the weekly sexual health clinic, the family advice session and breast feeding classes for young mothers only compound the time spent.

   All attempts to find the funding for a part-time worker from Connexions, the young person's advisory service which now runs youth work in the county have thus far come to naught. Even the idea of clustering several rural youth centres and funding a paid youth worker's post to cover all centres through the week has not borne fruit.

Transport is a vital resource and the source of a huge social divide: who has access to what transport and when. Increased mobility through the car has brought benefits for the majority in rural areas but at the same time has reduced the customer base for public transport and has thus created difficulties for those without access to a car. These numbers are considerable: half a million (14 per cent) rural households do not have a car and many people in households which do have a car do not have access to it when they need to travel (DEFRA 2003).

Loss of points for social contact

The withdrawal of services has been matched by the shutting down of informal points of social contact. The wave of closures of primary schools, chapels, public houses, post offices, local constabulary and banks have fused with constricted or closed community hospitals, health clinics and doctors' surgeries. Philips and Shucksmith have noted how changes in the housing market and labour market have particularly affected young people, older people and women who tended to have the fewest options in dealing with these widespread trends. These impediments to inclusion were closely bound up with failings of private and public services, most notably transport, social housing and child care and on friends and family. Migration and the loss of young people, also ruptured informal support networks and left older people socially isolated (Shucksmith 2000).

The extent of social exclusion in rural areas

Social exclusion in rural Britain is characterised by four groups: (i) older people living alone (predominantly widows) and older couples, often relying solely on the state pension – by far the largest single excluded group; (ii) children, especially of lone parents, or of households where no parent is working; (iii) young people who often have to migrate great distances for work or higher education; (iv) low-paid, manual workers' households (rural areas contain a disproportionate number of people in low-wage sectors, notably agriculture and tourism, and in small workplaces).

Collectively they face higher costs than urban counterparts for certain basic necessities such as transportation, food and heating. Distance and remoteness plays an important part in this. For example in the Western Isles in Scotland food takes on average nearly 25 per cent of a household budget over twice the UK national average. Housing and fuel together also costs twice as much. There is heavier reliance on pensions and less inclination among local people to give personal financial information in order to pursue a claim for benefits (Rural Poverty and Inclusion Working Group 2001). Yet the small scale and nature of rural communities makes it difficult to target services or resources at specific social groups.

The power of place

Hill farming (or 'upland' farming) in places like Northumberland, the North Yorkshire Moors, Cumbria, and Dartmoor covers some 18 per cent of English countryside with even greater percentages in Wales and Scotland. The natural beauty of the landscape hides many adverse social and economic trends that have accelerated since 2005 when subsidy arrangements were dramatically altered and geared to acreage and not numbers of sheep. Hill farming has become a rapidly ageing occupation with the average age of farmers now over 60. Many live below the poverty line, earning less than farm labourers and well below the minimum wage. Villages are not only losing their young people but have fewer children in them to lose as they grow up. A preliminary report from the Commission for Rural Communities has noted the extent of 'increased stress, depression, poor health and a sense of isolation' (cited in Hetherington 2009). To draw on an urban metaphor, upland farming is a factory for social exclusion.

ACTIVITY 8.2:   HILL FARMING IN THE SOUTHWEST

A team at Exeter University has looked hard at the financing of hill farming in the southwest of England. Their study concluded that 44 per cent of the total output is in fact subsidised by the European Union's common agricultural policy and is therefore wholly dependent on public funding – yet margins are 'hopelessly in the red' with incomes on average of just over £9,000 per annum. There are those who argue that this extensive subsidy should be put into other rural businesses and that hill farmers should be paid to leave their farms.

Do you think: (a) subsidies should be increased in order to raise standards of living; (b) left as they are; or (c) phased out and hill farmers paid for leaving their farms and finding work elsewhere? What would be the consequences of each option?

CASE STUDY 18: SMALL FAMILY FARMS
IN NORTHERN IRELAND

Small farmers in Northern Ireland face parallel problems where, it is estimated, income from the agricultural sector has fallen by 80 per cent in real terms since 1995 (Heenan 2006). As with upland farming the economic viability of family farming is under threat but it continues because of the commitment to the way of life and the tradition of family land ownership which goes back generations even as their children go elsewhere. In 2004 over 50 per cent of farmers in Northern Ireland were over 55 years old.

In the face of extreme economic disadvantage these farming communities retained the capacity to 'soldier on' and to 'suffer in silence' which they associated with strength of character. Mental health problems were generally kept hidden. Heenan has suggested that rural dwellers have more negative attitudes to mental illness than town dwellers, and among the farmers in County Down she found that mental illness was stigmatised and associated with weakness and shame. As one woman told her, the prevailing attitudes and norms meant there was little acknowledgement or understanding of mental health issues: 'Here it is all bottled up. You have problems but you don't talk about them. You are just expected to get on with it' (Heenan 2006).

In her study Heenan showed that access to health and social care among the farming families of County Down was influenced by economic, geographical, cultural and environmental factors, including the population's prevalent beliefs, expectations, attitudes and personal experiences of health and social care. Distinctive needs had combined with longstanding experiences and attitudes to create particular challenges to those designing and delivering services. Heenan provided compelling evidence that on the one hand needs are greater in those areas where people had farmed on their own for generations, but on the other hand precisely those same areas had lost support services following the centralisation of services and closure of cottage hospitals. Her conclusion is that if service development and access strategies are to be successful, they must be underpinned by a clear understanding of service-users' perspectives and attitudes (Heenan 2006).

SERVICE PROVISION IN RURAL AREAS

Social work in rural areas has generally followed what has been described as 'rural generalism' (Turbett 2006) which tended to reflect what was perceived as the communal elements of smaller towns and villages. Collier (1993: 40 cited in Turbett 2006: 9) wrote 'The generalist invents holistic ways to solve problems through refusal to be bound by disciplines or narrow job specifications. In rural areas such limitations almost always prove counter-productive.' The generalist model tended to harness the virtues of living and working within smaller face-to-face communities, relying on the capacity to cross professional boundaries easily and invoking models of community development models as a means for providing services.

Yet as Turbett has shown the rural generalist and community-oriented practice has found it difficult to survive in the face of powerful trends toward the specialisation and statutory procedural frameworks taking place at national level, though he noted continued efforts of practitioners in Scotland to maintain a community orientation and provide flexible responses to user need (Turbett 2006).

Tackling social exclusion in rural areas will in practice follow many of the same approaches as in urban-based social work. A child in need, a care leaver, a young person not in education, employment or training will have the same compelling case for services as if they were from an urban neighbourhood. But in providing these the practitioner faces a different set of forces that shape that practice.

Linking community development and social care

The exclusion of adult service users can in part be overcome by linking the objectives of social care with those of community development. They are in fact strongly complementary. The requirements for tackling social exclusion – partnerships, local approaches, community engagement and anti-poverty strategies – are also important elements in community and neighbourhood development. The Scottish government, Welsh Assembly and Commission for Rural Communities (CRC) in England have all pushed hard to tackle social exclusion in rural areas through community development (Welsh Assembly 2004; Scottish Executive 2001; CRC 2008.)

As Barr and his colleagues have asserted: 'Methods of community development can help achieve the objectives of progressive community care, whilst engagement with user communities helps community development to realise its vision of inclusiveness' (Barr et al. 2001). A community development framework places social care services and user involvement in a different light. People are motivated to learn, not by the invitation to join a consultation process for existing services but by the desire to solve real problems that beset them and their locality. Learning effective skills and understanding the process of practical action becomes a powerful form of education.

Community development approaches to social care emphasise:

• A focus on disadvantaged people and the redistribution of resources and power. It recognises that users and their carers are disproportionately poor. But the reverse is also true: that in disadvantaged communities there is likely to be large numbers of people with care needs. Moreover given the relationship between ill-health and poverty people are likely to become care users at relatively younger ages than the national average. The link between community care and community development brings a recognition that the needs of particular groups such as older people or people with disability are intimately linked to levels of employment and inadequate services like housing, public transport or education (McLeod and Bywaters 2000; Barr *et al.* 1997).

- A focus on the neighbourhood and communities of interest. Groups of care users may form communities of interest through their common experiences and needs which prompt them to act on a collective basis. Much of community care is based on the premise that users should be able to participate as fully as they are able; the task of community development is to help develop this participation. The principles of 'normalisation' and citizenship cannot be achieved without the active participation of care groups in the planning, provision and consumption of care services (Barr *et al.* 1997: 3).

Social care practitioners need several skills to fuse their work with community development. They need to engage with people in the community in setting aims and objectives. For example, in the setting-up of a carers' support scheme in a neighbourhood by a social worker with older people, consulting the community by advertising and holding a public meeting in the time-honoured way would likely have a poor response. It is more effective for practitioners to identify ways in which they are already in touch with members of the community through home-care service, low-cost day centres,

CASE STUDY 19: THE VILLAGE AGENTS SCHEME IN GLOUCESTERSHIRE

The Village Agents scheme provides support and information to older people in rural areas of Gloucestershire. A lack of available counselling was evident and the Village Agent concept was first identified as a recommendation from the Department for Work and Pension's research on rurality in 2002/03 which confirmed that 83 per cent of respondents in the county would be happy approaching someone they knew and trusted within the community for help.

The scheme, run by Gloucestershire Rural Community Council, operates throughout Gloucestershire covering more than 160 of the most rurally isolated parishes to 'bridge the gap' between the local community and statutory and voluntary organisations; agents provide information (but not advice), promote access to services, and identify unmet needs within their community. Support is provided across a wide range of areas, including health, social care, personal safety, fuel poverty and benefits/pensions. Although help and support are offered to any disadvantaged and isolated people, the agents predominantly work with older people in their seventies and eighties. Village Agents are recruited locally which enables them to connect with, and understand, their local communities. They come from a range of backgrounds (including former Citizens' Advice Bureau employees, counsellors, and some without direct experience or qualifications (adapted from CRC 2008).

lunch clubs or contacts with family and relatives. This allows them to pool useful information, to find articulate spokespeople for their interests and engage in lateral thinking around others' ideas. It also initiates discussion with potential partner services such as health visitors, general practitioners and voluntary agencies.

Living and working in the same place: implications for practice

There are challenges for practitioners who live in the very communities they serve. Face-to-face familiarity and the tracking of people's movements in work and out means that professional roles (of doctors, lawyers, social workers) overlap with face-to-face contacts that occur outside of those roles. This blurs public and private knowledge and communication with service users often holding concrete information on the personal lives of professionals – where they live, phone number, marriage status, their children. As Pugh writes 'Workers who wish to maintain a professional "distance", or some sense of "mystique", may find it difficult because their "otherness" and professional power may visibly be seen not to extend to other aspects of their context' (Pugh 2007: 75).

This lack of anonymity raises issues of privacy and confidentiality – and how they are tackled. Some of the qualities affecting rural social work (lack of anonymity) is based on the assumption of stable, long standing communities where information about individuals passes quickly from person to person. HIV sufferers for example in such a context may be reluctant to seek medical help. But there are considerable variations in types of rural communities – some are stable, others not; even the most stable are prone to movement and reconstitution. For example the postman/woman who knows many people even down to the receipt of particular letters may themselves fall to the rapid changes in postal service. (Of course cities are no longer the place where a person can lose themselves either; extensive surveillance in cities through CCTV and automatic modes for web and email surveillance may well prove more intrusive for urban residents than word of mouth information for rural individuals.)

ACTIVITY 8.3:   BOYS IN YOUR GARDEN

You live in the small town where you run a small, all volunteer youth centre for young people between the ages of 13 and 17. One day you come in from work and you find there is rubbish strewn all around your garden – tell tale signs of empty pop bottles, sweet wrappers, cigarette packs. That night starting at 4 a.m. in the morning you get a series of phone calls with weird put-on voices asking for different individuals accompanied by some fits of laughter. Although most of the callers had their numbers withheld, one or two did not and you are able to identify these numbers as belonging to two of the young people who attend the centre and who you know as living right around the corner.

Would you report these events to the police? Go to the parents of the young people who you knew had made the phone calls? Talk to the young people themselves when you next encountered them? Say or do nothing on the assumption that it was out of character behaviour and was unlikely to happen again? Make a list of the pros and cons of each of these responses to the situation.

CASE STUDY 20 AND ACTIVITY 8.4: CHESTER RURAL CHILDREN'S CENTRE

The Chester Rural Children's Centre, based in a small town some 10 miles from Chester, delivers services over a wide area in mid-Cheshire. Two staff, both female, hold clinics in smaller towns and villages offering guidance on breast feeding and stimulating children's development for parents who drop in. Other staff provide a family café in the same locations where they offer advice and reassurance to young parents concerning a child's tantrums or eating healthy foods. In addition the Centre funds St. John's Ambulance to put on a series of first-aid training sessions, 'Baby Safe', that teach parents of new-born infants, what to do if their infant should have an accident or suffer some other physical emergency.

The centre delivers its programme in small halls and youth centres. The resources to provide the advice session on breast feeding alone are as follows:

- Time required to drive from the centre and back: 1 hour × 2 staff members.
- Expenses claim for car mileage: 18 miles.
- Time staffing the advice session: 2 hours.

The service also relies on local volunteers to open and close the youth centre in which the sessions take place. As manager of this service how many mothers would you want to see attending the advice sessions to justify the resources used?

CASE STUDY 21: TRANSPORT IN COUNTY DOWN

The would-be health service users that Deirdre Heenan talked to mentioned the lack of transport as the chief barrier to practice. She reported that there was only one daily bus service from the study area into the local town. As she wrote,

> This bus was a 'school run' and left at 8.30 am and returned at 3.30 pm, and there was no service during the school holidays in July and August. There were no community transport schemes and no special provision for the rural area. Twenty-two of those interviewed were entitled to a free bus-pass (being over 65 years of age), but only one had applied for the pass; the others simply regarded it as a waste of time. As one said, 'It's a joke when you think about it, a free bus-pass but no bus'. (Heenan 2006: 382)

She concluded that free public transport is meaningless in a rural area where there is scant public transport in the first place. In towns social services would organise bus transport to services; in the country people are expected to organise their own. Services never come to them; 'the onus is always on them to get there'.

CASE STUDY 22: BENEFIT TAKE UP SCHEME IN A RURAL AREA

Powys benefit take up scheme uses workers who are based at home and take referrals there, link with host venues and referral agencies providing office facilities for administrative work or seeing users.

CASE STUDY 23: CAR CLUBS

Lack of access to transport in rural areas is a major cause of social exclusion; public transport services are such that car ownership is often a necessity. For reasons of age, disability or financial hardship, a significant minority of people cannot use a car and suffer socially and economically as a result. The government's rural white paper and a Social Exclusion Unit (SEU) report both recommended ways of improving transport in rural areas (DEFRA 2003; SEU 2003).

Car clubs provide a community with access to a group of cars as a shared facility, with low overheads for each club member. The Rural Transport Partnership (RTP), funded by the Countryside Agency, ran a programme of pilot car clubs in rural areas of England and Wales called the Rural Car Club. An evaluation showed the Club to be successful in a number of different ways. Another scheme, Kickstart Norfolk, has helped people in disadvantaged areas to access job and training opportunities by lending out mopeds.

Several factors have been identified as helping rural car clubs develop, including: the presence of a local champion; the existence of some public transport to ensure that private car ownership is not essential; residents' perceptions of congestion problems; the popularity of 'green' lifestyle choices; a mixed-income community; and effective partnerships between local organisations. Factors which may act as a barrier include: the length of time it can take to set up a car club; the up-front costs for potential members; finding people to run the club; organising vehicle pick-up and return in remote areas; and insurance restrictions on who can drive.

Forming partnerships in rural areas

Working in rural areas, especially if full time, can be an isolating experience. Recognising that this applies to all service practitioners, workers need to take a more proactive stance in articulating a need for a particular service development, promoting partnerships for specific initiatives. If not quite likely the rural dimension will go by default as pressing claims – both political through the service hierarchy and from service users and perhaps local media – will force attention back to urban-based problems.

In large geographical areas with dispersed populations supervision and peer contact may be patchy. It is likely that there will be few or no co-workers on hand and line management may well be miles away. Specialist knowledge will be hard won – based on what the worker has accumulated on their own.

Ellis (2002) explains how social exclusion happens as a matter of course in engaging rural communities. She notes that the mechanisms for participation and involvement will assume:

- the definition of 'community' by the development agencies assumes levels of social capital that are not necessarily there
- the displacement of existing organisations and community groups by the mobilisation and enrolment of individuals.

Her research suggests policy making has been naive in assuming that bottom-up rural development will necessarily lead to more extensive local participation. Rather her study shows that even bottom-up development will be controlled and shaped by external gatekeepers, and will almost in spite of itself serve the needs and interests of the more powerful sections of the rural population – unless practice becomes sensitive to processes of exclusion and power relations in rural society.

Accessibility and delivery of service over distance

The brute fact of distance will impact a practitioner's work and own caring responsibilities. Overcoming distance requires time and expense, a cost too high for those on low incomes or with caring responsibilities. That there is an inverse relation between the distance users have to travel to access a service and utilisation of that service (referred to as the 'distance decay' of usage) has been widely observed. Heenan (2006) cites research in Northern Ireland, noting that distance was the single most important factor on attendance at hospital accident and emergency departments, while access to 'out-of-hours' doctors demonstrated that increasing distance from the health centre reduced the likelihood of using the service. There are clear parallels with social care.

To overcome problems of distance and less dense populations the Commission for Rural Communities has suggested piggybacking one or more services on other delivery systems. Developing community transport, utilising different local community buildings and venues in which to provide services, deploying mobile information and communication technology are at the core of their suggestions. All of these are means of delivering information, advice, services and can be combined with information and communication technology points to connect residents with support organisations and wider learning opportunities.

WORKING WITH EXCLUDED GROUPS IN THE COUNTRYSIDE

Difficulties facing young people in rural areas

Although as noted above a practitioner living and working in a small rural setting may feel more personally exposed than urban counterparts it is important to remember that sections of the population as well as service users may well feel the same sense of exposure. The older teenagers who spoke to Glendinning *et al.* (2008) about their social lives, family and social networks, and their community, noted both as close-knit and caring and as intrusive and controlling. Surprisingly it was evident that community links were important to young people's sense of wellbeing but getting the balance right between intrusiveness and support and attachment was difficult. This is particularly true of young women and people who often lack a social and geographical space where they can associate and identify as their own. Young people are highly visible in their communities, and subject to adult scrutiny and in many cases disapproval, viewed as a problem rather than as contributory members of their communities.

Dealing with this scrutiny is not easy. Marginalisation also arises from being denied one's own space for social interaction, not because of physical distance and lack of transport but as a result of power-laden interactions with peers and adults within the village. 'For rural youth, marginality is in part founded upon adult surveillance and regulation of activities and spaces within the countryside' (Leyshon 2003: 236 cited in Shucksmith 2004).

Gender is a key dimension affecting young people's feelings about their communities with significant implications for wellbeing, and out-migration. Stereotypes still abound:

> Young men drinking in village pubs gained affirmation of their rural identity from peers and older males through adopting an exclusive, hierarchical, homophobic and sexist discourse which serves to marginalise young women and other young men whose identity as 'rural' is thereby called into question. (Shucksmith 2004: 3).

In the transition to adulthood and particularly in finding a place in the labour market further difficult choices await young people in rural areas. They tend to become integrated into one of 'two quite separate labour markets – the national (distant, well-paid, with career opportunities) and the local (poorly paid, insecure, unrewarding and with fewer prospects)' (Shucksmith 2000: 26). Social class and education are two major determinants – as they are in urban Britain – that give some young people access to national job opportunities. Significantly for those whose lack of educational credentials confine them to local labour markets, further education and training are much less available than for their counterparts in towns, and their life-chances correspondingly reduced (Shucksmith 2000: 4).

A range factors associated with rural school systems further hobble work to tackle the social exclusion of young people:

- insufficient resources to recruit and retain specialist staff around important resources such as special educational needs (SEN), English as an additional language and pastoral support;

- • a lack of alternative provision for excluded pupils owing to travelling distances;
- • a lack of employer engagement and inconsistent or patchy provision across institutions of the 14–19 Diploma programme;
- • insufficient availability of apprenticeships and an almost complete lack of GCSE evening classes outside major towns, making it impossible for poor rural households to gain or improve their qualifications once they have left school (Association of Teachers and Lecturers 2008).

The development of youth services provides a good example of the impact of 'partnership marginalisation' and the shrinking role of the local authority in service provision. In the mid 1970s, shire county youth federations offered widespread funding for local youth services in rural and urban areas. There was in place a system of training volunteers at local colleges who could gain entry level qualifications for youth work as well as opportunities for observation and mentoring at other youth clubs. To assist smaller clubs a roster of staff was available to underpin the work at local clubs.

These once robust federations are a pale shadow of their former selves employing far fewer staff who are confined largely to supplying training, a trend that has only accelerated after the youth service was subsumed with Connexions the youth advisory organisation. The activities of extended schools means that schools too are competing to host activities in order to show how their facilities are used by the community and after hours. In rural schools young people's friendship groups may be distributed over wide catchment areas and may be further undermined at sixth form as the choice to attend a sixth form college becomes available. The means of transport for young people rests wholly on parents' driving, or on a patchy bus service. Understandably young people are eager to learn to drive themselves and to acquire their own vehicle. Driving competence becomes an essential skill since 'bridging' contacts that enable young people to move to higher or further education or the job market are built on their own resources and not least on the capacity to drive.

But driving also brings into play a serious risk: safety and survival on the road. The combination of young drivers and a network of minor roads and lanes have lethal consequences for the careless, the aggressive and the innocent. There is a telling statistic from one of the more affluent shire counties: in Chester district in 2003 (before it was moved into the new Cheshire West unitary authority in 2009) 60 per cent of road accidents involved drivers and passengers who were either killed or seriously injured – whereas the national average was some 20 per cent (Office of National Statistics 2009).

Working with lone parents in rural areas

The number of lone parents in rural areas is rising though still more prevalent in urban areas. Hughes (2004) notes how the term 'lone parent' in fact skews perceptions of their parenting and ignores the range of supports and resources, both material and emotional, which they can draw on from their social networks. She argues that a significant proportion of lone parents are far from alone, that by leaving unsatisfactory relationships, they actually receive more opportunities and a greater level of support and help than they had when they were part of a couple.

The 2001 census showed that some 300,000 lone parents with dependent children lived in rural districts – nearly 5 per cent of all rural households not much less than

SECURING FUNDING FOR RURAL YOUTH PROJECTS

Obtaining a secure source of funding is vital to the success of any community youth programme. Emily Bain (2002) notes that the rural youth projects she reviewed were more likely to succeed if they had considered the following:

- Convincing would-be funders that the project did not present extra risks.
- Able to obtain longer term funding by planning to work around financial constraints and by employing permanent staff, which improved the quality of the projects.
- Emphasise to funders that rural communities without financial resources, physical facilities or trained professionals would require a greater initial investment and incur additional maintenance costs to address the needs of young people.
- Rural youth projects had to be able to work creatively around time-limited grants, and the need to apply for future funding, while attempting to run ongoing programmes.
- Projects allow time for trust and rapport to be established, particularly services dealing with sensitive issues.
- Projects focus on an issue that rural young people themselves identified as important. Resources can be wasted if young people are not involved in the design, construction and operation of a programme.
- An internal evaluation system necessary to demonstrate the value and achievements of any project. However, evaluation systems need to be designed to focus on project achievements rather than numbers of young people involved due to the smaller numbers of young people in rural communities.

the 6.4 per cent for the UK as a whole (Hughes 2004). This represented a significant increase over the previous ten years and for many rural areas a doubling. Rural lone parents are more likely to have become so through marriage breakdown (as opposed to breakdown of non-married partnership or never partnered); more likely to experience geographical relocation; more likely to receive maintenance for children from former partners.

Earlier research had highlighted lower levels of labour market participation among rural women, in general stemming from a lack of expectation of obtaining secure employment as well as giving priority to a domestic and caring role. There were reasons for this choice: jobs in rural areas are low wage and insecure with no sick pay or paid leave. It is also more difficult to find employers who are prepared to work around school hours – they remain 'unenlightened' about work–life balance. The likely work would be administrative positions and clerical jobs, such as school secretaries, receptionists and office clerks, and personal service work such as care assistants in nursing homes, learning support workers, teaching assistants and carers for adults and children with learning disabilities.

The dilemmas facing lone parents and the social workers about taking on work are similar to those discussed in Chapter 4 but compounded by some of the limits of the rural labour market. Hughes noted that there is little correlation between age of children and number of children on the decision to take on paid work but the ill health of children had a profound effect on the decision of lone parents. In the rural areas she studied she found that day-care centres would not take disabled children since care for the disabled child is more expensive: it is labour intensive and expertise difficult to find. In general those without educational qualifications were less likely to be in work than those with a qualification by a ratio of 2 to 1. In supporting low incomes mothers saw the working tax credit as a major boost since child maintenance is disregarded (Hughes 2004).

KEY POINTS

❑   The countryside is changing rapidly as agriculture loses it dominant position, young people leave and a more affluent middle class moves in.

❑   Social exclusion affects a large proportion of those living in rural areas but it is more dispersed and less readily 'visible'. Many of the government's programmes for tackling social exclusion were intended for disadvantaged urban areas and were field tested there. They have not transferred to rural areas easily.

❑   The national trend towards separating purchasers of services from the providers, and towards delivering services through broad partnerships involving public and voluntary sector agencies have had the effect of thinning out services to rural areas. Statutory services which once underpinned a guarantee of provision have withdrawn from rural areas.

❑   The plight of hill farming families, lone parents, young people and older people in rural areas is multi-dimensional with certain costs – for transport and food in particular – weighing on the budgets of those on low income.

KEY READING

R. Pugh, *Social Work in Rural Areas* (Russell House Publishing, 2000). The standard, and only, text on social work in the UK countryside.

M. Shucksmith, *Exclusive Countryside? Social Inclusion and Regeneation in Rural Britain* (Joseph Rowntree Foundation, 2000). Gives a thorough account of the extent of social exclusion in the countryside.

D. Francis, and P. Henderson, *Working with Rural Communities* (BASW, 1992). Povides a community development perspective with insight.

CHAPTER 9

RACISM AND SOCIAL EXCLUSION

OBJECTIVES

At the end of this chapter, you should be able to:

▪ Identify the various exclusionary effects that racism causes in the UK.

▪ Understand the concept of institutional racism and the implications it has for social work practice.

▪ Recognise the various ways in which practitioners can combat racism within social work practice, such as anti-bias work with children and young people.

▪ See the links between racism and asylum seekers and how practitioners can develop a practice to advance community cohesion.

This chapter sets out to highlight the inflammatory role that racism plays in underpinning the social exclusion of different ethnic groups in Britain and looks at ways that its damage can be overcome in practice.

Social exclusion, as used generically by government, has been criticised as 'colour blind' since it often ignores ethnic difference (Parekh 2000: 82). Yet ethnic difference is a powerful determinant of exclusion and racism, the mass intimidation of a people based on their skin colour, even more so. Racism is not singular but plural. 'There are', writes Tariq Modood, 'colour or phenotype racisms but there are also cultural racisms which build on "colour" a set of antagonistic or demeaning stereotypes based on allied or real cultural traits' (Modood 2007: 44–5). Islamophobia for example is as much about 'race' as it is about faith.

Racist concepts and the hate movements founded on them have provided fuel for the mass intimidation of, and violence against, designated groups of people such as asylum seekers, Roma travellers, immigrants and refugees. The civil disturbances in northern cities such as Oldham and Bradford in 2001 were in the main conducted along ethnic lines fuelled by white antagonism to perceived injustices as well as by the gulf of separation between different communities. The British National Party electoral success in 2008 in Stoke-on-Trent, based as it was on resentment to new arrivals in the city, is another strong indicator that racism and its coded accessories are still a powerful influence. Racism remains the agent of intolerance.

UNDERSTANDING 'RACE AND RACISM'

'Race' is a bogus concept, nineteenth-century in origin, deployed to suggest a sense of inherent physical and cognitive superiority and inferiority among different peoples. It is a purely social construct without biological foundation which is why most writers now use the term in inverted commas. The paradox lies in the fact that on the basis of this false concept there are nevertheless groups and individuals who use it to justify overt discrimination, prejudice, violence and hate crimes. In short, there is racism though 'race' does not exist.

Disadvantage and social exclusion dominate many minority ethnic communities and racism has a good deal to do with this. Minority ethnic communities are more likely than the rest of the population to:

- Live in poor areas and in poor housing: 56 per cent of those from minority ethnic communities live in the 44 most deprived local authorities in the country; two-thirds live concentrated in four conurbations – London, West Midlands, Greater Manchester and West Yorkshire. Over two-fifths of Bangladeshi and Black African households were overcrowded in 2001, seven times the rate of overcrowded white British households (Sellick 2004). Forty three per cent of Muslim children in Britain live in overcrowded households, of these some 56 per cent of Bangladeshi children live in overcrowded households (*ibid.*).
- Be unemployed. In 2004 Pakistani women had the highest rate of unemployment of any social group in Britain – 20 per cent – while women from Black African and mixed ethnic groups had unemployment rates of 12 per cent, three times the rate for white British women. Men from black Caribbean, black African, and Bangladeshi households had unemployment rates of 14 per cent, three times that of white British men (at 5 per cent). In 2004 a third of all Muslim children lived in households where no adult is working (Sellick 2004).
- Live on low incomes: over 40 per cent of African Caribbean and Indian people live in households living on less than half the average national income compared with 28 per cent of all people nationally.
- Be excluded from school. The number of pupils permanently excluded from schools has fallen, from roughly twelve and half thousand in 1996/97 to just over

DEFINING 'RACE' AND RACISM

Race is a biological and cultural construct to classify one group of people from another, using such criteria as skin colour, language or customary behaviour. It is also used to denote status and lineage (Burke and Harrison 2001: 282). Racial and ethnic categories vary over time in meaning and importance. Generally they imply a distinction between 'whites' and other minorities of colour (Bobo 1998: 7).

Racism: 'consists of conduct or words or practices which disadvantage or advantage people because of their colour, culture, or ethnic origin. In its more subtle form it is as damaging as in its overt form' (Macpherson 1999: 20).

'Whiteness' – refers to white people's favoured position in the social order relative to other racial groups. It describes the automatic, unmerited advantages and benefits conferred upon ownership of white skin by society. It does not mean that every white person is materially or otherwise more advantaged than black or Asian people (from Lawrence 2001).

nine thousand in 2005/06. However, throughout this period a larger proportion of Black Caribbean and White and Black Caribbean pupils has been consistently excluded than White British pupils. (Parsons 2008).

INSTITUTIONAL RACISM

The concept of institutional racism was advanced in the Macpherson Report (Macpherson 1999) into the death of a young black man, Stephen Lawrence. It denotes the built-in tendency of services, especially the police, to not see the racialised dimensions of their own practice. It also reinforces a key pillar of exclusion by building a wall of suspicion and distance between a service essential for a sense of community safety – the police – and local residents. The focus of institutional racism is on the ways in which services and practices produce discriminatory results intentionally or unintentionally, and one of the great strengths of the Macpherson Report was that it required examination of the unintended consequences of the activity of public institutions and service agencies, and provides a new set of instruments with which to monitor and oppose racist activity of all kinds. The report defined a racist incident, for example, as 'any incident which is perceived to be racist by the victim or any other person' (Macpherson 1999: 328). (Much of the criticism of the report centred on this subjective definition of what a racist incident is, which, its critics said, meant that an allegation of racism was its own proof because in the view of the victim it had happened.) Further, it made clear that all local government and relevant agencies and not just the police should adopt this standard. The subsequent Race Relations Amendment Act of 2000 did indeed make this standard mandatory for all public agencies to uphold.

DEFINITIONS OF INSTITUTIONAL RACISM

The collective failure of an organisation to provide an appropriate and professional service to people because of their colour, culture, or ethnic origin. It can be seen or detected in processes, attitudes and behaviour which amount to discrimination through unwitting prejudice, ignorance, thoughtlessness and racist stereotyping which disadvantage minority ethnic people (Macpherson 1999: para 6.34).

Institutional racism refers to characteristics of formal political, economic and organisation structures that generate racialised but nevertheless widely legitimised outcomes – outcomes that cannot be traced to obvious racial biases in the practices themselves or to acts of individual racism by staff or officials in these institutions. 'Nevertheless these institutions maintain cultures and practices that, in the end, disregard the particular needs of disadvantaged racial groups or facilitate unequal outcomes for different racial groups' (Lawrence 2001: 45).

The report also made a sustained attempt to see overturned the unwitting prejudice and thoughtless deployment of racist stereotypes embedded in the norms and values by which police officers defined their roles and the legitimacy of their activities. As Lea (2000) observes, the Report saw prejudice as something into which individuals are socialised. It is not the kind of contact between predominately white police and black people that is the issue 'but rather the *lack of other contact outside that relationship*' (Lea 2000: 222; emphasis in the original).

Social work and institutional racism

Social work has long sought to overcome exclusion based on racism and to its great credit had tackled institutional racism well before the Macpherson Report. It was also among the very first professions to focus on racism as a means of exclusion and to make anti-racism central to its practice. From the late 1980s on the old Central Council for Education and Training in Social Work (CCETSW) explicitly brought in a black perspective to its deliberations and worked out a set of competencies for anti-racist practice (CCETSW 1991). Sometimes these policies caused unease because of the Council's categorical and top-down approach (Penketh 2001). More important was the new thinking within social work in which 'race' was not viewed as 'essentialist', that is innately embodying fixed qualities whether positive or negative, and more as a product of social relationships (Stone and Butler 2000).

The clear acknowledgement is that racism in public agencies is only eradicated through specific co-ordinated action within the agencies themselves and through social institutions at large – particularly schools from pre-primary school upwards. Social work has much to contribute here through its involvement in early years work; anti-racism is foremost a matter of heart and mind and it begins in the early years (see below).

RACE RELATIONS (AMENDMENT) ACT 2000

The Race Relations (Amendment) Act 2000 embedded the major concepts of the Macpherson Report by amending the Race Relations Act 1976 in two major ways:

- It extended the public's protection against racial discrimination by public authorities.
- It placed a new, enforceable, positive duty on public authorities not to engage in racial discrimination in any of its practices. This lays on each authority the urgent task of examining their practice to ensure that the forms of institutional and unwitting racism, as much as the intentional racism of individual officers, are eliminated from their practice. While the act applies formally only to public authorities it is also clearly intended to apply to private and voluntary organisations and other bodies such as multi-agency partnerships.

COMMUNITY COHESION

The concept of community cohesion provides the other main prong for setting antiracist strategy and practice. The conflict that occurred largely along ethnic divisions in several northern cities in the early 2000s shook both central and local government. They seemed to prefigure a Britain that was built on segregation and violent discord between south Asian communities, the police and some white communities. The sources of conflict as identified in the official inquiries that followed (Cantle 2001; Ousley 2001) stemmed from the consequences of communities living in isolation from one another. These investigations highlighted what they considered to be strong evidence of the extent of social exclusion arising from segregation of ethnic communities through separate housing, the lack of common leisure, recreational, sporting and cultural activities and schools dominated by a single culture or faith. In this context policies for promoting community cohesion were rapidly assembled but proved remarkably durable. The National Action Plan on Social Inclusion defined community cohesion as a central aspect of its wider social inclusion agenda, suggesting that areas most at risk of community tensions are also those with high levels of social exclusion (Department of Work and Pensions 2005).

The policies that followed sought a wider sense of inclusion by reinforcing ideas of common citizenship, diversifying schools which by design or default were based on a single culture or faith, and developing integrated housing schemes and institute programmes to promote contact between faiths and ethnic groups. Whether such policies can achieve these objectives rests on the assumption that common principles and shared values can ultimately be found in a multi-ethnic and multi-faith society. Yet in diverse communities this is by no means certain and trying to prescribe certain outcomes no matter how desirable may have unintended consequences. As Madeleine Bunting has written:

> A comfortable multicultural society is … made on the street, in the school – in the myriads of relationships of friends, neighbours and colleagues. That's where new patterns of accommodation to bridge cultural differences are forged; that's where minds change, prejudices shift and alienation is eased. (Bunting 2006).

Such bridges cannot be constructed through central government insisting that it be so.

Community cohesion policies have attempted to deal with both elements of communal segregation: both trying to diminish spatial segregation – or what Briggs calls 'cure' strategies – and at the same time trying to soften the negative impact of segregation on social outcomes – what Briggs calls 'mitigate' strategies – without trying to change patterns of geographical residence (Briggs 2004).

Pursuing cohesion has significantly changed the orientation of the government's anti-racist strategies and to some extent have overshadowed the more radical perspectives of the Macpherson Report (Worley 2005). While continuing to promote respect for all cultures it now places greater weight on social integration and shared values playing down both racism and economic deprivation as potent elements in community discourses (Worley 2005; McGhee 2003). The strong commitments to tackling institutional racism embodied in the Race Relations (Amendment) Act of 2000 have been downgraded.

The perceived dangers of segregation overlap with divisions between faith communities that are themselves entwined with ethnic and class divisions. Ted Cantle, author of the key report on the disturbances in 2001, has described these as 'layers of separation' – around language, education, use of leisure time, housing, lifestyle and familial and social structure (Cantle 2008). Awareness of how profound these divisions are has reawakened debate about the viability of multi-culturalism. Multi-cultural definitions of citizenship, formed in the 1980s and 1990s and particularly embraced by the social work profession acknowledged that different groups have different values, interests and needs and should enjoy rights of 'recognition' and respect. While there were problems with this approach, namely that it often ignored differences *within* particular cultures and overlooked the fluidity of boundaries between ethnic groups including White British, it nevertheless provided a framework of separate cultural rights as part of a larger mosaic of cultures. Now, in the wake of concepts of community cohesion members of ethnic minorities (remembering of course that in many urban areas they are majorities) are facing a narrower definition of citizenship and being asked to adopt a set of shared national values.

The intention of such policies is to build inclusive communities where people feel confident not only that they belong but that they can mix and interact with others, particularly people from different racial backgrounds or people from different faiths. But the difficulty is that a prescribed notion of 'shared national values' may derive largely from a received idea of 'national heritage' formed at a time before Britain became a place of cultural diversity. In practice this could be highly constricting and antagonistic to cultures, particularly those associated with faith, that have distinct views on say raising children and the place of religion in public life. To require all citizens to sign up to 'non-negotiable' value statements is not in the spirit of open, plural citizenship. A national identity, argues Tariq Modood emerges from that debate and cannot be reduced to a list (Modood 2007). 'In this way', he writes, 'racism and other forms of stigmatised identities can be challenged and supplanted by a positive politics of mutual respect and inclusion' (*ibid.*).

Recent investigations have discovered that in practice most people think that cohesion does not require total unanimity on values and social priorities but is founded on a balance between expressing difference and unity within specific localities. They also found that local people who thought of a locality as belonging to them in particular were more likely to blame new arrivals for problems that already existed while those that thought a locality belonged to everyone were more receptive to new arrivals (Hickman *et al.* 2008).

In Northern Ireland there is a difference between 'single identity' and 'cross-identity' approaches to community relations. Each is appropriate depending on objectives. Single identity approaches help individuals develop deeper understanding of culture and identity and self-awareness of a particular group *before* engaging in dialogue and exchanges with members of other groups. It is a useful approach particularly when there exists a wider atmosphere of antagonism, or when there are risks to cross-community approaches or when the sense of identity may be relatively weak within particular groups (Kelly and Philpott 2003). An example in England is the 'Healing History' project in Mansfield, a predominantly white working-class town in the Midlands, that examined the once strong working-class culture that formed around the mining industry and the contemporary impact of that culture on attitudes towards race and minority ethnic groups after the mines had all closed (Cantle 2008: 203). On the other hand, such approaches may only encourage stereotyped views of one's own culture, creating 'better informed bigots' when the overriding aim should be to encourage greater critical self-awareness of culture and to enable individuals to understand what is positive and what is problematic in their beliefs and values. It should build in steps to enable members of a group to recognise how and why identities are formed, to understand the notion of multiple identities and to recognise both similarities and differences with others (Kelly and Philpott 2003: 37).

Another useful distinction is between 'associational' and 'everyday' forms of cross-cultural networks. Associational networks are formed through relationships based on organisations and provide a strong element binding local civic and commercial life together, particularly between religious communities. Everyday networks on the other hand do not require organisations but are founded on individual relationships and are more prominent in rural areas. Varshney (2002, cited in Cantle 2008: 190) in his explanation of this distinction argues that associational networks provide a 'sturdier bulwark of peace'. In the conflict between Hindu and Muslim communities that he investigated Varshney cited the 'pre-existing local networks of civic engagement between the two communities ... as the single most important proximate cause' of maintenance of peace even in a period of heightened antagonism, by facilitating communication, proving rumours false, and providing information to the local administration. Where such networks are missing 'communal identities led to endemic and ghastly violence' (*ibid.*: 190).

Predominantly the work on community cohesion has been cross-cultural in several different fields, such as twinning schools that are dominated by one culture and encouraging mixed intakes, creating residential areas mixed ethnicity, creating cross-cultural employment opportunities in public sector work and in policing and community safety (Cantle 2008: 206). 'Mono-cultural' schools – often faith based – pose a particular difficulty. They are not intentionally acting as agents of social exclusion or deliberately drawing intakes from segregated residential patterns but rather on what Cantle has called a 'critical mass' model where a given community is clustered in a particular area and sufficiently large to maintain strong cultural institutions but interaction with other groups and cultures nevertheless take place. To be successful school twinning schemes, such as those in Bradford and Oldham (where 50 schools are twinned) need to be buttressed by joint teaching programmes and shared extra-curricular activities, especially ones involving cross-community parental links (Cantle 2008: 221)

ANTI-RACIST PRACTICE

Anti-bias approaches in work with children and young people

Racism can have a profound effect on the later development of children through loss of self-esteem, faltering self-belief and inhibiting a positive view of the child's own origins. For these basic reasons developing programmes to counter prejudice and bias in children provides a key component in an agency's efforts to tackle exclusion among children.

Bias has been defined as an attitude, belief or feeling that results in and helps to justify unfair treatment of an individual or group (Save the Children 2000a). As a term it implies less structure and intensity than its cousins such as racism or homophobia and is probably the more appropriate word to describe the sort of prejudice found among young children. In their study of mostly white primary schools Troyna and Hatcher found that white children deployed a variety of discourses when it came to discussing race. They observed that 'Many children display inconsistent and contradictory repertoires of attitudes, containing both elements of racially egalitarian ideologies and elements of racist ideologies' (1992: 197).

ACTIVITY 9.1: DID YOU HEAR WHAT SHE SAID?

A white mother is riding with her white three year old daughter on the upper deck of a bus in central London. Suddenly the daughter turns to her mother and says in a loud voice, 'Mummy, I don't like black people. Do you?'

Write down what you imagine might be the range of responses from that mother and how effective each would be. What would your response be?

Young children will begin to show bias against children different to themselves from as early as two unless they have accurate and positive information. They are certainly aware of differences of gender and ethnicity and begin to develop their self-identity and attitude towards others from that age. If we ignore their questions or pretend that differences do not exist or fail to provide sufficient sources models for diversity we simply allow this bias to take root (Save the Children 2000a; Siraj-Blatchford 1994).

The differences they observe in others – physical impairment or difficulty in communication, difficult behaviour, a learning disability, different cultural background, ethnicity or race – can become the focus of distancing, annoyance and ostracism. They will also absorb how their parents, friends, their friends' parents and local society view and value (or not) other children and adults who may be black, disabled, boy or girl.

ACTIVITY 9.2: WHEN DO CHILDREN START TO LEARN ABOUT DIFFERENCE?

If you work with young children or if you liaise with a children's centre or pre-school discuss with a colleague at what age you think young children start to learn about:

- gender and what being a 'boy' or 'girl' means
- noticing and applying names of colour to skin colour
- the differences between genders and how 'boys' and 'girls' might be different
- physical disabilities
- learning disabilities.

At what age do you think they begin to attach positive or negative values to the above? Think back to when you were a child of comparable age. How do the children's values compare with yours then? And now?

(adapted from Save the Children 2000a: 19)

As a social worker you may be working directly with young children in care settings or responsible for advising or otherwise participating in creating positive atmospheres for children in their early years, perhaps with a family centre or family support worker. Either way knowing something about approaches to correcting bias is important. Two ways of doing this have been tried and tested: the home corner and story telling.

The home corner

Home corners or real-life play areas are special places where children can play out different roles they have seen in the adult world around them. They both explore those roles in relation to themselves and others their age and help make sense of the world they live in. Using the home corner idea:

- Think about how you could change it so that it reflects the communities the children live in, or others that they might one day live in.

- Decide with children what the home corner should look like, perhaps after looking at some pictures, a walk around the community itself or visits to other neighbourhoods that are different.
- Create a more diverse community by using specific props to build different work-places, with different kinds of tools and implements so that a diversity of gender and culture (for example in cooking) and physical abilities is represented. The aim should be to avoid a narrow definition of the typical. To do this simply ask yourself what the home corner would look like from different points of view: girl, boy, person with disability, ethnic, religious or racial group, travellers?

Stories

Stories offer many opportunities to examine bias and create a broad positive aware-ness of the many different kinds of people there are and how they may see things in a way that is new. There are many options from story books which promote this vision in addition to making up scenarios, skits or story books with children. The many ways of doing this are considered in several key publications mentioned at the end of this chapter. (For more on the home corner and stories see Save the Children 2000a.)

Identity project on 'myself'

This approach, based in an early years care and education centre run by a local education authority, began when staff in the nursery noted a number of pre-schoolers who were struggling with or were unaware of their cultural and racial backgrounds. Essentially the work with parents and children is based on concepts of identity. Children, parents, carers and key workers at the nursery are involved in completing a series of activi-ties that explore the ethnic origins and religion of the children and their parents. The exercise is carried out in the form of regular activity sheets prepared in advance and sent home together with requisite materials for completing them. Where parents had difficulty with reading or comprehension they were able to complete the activity with the help of nursery staff (Sawyerr 1999).

Whiteness and young white people

Failing to understand 'whiteness' has been one of social work's great omissions in practice.

There was a tendency to treat with suspicion claims for recognition by young white people, even those from the disenfranchised poor white youth of excluded urban enclaves and to view such claims as a source of exclusion of black and Asian residents. Little was done to explore white ethnicity among young people; in part because of this anti-racist approaches ignored the needs and perspectives of white working-class students. In the words of the Burnage Report (MacDonald 1991) into the murder of Ahmed Iqbal Ullah in Manchester, the anti-racist initiatives of the time regarded white youth as 'cultureless, wandering spirits' (cited in Nayak 1999:

THE SPECTRE OF WHITENESS

My involvement with radical politics on the left, had taught me to disavow the racial exclusivity of white ethnicity, but never to analyse or try and understand it ... The problem with intellectually disowning English ethnicity was that the left never got around to work out what it was ... (Rutherford 1997 in Nayak 2003).

178). Ironically, the racism of white working-class youth brings that class scant social advantage. It breeds ever-deeper engagement in psychic conflict and in what young white male racists see as identity-confirming violence. They do not see, however, that every act of violence further cements in place the one-dimensional view of would-be employers that they are a violent, disreputable underclass that should not be let anywhere near the job market.

There has been a lack of anti-racist initiatives responding to young, white working-class people who, as Nayak (2003) explains, can be agitated and insecure in what their own racial grouping ought to signify, or indeed what Englishness might mean. In the perspective of these earlier anti-racist initiatives whiteness is linked with racist energy but not with the social insecurities of white youth.

Nayak concludes that these descriptions of anti-racist practice suggest that the young white people he interviewed perceive them as a largely proscriptive, often negative set of values with the feeling emerging that white ethnicity was being unfairly regulated. This sense of unfairness he regards as a major obstacle to anti-racist initiatives because it functions as 'a screen which filters out the possibility of some whites fully understanding the meaning of racial harassment, and generates an almost impermeable defensiveness' (Hewitt 1996 cited in Nayak 2003).

Nayak suggests that a more positive strategy for engaging with white ethnicity is required. He found projects around local white identities, drawing on life-history and family-history accounts to be particularly effective. Settings where young people could explore and then tell their family stories, share personal biographies or trace their ethnic and social class lineage provided a way of deconstructing whiteness. Tracing their family past was a means of personalising history, making it relevant to their life experiences to date. Once this is under way, the solidity of the 'Englishness' of the Geordie white youth gives way to a broader, more inclusive sense of national origins and ethnicity (Nayak 2003). Racist groups are hate groups so another line of engagement is to work with young people around the notion of 'hate', exploring with a group particular topics:

- How hate groups function and how they use vandalism to intimidate whole areas.
- How specific laws, such as those prohibiting harassment and trespassing, can be used to forestall the activities of hate groups.
- The reasons people join hate groups, such as having low self-esteem.

A wide ranging survey conducted in 2005 found that a significant minority of young people with different backgrounds expressed dislike of specific groups such as refugees and asylum seekers, Muslims, Asians and white English. The influences that shaped these attitudes largely stemmed from friends and family, events and circumstances within the locality and the media reporting on local, national and international events. This multiplicity of influences produced inconsistent, contradictory perceptions of other groups (Lemos 2005).

Lemos found in his review of projects designed to further tolerance among and between different ethnic groups that a significant minority of young people harboured

---

DISCUSSING RACE WITH WHITE YOUTHS ON TYNESIDE

In his discussions with white Geordie young people Anoop Nayak first hears some standard complaints about positive discrimination ...

Nicola: And there's these dolls that you're not allowed to 'ave.
Sam: Gollywogs.
Nicola: Aye. And on the news now [it says] every child has gotta have a black doll.
Anoop [the interviewer]: Hold on, are you saying that every child by law has got to have a black doll?
Nicola: Yeah, so they grow to accept black people.
Sam: Y'kna how they've started making black Sindys and that, and Barbies?
James: And black Action Man.
Michelle: Aye, black Action Man!

(from Nayak 2003)

But as the conversation develops the young people show they are aware of the complexities of ethnicity ...

Danielle: Mine parents were born in Germany, cos me nanna used to travel o'er abroad.
Brett: I used to have Italian grandad.
Alan: Me next name's O'Maley and that isn't English.
Nicola: I tell yer I'm English, but I'm part German. My grandad came over as a prisoner of war, he was working over at Belsey Park and my grandma was teaching.
James: Some white people have got black people in their family. Like say my aunty married a black person and had babies.
Michelle: I've got one in my family.
Sam: I'm a quarter Irish, a quarter Scottish, a quarter English and a quarter Italian.

(from Nayak 2003: 162–3)

dislike of other ethnic groups. Boys were more likely to express 'dislike' of other ethnic groups than girls and there was evidence that young people in multi-cultural areas were more likely than others to hold negative views (Lemos 2005). Refugees and asylum-seekers were prominent among the 'disliked' groups, with some young people believing they received preferential treatment or posed a security threat. He found that misunderstandings, confusion and outright false myths were common among young people about other ethnic groups. When he probed where this mix of ideas came from he found that they came from their own experiences but these had been framed by the views of family, friends and the media.

YOUNG PEOPLE EXPLAIN IN WRITING

Below is some of the written testimony that Lemos gathered from young people when he put to them the question – Which groups do you dislike and why? Their responses revealed their confusions and myths regarding other ethnic groups (original spellings and punctuation are retained):

'the eraceys and asuman binlanden – because of September 11 and war' (signed: 'I am white and taned', male).

'Bin laden folloners, Zidane Husain – because they are causing death and making weapons for no reason' ('White quarter scotish 3/4 English', male).

'Pakies – because they are going to war and killed lots of people' ('White and British', female).

'Terrorists from Irak and Pakistan – because they experiment different weapons of mass distrucksion and hate our way of life.'

'Muzlims, Indians, pakistans Iraquies – Because they have there own country and they try to sneak in our country (theres to many)' ('ENGLISH! White' male).

'Pakistanis, Muslims, Indians, Iraquis – because they do nothing at all for our country and get free housing, food and they have there own country ('English [white] christian', male).

'I am not that keen on idians because they give you evil looks, they look at you in a horrible way' ('Black come from England', female).

'I am not that keen on pakistanies – Because they are vishious.'

(all from Lemos 2005).

One of Lemos's most important conclusions is that young people had a poor sense of their own identity but a strong grasp of the different ethnic groups in their town. In his review of five different community projects to forge links between groups he noted that the success of these projects was based on: (i) having well-defined objectives, (ii)a clear structure, (iii) a sustained programme of varied activities, and (iv) an emphasis on learning through 'doing' and 'experiencing', rather than just listening and talking.

SHOW RACISM THE RED CARD: SCOTLAND

Show Racism the Red Card is an anti-racist charity, begun in the northeast in 1996, and now with a presence in all Scotland, Wales and England. Its produces educational resources, particularly films, that draw on professional footballers to put across the message that racism is destructive. Stadium events where young people interact with the players is their signature, giving those young people a chance to talk with their role models.

In Scotland – where there has been a steady increase in reported racist incidents – Show Racism the Red Card holds an action fortnight every October involving all 42 professional clubs as well as other grassroots organisations. It also puts on educational workshops combined with football training sessions specifically aimed at acquainting young people with the issues around asylum. Called 'Coaching with a Conscience: A Safe Place' it is delivered by a footballer and includes a screening of a film raising awareness, distribution of football posters and magazines and concludes with a football skills training session (Show Racism the Red Card).

REFUGEES AND ASYLUM SEEKERS

Refugees, asylum seekers and new arrivals from eastern Europe and Africa are among the most excluded groups in Britain. They often face similar experiences to that of ethnic minorities – dislocation, powerlessness and discrimination – while having fewer support systems to call on. Tension between new arrivals and the settled community is sometimes reported by local newspapers in ways that are often xenophobic and tacitly racist such as those that announced the arrival of Polish and Romanian workers in the early years of the twenty-first century.

There are of course major reasons behind the movement of vast numbers of people from poor countries to developed nations, including impoverishment, climatic destruction and civil violence. The impression that refugees, clandestine immigrants and asylum seekers can be easily sorted out among the genuinely persecuted and those looking for work, is erroneous. Whatever their 'category', great numbers of people are prepared to take enormous risks and their movement continues. The concept of 'forced migration' captures the mix of severe economic pressures, civil war, warlord and gang activity, and abrupt climate change such as desertification that drives global migration.

DEFINITION OF REFUGEES

The United Nations Convention 1951 defines refugees as those who have to flee their home 'owing to a well-founded fear of being persecuted for reasons of race, religion, nationality, membership of a particular social group or political opinion'. Asylum seekers are defined as people who have had to flee their homes and cross an internationally recognised border in search of a place of refuge and safety. The Organisation of African Unity (OAU) have improved these definitions – acknowledging the complexity of racial, ethnic and economic factors, in particular inter-communal violence, cross-border raids and intimidation. The OAU definition reads: 'Refugees include people compelled to leave their home countries by "external aggression or domination" or by events seriously undermining public order' (Rutter 1994: 5).

Long-term development facilitated by trade, intergovernmental assistance and debt relief is one answer but in the meantime many countries, both developed and developing[9] have had to put in place policies that attempt to manage the problem in response to what it sees as a strong public current that it is dangerous to attempt to reverse. The world of globalisation, multi-national institutions and mass migration is bewildering for many people who are anxious about losing their sense of place; they feel abandoned by their own leaders. As in Britain and across the developed world nativist political movements and far-right agitational groups are seeking to capitalise on this confusion.

To relieve pressure, ostensibly on social housing in London and areas around the ports, the National Asylum Support Service (NASS) was introduced in April 2000 as part of the Home Office, to replace the asylum teams from local authority social services departments. The change meant that resettlement policy was decided nationally with specific towns, such as Stoke-on-Trent, designated as places where new arrivals would be dispersed. There is legitimate debate about the extent that racism plays in the reaction of these settled communities to the arrival of newcomer groups and concerns about how local services – particularly housing and schools – can cope particularly when disadvantaged communities are already dealing with serious pressures on resources.

For 'persons subject to immigration control', Section 115 of the Immigration and Asylum Act 1999 removes entitlement to means-tested benefits such as income support, income-based jobseeker's allowance, housing benefit and council tax benefit, as well as a range of family and disability benefits such as child benefit and disability living allowance. Some exemptions are allowed, however, such as asylum seekers who claimed asylum on arrival before 3 April 2000. Importantly for social workers, provision of family support under Section 17 of the Children Act is not available to a dependent child and members of the child's asylum-seeking family

---

9   The majority of large-scale movements of refugees take place within the developing world.

where adequate accommodation or essential living needs are being provided under the Act's support system. From 2007, all new applicants have had a named 'case owner' who will be responsible for dealing with all aspects of their case from initial interview to final integration or removal. To bolster public confidence the application process is subject to tighter timescales and more rigorous reporting of decisions taken at each stage.

Barriers to social housing for new arrivals

Exclusionary barriers begin with housing which refugees and other new arrivals find difficult to obtain: lack of awareness of housing options, difficulty completing forms and providing supporting documentation, wanting to be placed in areas which are already oversubscribed, lack of networks and word-of-mouth contacts on which information of local services and support depends all contribute.

The Immigration and Asylum Act 1999 can place social workers, social care managers and social care officers in the midst of some uncomfortable dilemmas. As Steve Cohen has indicated the system of immigration control is underpinned by compulsion of those individuals who are unwanted here. This coercive element is part of a total system which includes policing (and economic policing through tying welfare provision to immigration status). Housing, education, social services and health services are all part of the control apparatus, compounded by social workers general ignorance of immigration law (Hayes and Humphries 2004).

Since providing services through the National Assistance Act 1948 or the NHS and Community Care Act 1990 is dependent on immigration status, this requires practitioners to investigate the immigration status of a person asking for a service contrary to their professional code of ethics. There is also tension between asylum law and the Children Act 1989. That act stipulates that the child's welfare is paramount in decisions affecting children, yet this principle does not automatically apply to children in immigration-linked cases. Nevertheless the Home Office in making decisions regarding children of parents whose immigration status is in doubt, is obliged 'to consider' the matter of the child's welfare when deciding to expel children or parents. As Cohen (2001) reminds us, it is imperative for social workers to write welfare reports that address each of the points in the checklist of the child's welfare contained in the Children Act in cases of deportation.

Children as unaccompanied child asylum seekers

In 2003 the United Nations estimated that world wide there were some 17 million refugees, asylum seekers and people displaced within their own country. Of these 43 per cent, some 7 million, were children. Only a tiny proportion of these – just over 3,000 – made a claim for refugee status or asylum in the UK in 2003 (Kohli 2007: 9), predominantly from Somalia, Afghanistan, Iraq and Serbia. While few were granted formal refugee status a large proportion were granted leave to remain on humanitarian grounds. In 2003, some 12,500 refugee children were deemed 'children in need' by local authorities or 6 per cent of all children in need. Of these some 2,400 were looked after by local authorities (DfES 2003, cited by Kohli 2007: 10–11).

Of these some 10 per cent were able to live independently with cash payments from local authority social service departments through Section 17 of the Children Act while the others were fostered (70 per cent) or accommodated in children's homes or hostels (20 per cent; *ibid.*: 12).

ACTIVITY 9.3: SOCIAL WORK AND THE UNACCOMPANIED CHILD

Bahri is 15 years old and is an unaccompanied refugee from Kosovo. His social worker gave him a travel card to go between his foster placement and his school – a journey involving a train and two buses. When his first foster placement broke down he had been offered a place at another school closer to where his new foster parents lived. This he declined and his school agreed that he should continue to attend there even though it acknowledged that he was unsettled in his behaviour. One day Bahri had a fight with a local boy who tore up his travel card. As a result Bahri had to walk home which took him three hours. The next day he took a skewer to school and used it to threaten the boy who tore up his card. He was immediately suspended from school. Bahri said: 'He is the one who is to blame because he committed a terrible act on me [and] I was defending myself' (adapted from Kohli 2007: 140).

As Bahri's social worker what would your first tasks be? How would you talk to Bahri about the incident? Would you seek to move Bahri to another school? Would you seek to change the school's understanding of how to respond to Bahri? Would you bring in other resources or services to support or discipline Bahri?

THE CHILD AS REFUGEE: THE UN SPEAKS

Article 221 of the UN Convention on the Rights of the Child (1989):

'A child who is seeking refugee status or who is considered a refugee ... shall, whether unaccompanied or accompanied by his or her parents or by another person, receive appropriate protection and humanitarian assistance ... including help to trace the parents or other members of the family ... in order to obtain information necessary for unification.'

Promoting inclusion with refugees and asylum seekers

The skills needed for effective work to reduce the exclusion experienced by refugees and asylum seekers are those needed in the other realms of this work: communication, assessment, building networks, resource finding, advocacy, mediation, support and counselling. The ecological model has clear implications for practice by getting you to focus on the relationship with family and community with perhaps school or early years centres as crucial institutional sources of support for children. Although obvious in one way Figure 9.1 may help you to visualise how scanty the network of a child refugee actually is.

Kohli (2007) has conceptualised three domains for social work practice. While he has developed these in relation to unaccompanied children seeking asylum in Britain they are useful in mapping the practice terrain for all refugees and asylum seekers.

The first is the *domain of cohesion* in which the primary focus is on the 'here and now', the practicalities of settlement such as providing shelter, care, food, money, schooling, medical support, welfare advice, a support network and ensuring good legal representation in relation to any claim for asylum. Social workers in this domain follow humanitarian efforts of non-governmental organisations (NGOs) abroad, offering material and practical help. Kohli describes them as 'realists, pragmatists' who want 'to deal with the present first, the future next and the past last' (Kohli 2007: 156).

The second is the *domain of connection* which focuses on resettlement of the 'inner world' of the refugee. Here social workers respond to the emotional distress of leaving the country of origin and helping the person connect events, people and feelings that will assist in making sense of them. Kohli's observation of the young people he interviewed applies to many refugees and asylum seekers: while few needed psychiatric or therapeutic services many were 'psychologically dishevelled as a consequence of dislocation and the shredding of roots' (*ibid.*: 156). The social work then is mindful of making connection between past and present and between inner and outer worlds, to free up emotions to cope with resettlement.

The third is the *domain of coherence* in which social workers framed the experiences of asylum seekers within a broader view of how children (and adults we can add) cope with extraordinarily adverse circumstances by making the best use of their own strengths and capabilities. These workers – Kohli dubs them 'the Confederates' – looked for and found resilience, expressed fondness and attachment towards them making 'the line between friendship and professional help less distinct' and in so doing tried to make the young person feel more at home (*ibid.*: 157).

Housing and community links

Housing is a key resource in the resettlement of asylum seekers and refugees. This is an area in which refugee community organisations may already be at work, particularly in London but also in the cities designated as dispersal areas, with social housing landlords and others in setting up and managing accommodation schemes for refugees. These may start out by managing short-life property from local authorities to which they then add systems of social support. The twin objectives of such schemes is to support tenancies and to help resettlement in the local community. In this local colleges

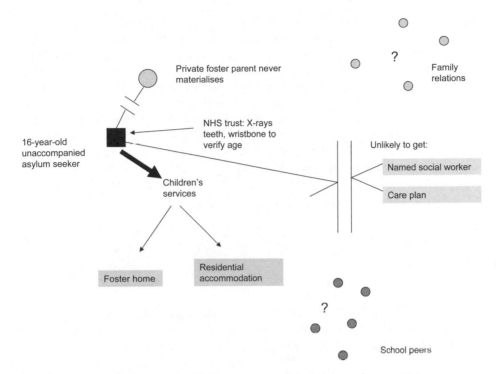

FIGURE 9.1   Thin network of the unaccompanied asylum seeker, age 16

are vital – they provide access to training, education and employment. (In Stoke-on-Trent for example housing requests often focus on the area around the local college.) Placing people in safe areas is paramount. If settlement involves interim housing then resettlement to permanent accommodation should be part of the broader plan. Some housing providers may be reluctant to take refugee tenants unless they know that there is a support package in place; any housing assistance should be tied to helping people negotiate their way around agencies.

CASE STUDY 24: WOLVERHAMPTON ASYLUM AND REFUGEE SERVICES

Wolverhampton Asylum and Refugee Services (WARS) and now known as the Refugee and Migrant Centre, was founded six years ago by two refugees who had arrived in the town and wanted to provide advice and support for those in the same position. With funding from the Barrow Cadbury Trust, WARS has assisted asylum seekers and refugees from 84 different countries. Ninety-five per cent of those in touch with WARS speak almost no English on arrival. Yet astonishingly WARS have been able to interpret up to 90 per cent of the languages spoken by their clients. The most pressing issue for new arrivals is usually to help them negotiate their way through the asylum policy maze – translating official letters and intervening if, for instance, support is suddenly withdrawn due to an unregistered change of address. Refugees that are granted refugee status and indefinite leave to remain need help with sorting out accommodation, validating their qualifications, understanding their benefits entitlement and finding employment.

In 2006, WARS successfully campaigned against a change in the law that meant that only those that immediately lodged a claim within the first few hours of arriving in Britain were eligible for asylum. As founder Arten Llazari says, 'When the need comes through your door – and you are not the only organisation in the country that are noticing it – you realize that kind of campaign becomes a priority' (Barrow Cadbury Trust 2009).

KEY POINTS

❑   A range of data on housing, education and income show that ethnic minorities suffer social exclusion disproportionately to white people. Racism plays a powerful role in the social exclusion of ethnic minorities and of the areas where they live.

❑   The Macpherson Report on the death of Stephen Lawrence brought the concept of 'institutional racism' into the heart of practice – for social workers as well as all public service agencies.

❑   The concept of community cohesion is, to an extent, at variance with the earlier focus on institutional racism in that it problematises cultural and ethnic differences as cohesion policies press for uniformity around standards of citizenship and what it means to be 'British'. On the other hand there are strategies that utilise the concept in order to build bridges between different ethnic communities.

❑   There are a number of approaches that social work can develop in its anti-racist practice:

  ○   in family support services

  ○   against bias in the early years

  ○   around 'whiteness' and understanding ethnicity with young white people

  ○   in community cohesion initiatives.

❑   Refugees and asylum seekers face a highly charged and racialised public context as they enter the UK. Given the legal restrictions they face and the lack of support available to them they constitute the most excluded of all groups. This poses extreme dilemmas for practitioners, who have to choose between two conflicting sets of values.

KEY READING

Ravi K.S. Kohli, *Social Work with Unaccompanied Asylum Seeking Children* (Palgrave Macmillan, 2007). A source of reflection on how social work can support or let down children arriving unaccompanied to this country.

Debra Hayes and Beth Humphries, *Social Work, Immigration and Asylum Debates, Dilemmas and Ethical Issues for Social Work and Social Care Practice* (Jessica Kinglscy Publishers, 2004). Explores the dilemmas facing practitioners at every turn.

Tariq Modood, *Multiculturalism* (Polity Press, 2007). Modood is one of the shrewdest observers of community relations but one who backs his views with analysis.

Ted Cantle, *Community Cohesion: A New Framework for Race and Diversity* (Palgrave Macmillan, 2008). The standard work of the author who effectively developed the concept of community cohesion.

CHAPTER 10

SOCIAL EXCLUSION AND THE LEARNING ORGANISATION

OBJECTIVES

By the end of the chapter you should be able to:

■ Understand the changes in organisational culture and practice required to enable your organisation to attack social exclusion as a core activity.

■ Develop your agency as a learning organisation that gathers knowledge about the impact of programmes and establishes reliable feedback loops.

■ Develop approaches to evaluating complex initiatives.

Tackling social exclusion requires continuous learning for the organisation and refitting itself with new skills. This chapter discusses how the responsive agency, can undertake that learning through effective evaluations of initiatives as part of a strategy to improve practice.

A lengthy academic commentary going well back into the twentieth century portrays bureaucratic and professional cultures as resistant to change. And there is some truth to this broad analysis from which social work organisations are not exempt. While social service agencies have an undoubted commitment to public welfare, a high degree of probity and a value-base dedicated to promoting inclusion, one of their tacit aims is also to defend and control budgets (Pollitt *et al.* 1998). It is wholly understandable why this should be so: their budget is their oxygen and without it the organisation withers and conditions of employment decline.

But protecting budgets sets in motion behaviour within the organisation that is often cautious, defensive and apprehensive of new initiatives, especially if they hint at loss of sector responsibility and are bent on controlling information, releasing only that which will have favourable budgetary impact. This is one of the main factors in bolstering the 'big silos', in which the major services such as health, education, housing, social services and police have over a long period developed separate cultures, values and management styles. Even in an era of collaboration, say within joint working parties, people act as departmental representatives rather than as 'co-colleagues working towards a common picture' (Wilkinson and Applebee 1999: 33). The big silos in effect have bequeathed us a set of structures, professions, skill mixes and job demarcations for a way of understanding social problems that has long since passed (*ibid.*: 34). A negative consequence of the silo culture has been that issues and social problems are largely seen as 'out there' and 'not down to us', or to do with 'economics – which we have no control over' or 'community development which is not our role' (Wilkinson and Applebee 1999).

The distinction between 'strong tools' and 'weak tools' helps clarify what roles practitioners might adopt. The former includes matters such as pooled budgets, budgetary incentives, inspections and sanctions, and whole organisation directives that are more characteristic of large, formal partnerships and will of necessity require senior management engagement. Soft tools however include persuasion, sharing information, training and learning, building networks, evaluation and changing cultures – the very tools that you, your colleagues and middle managers in the organisation can adopt to facilitate anti-exclusionary practice. Building such practice is incremental, moving on from existing approaches and professional relationships step by step in which you:

- build constructive relationships with different institutions such as schools, community groups, children's centres, social housing associations, tenants and residents' association or primary care groups;
- think in terms of 'coalitions' and include other public agencies, community groups, local citizens and motivated professionals;
- factor in joint activity with local participation – whether a survey of local need, setting up a project, writing a report or news release for the local media or evaluating outcomes.

Waiting for top-down initiatives from within or without your organisation could well be counter-productive. Wilkinson and Applebee note that the single greatest danger with the move towards holistic services is a wave of top-down, corporately led initiatives which are complex, time-consuming and slow to get off the ground. Senior managers on their own construct partnerships with an emphasis on managing and planning mechanisms. They write:

Means will become ends. Process improvement will be detached from outcomes and the focus will go internal. The predominating interest will once again be on inputs and top-down indicators of success. In no time we will have an array of indications that purport to measure the effectiveness of partnerships but that are themselves quite disconnected from the real need for partnership on the ground (Wilkinson and Applebee 1999: 15–16)

CHANGING CULTURE IN THE ORGANISATION

Overcoming this sense of distance from the deprivation and isolation of social exclusion as experienced by users and local people in disadvantaged neighbourhoods is an
important step. So too is overcoming some of the limitations of a traditional 'bureau-
profession'. In essence this is accomplished by building up experience through small
initiatives and informal partnerships and in this task accumulating and banking
knowledge through evaluation is an essential step. Discussing impact and the lessons
learned from implementing specific programmes or initiatives within team meetings
and assembling data and evaluative material to reflect on, sets up the 'continuous feedback loop' so prized by theorists of a learning organisation.

The process of continuous knowledge-building is underpinned by a capacity to
understand the role of evidence and evaluation and all practice should be part of a
greater cycle of accumulating evidence and evaluating that evidence to improve that
practice. This is rarely a straightforward process, particularly in the field of initiatives
tackling social exclusion involving multiple resources, multiple partners in delivery
and a long time frame for marshalling these in the field. All the more then is it necessary for a learning organisation to be able to appraise different kinds of evidence and
also to be able to understand how different factors influence decision making and how
they impact what actually happens in the field.

In general social work in the past has been notoriously eclectic in its method-
ologies: counselling and 'brief therapy' techniques with crisis intervention, systems
intervention, family therapy, and task-centred work jostle side by side, leaving the
matter of which 'method' to choose at the discretion of individual practitioners. The
profession has also been casual in its attitudes to evaluating specific approaches –
only task-centred work and cognitive behaviour therapy have had regular and positive
evaluation.

Sheldon and Chilvers make a number of suggestions that agencies can adopt to
enhance respect for information and evidence:

- Staff development systems, including supervision, should regularly draw on
  research to inform decisions about work with users or in projects. Questions
  should be regularly asked: 'so why are we proceeding in this way?' and 'on what
  evidence are you making this decision?'.
- Make a range of support facilities available to assist staff in their efforts to keep
  abreast of relevant research in their field with document supply facilities and
  summaries of evidence available.
- Practitioner attitudes need to include some personal responsibility for searching
  out and drawing on evidence of effectiveness.
- Develop collaborative arrangements between social service agencies and local
  universities and research institutes so that each influences the work of the other
  through joint seminars and work experience, and so that common purposes
  around social exclusion practice are understood and mutually interrogated.

(Sheldon and Chilvers 2001)

Understanding complexity

Tackling social exclusion is difficult and long term – it is after all a product of the entire social and economic environment in which changes do not occur in linear fashion. Small changes in that environment, introduced by an initiative may produce small changes, or very large changes or no changes at all. It is all too easy to look at the social environment for example of a disadvantaged neighbourhood and break it down into a collection of factors – poor housing, anti-social behaviour, under-stimulated young children. So strong is our belief in analysis that we take these to be the reality of that environment and lose sight of the total social system. In this system outcomes are determined by multiple causes and these causes can combine in unpredictable ways either reinforcing (for a large effect) or cancelling themselves out (for a negligible effect) (Byrne 1998).

The difference between 'complicated' and 'complex' is part of the reason we find it difficult to understand how social interventions work. A task may be complicated, that is involve a sequence of many different steps which are intricate and detailed in themselves. Building an airliner is complicated, so too is taking an emergency protection order (EPO) – there are rules, protocols and standards that must be scrupulously followed by law. While they take some time to master *once* they are mastered making the airliner or the taking of an EPO can be done over and over again because the rules stay the same.

Complexity is not like that. It involves multiple potential outcomes including those unforeseen, an ever-changing mix of resources and human inputs, and hidden relationships between circumstances and human agents as they struggle to reverse the many effects of long-standing social disadvantage. Deciding whether to take an emergency protection order or not on a specific child is complex – the actual outcomes of the decision are going to be multiple and not wholly predictable.

So too an initiative to promote the inclusion of a particular group of people into a social environment – for example young people congregating in a park every night; practitioners and indeed local residents may be expecting a defining set of outcomes only to find that they have achieved others.

CASE STUDY 25: COMPLEXITY: WHEN DO BURGLARIES PEAK?

A community safety neighbourhood forum on an estate reported that a number of youths were clustering on particular streets around 7 p.m. in the evening. This seemed to coincide with an increase in burglaries in the area according to residents and the forum appealed for extra policing on the streets and even called for dispersal orders to be issued. It was only sometime later that a record was kept of when burglaries were happening and not just where. Examining the record after two months, the forum revealed that the peak time for burglaries was around 3.30 to 4 p.m. – just after school let out and concentrating police activity in the evening had inadvertently contributed to that.

EVALUATING EFFECTIVELY

Tackling social exclusion draws on large-scale public efforts intended to be participative in process while at the same time committed to producing results. These efforts require the support of a wide range of stakeholders, all of whom need to be kept informed of progress and outcomes and to have evidence that their investment – whether of time and energy or funding – is achieving something. Neighbourhood residents in particular need to know whether the promises and hopes extended by particular initiatives are bearing fruit.

But several factors can make evaluation a contested, even messy process. With many stakeholders in a programme sharp conflicts of interest can emerge. Evidence can be used selectively, deployed for particular purposes and not others. Politicians or local officials will want quick and visible wins, academics will be looking to augmenting their research profiles while agencies will be prone to cherry-pick from the evidence base that best suits their service and defends their turf. Add to this mix the limits of evaluation 'science' and you have in the words of Coote and colleagues: 'not the component parts of a single jigsaw ... but bits from many different puzzles, most of which are incomplete' (Coote *et al.* 2004: 47).

Nevertheless evaluation with all its limits must be a major tool for both practitioners and their organisations as they strive to improve the impact of the work they undertake. Whether it is in the form of 'technical assistance' or in a broader flow of 'knowledge building' some appraisal of work undertaken through a transparent, trusted and widely understood process is the only way to meet this objective (Hughes and Traynor 2000; Kubisch *et al.* 2001). Where conflicting interests and competing philosophies are openly acknowledged.

Rossi *et al.* (1993: 5) assert that evaluation 'is the systematic application of social research procedures for assessing the conceptualisation, design, implementation and utility of social intervention programmes'. Despite the confident ring in this definition there is no one way to evaluate a programme or initiative and all approaches have limitations. Just as it is quite possible to have unrealistically high expectations of what a programme can achieve so it is unrealistic to expect that an evaluation will be able to assess exactly how well a programme has worked and why. Organisational learning is a two way street: it requires evidence that is capable of generating learning as well as the organisational and practitioner capacity to learn from that evidence (Coote *et al.* 2004: 30).

Coote and her colleagues have summarised some of the perplexities that can beset practitioners in using and learning from evidence. One is the difficulty in weighing up the relative merits of different sources and types of knowledge. For example when is practice experience or tacit knowledge a more reliable basis for judgement than published research findings or the opinion of an external evaluator? Another is the form that much evidence takes – both abstract and removed from the day-to-day demands – often means challenging practitioners.

Practitioners tend to give priority to delivering the practical outputs required by a programme and attempt to meet targets and other performance indicators rather than to reflect on longer term broader outcomes and academic research (Coote *et al.* 2004: 33). In numerous interviews Coote and her colleagues found that practitioners needed more guidance on how to use evaluations and evidence and greater consistency across programmes in their approaches to evaluations. Evaluations need to be geared more closely to practice needs with researchers focusing on questions that practitioners need answering rather than, as all too often, practitioners having to comb published evaluations for anything that might be relevant to their work (Coote *et al.* 2004: 35).

The development of evaluation as a tool

Essentially from the late 1960s on evaluations aimed to establish that observed outcomes were caused by or in some way related to the particular programme being evaluated. To do that they needed to estimate what would have happened had the programme not been implemented. To establish this a staple of many evaluations have used 'before and after' estimates drawing on baseline data and then gathering fresh data after a programme has run for a period of time (Hollister 2009). Many of the national evaluations of major government programmes such as Sure Start local programmes, the new deal for lone parents, and the Children's Fund employed this basic approach.

CASE STUDY 26: EVALUATING AN ANTI-SMOKING CAMPAIGN

To evaluate a smoking cessation programme aimed at parents with young children the first step could be to establish the rates of smoking among parents with infants under 12 months before the programme is launched in a particular locality and then to compare these rates with after the programme had been running for say a two year period.

If it is found that a reduction in parent smoking rates had taken place it would at least suggest that the programme had not violated a 2,500 year old cardinal rule of physicians' code of ethics – 'to do no harm'. On the other hand it would not necessarily mean that the programme itself was responsible for the reduction in smoking rates since this could have been caused by other factors. For example running parallel in time the increased general awareness among the public at large about how bad smoking is for health might have contributed to the reduction; the prohibition on smoking in pubs and restaurants could have called attention to the seriousness of secondary smoking.

To do this evaluators constructed comparison groups – that is groups of individuals with characteristics similar to those who were participating in the programme – and to then compare the outcomes for the two groups, those who had been part of the programme and those who had not (Hollister 2009).

As with any evaluation there are difficulties in trying to evaluate the kinds of programmes that tackling social exclusion requires. First, there are many different stakeholders in the form of service agencies' managers and practitioners, local politicians, a range of local organisations and their leaders and residents with different interests and commitments. How do they arrive at agreed standards for evaluation?

Second, initiatives themselves are complex, with large social objectives – bringing about social change – that calls for a range of actions and resources. The effects of such initiatives are often difficult to track. How can you identify which input, resource or activity is responsible for any given outcome? Third, initiatives take place over a much longer time-frame than the usual techniques are accustomed to handling. How can you link with certainty the outcomes in year four of an initiative to resources put in place in year one? There is presumably some relationship but of course other unplanned factors may have influenced outcomes three years later.

There is one further impediment to effective evaluation: the tension between 'process' and 'product' with which every multi-pronged initiative has to grapple. *Process* refers to building participative structures, agreeing the rules of the game for partners and for establishing governance over the initiative, and building trust among collaborating organisations. This takes time, does not easily yield to deadlines and is not easy to pin down or evaluate. *Product* refers to the specific outputs of a programme – the rise in the percentage of care leavers achieving GCSE passes with grades A–C, reduction in teenage pregnancy or the number of young offenders brought successfully through a local final warning scheme. Managers, councillors, funders, and certainly politicians will be more interested in the latter than the former (Kubisch *et al.* 2001). But for local people an excessive emphasis on output or product and neglect of process can be disempowering. Taking the time to establish participatory channels, to build confident working relationships and to equip residents for governance of a project are all part of the 'process' which can be undermined by tight deadlines and constant emphasis on concrete outputs.

Even in basic definitions of evaluation one can see the potential for conflicting views and interests to emerge. Nevertheless any evaluation, including self-evaluation, should undertake four basic functions.

• Audit: did the programme do what it set out to achieve within budget?
• What was the level of satisfaction with the results – such as specific outputs and outcomes?
• Value for money – did the programme have an impact, did it make a difference in changing the set of social conditions it was targeting? Can it be clearly established that the programme was responsible for the changes effected?
• What were the elements of 'best practice' within the programme? Can comparisons be made with programmes elsewhere – or with what would have happened had no programme been introduced in the first place?

Approaches to evaluation: logic models

There are many approaches to evaluation and to gathering information on the effectiveness of programmes. Evaluations differ in many dimensions – for example in intent: is the purpose of an evaluation truly objective or is it a tool for advocacy? Or on its philosophy: is it qualitative or quantitative? Or in its design: is it to be participatory, drawing on users views of how it should be constructed or quasi-experimental?

Necessarily then a broad pragmatism is involved in choosing approaches to evaluation and key decisions need to be made at the outset about what information is to

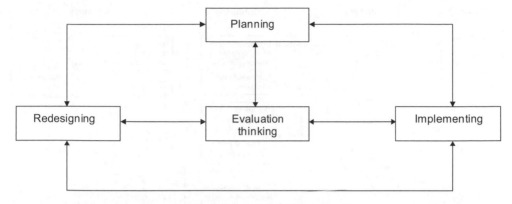

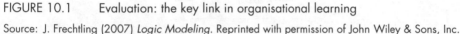

FIGURE 10.1   Evaluation: the key link in organisational learning

Source: J. Frechtling (2007) *Logic Modeling*. Reprinted with permission of John Wiley & Sons, Inc.

be gathered and how that information is to be assessed and interpreted. Moreover evaluation is more than simply answering the question did a programme work or not (a summative evaluation); it should also inform improvement or modification as the project is unfolding (Frechtling 2007).

Experimental design, following models of the natural sciences are difficult to put into practice for the obvious reason that one cannot control the experimental conditions as one can in a research laboratory. In a sense, however, it remains the 'gold standard' and the most sophisticated evaluations of large national programmes, for example of the Children's Fund (see box below), attempt to introduce quantitative evidence that introduces an element of objectivity.

More widely used are logic models of evaluation and in this section we focus on them as a template for evaluation. Logic models are a systematic and visual way of uncovering the relationships between the resources of a programme, the activities that the programme intends to carry out, and the changes or results it expects to achieve (Hollister 2009). The most basic logic model constructs a picture of how a programme is supposed to work. It uses words or pictures or both to describe the sequence of activities thought to bring about change and how these activities are linked to the results the programme is expected to achieve.

Achieving better community development

The ABCD model – Achieving Better Community Development – offers perhaps the more straightforward pathway to sound evaluation. Within this approach Barr and Hashagen (2000) have incorporated many of the techniques required for evaluating projects with multiple outcomes achieved over time and an important role for services in achieving them.

The ABCD model works, as any logic model does, on four variables: inputs, processes, outputs and outcomes. Inputs are the range of resources and tools that are available from within the community or brought in by outside agencies working in support of community development. Such resources move well beyond funding to include:

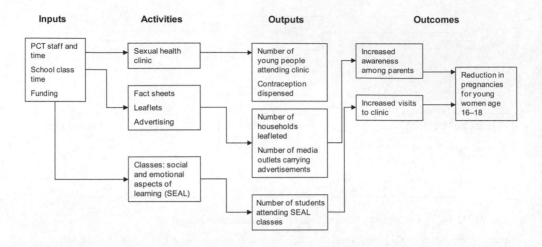

FIGURE 10.2   Logic model for a programme reducing pregnancies in young women, 16–18

- people's time, motivation and energy
- skills, knowledge and understanding
- trust within the neighbourhood
- networks
- leadership.

Stakeholders from outside the community bring resources such as a policy framework, expertise and training, additional funding and co-ordination.

Processes are defined as those actions that need to take place to direct inputs towards specified outcomes. In this framework the central process is one of 'community empowerment' which embraces four components: personal development for individuals, 'positive action' for social justice and social inclusion, community organisation and the effectiveness of community-based groups, and gaining power and influence at local level. This empowerment process can be seen as the way in which inputs are used to develop the ability of the community to achieve change (Barr and Hashagen 2000: 61).

Outputs are the product of community empowerment, the specific actions that relate to economic, social, environmental or political issues of the locality. These outputs may include social service development, a safe and healthy community or increased citizen control over services and political developments.

Outcomes are the consequences of the outputs relating to the improvement in the quality of life of the locality. Evaluation poses critical questions for each stage. What are the inputs to community development activity, and how do they change with the progress of action? How well are the inputs applied to the process of community empowerment? What are the outputs and outcomes? How is empowerment used to influence the quality of community life? (*ibid.*: 62).

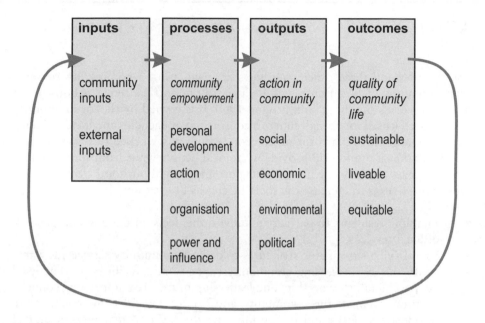

FIGURE 10.3   The ABCD model of evaluation

Source: Barr and Hashagen 2000

To answer such questions some notion of a starting point or baseline has to be established as well as a number of indicators that will provide yardsticks as to what is being achieved. Once a baseline has been established the evaluation task then requires information to be gathered and assessed. Gathering information is the crucial stage requiring advance planning. You need to know what type of information is required, for example whether facts or opinion, and who you want to obtain information from, for example from users, local residents or community representatives. Information can be obtained by:

- Observation, that is having an observer present when key events occur either as a participant–observer or as non-participant.
- Asking questions – through questionnaires, face-to-face interviews, consultations or focus groups. Barr and Hashagen have sound advice as to how to gather information for evaluation:
  - be focused by asking relevant questions about specific activities
  - keep it as simple as possible
  - look for emerging themes by interpreting findings
  - offer choices and options to those you are seeking information from such as ranking the importance of items
  - use innovative techniques such as tapes, photographs, exhibitions, physical representations, diagrams or story telling.

(Barr and Hashagen 2000)

ACTIVITY 10.1: EVALUATING A COMMUNITY RESOURCE CENTRE

Assume you and three other colleagues are evaluating a community resource centre on a low-income housing estate in east London. The centre is housed in a one-storey brick building, built around 1960. It is owned by the local authority but has been leased for a small sum to a consortium of agencies and local residents who have ambitious plans for it. The consortium has worked out a number of objectives that it thinks will provide what local people want from such a centre; it also reflects much of the new thinking around 'neighbourhood renewal'. One set of objectives is to increase the social strengths of the estate by:

- Enabling residents to participate fully in the decision making and delivery of local services.
- Establishing sustainable structures to deliver community services. It wants to do this by increasing community capacity and facilities so that local people can take 'ownership' and leadership of the area, improving communication between the community and service providers to create more responsive services and to develop a neighbourhood management model for those services.

The only member of staff is a part-time caretaker. The resource centre is well used although the activities that take place there do not always seem to further the consortium's objectives. Among the activities that take place within it are the following:

- a luncheon club for older citizens four days a week
- occasional cultural activities for the substantial local Bengali population in the evening
- an after-school club for children up to the age of 14
- a training course in IT skills for women
- a youth club two nights a week
- a venue for local community groups to meet.

With your three colleagues plan a brief evaluation of the centre. Who do you think would be among the principal stakeholders and involved in the evaluation? What and who are the inputs? As far as the set of objectives is concerned what indicators would you look for to measure any progress? What kind of information or data would you need and how would you go about collecting it? How would you present this information to users of the centre and to members of the consortium itself to make it a useful learning tool?

Theory of change

Theory of change is an approach to evaluation that shares many elements of a logic model. It acknowledges the complexity of a multi-pronged, multi-agency programme by pinpointing the specific interventions of a given programme and how they are intended to deliver the long-term outcomes. Essentially the theory of change approach asks certain questions of all participants in a project that tackles exclusion:

*   Why is this project going to work?
*   What are the theories that in your view will make the project effective and achieve the (often complicated) social objectives that the project aspires to over the time span?
*   How will you be able to show the outside world that the project has succeeded?

The phrase 'theory of change' means simply making clear and bringing into the open those theories on which the initiative is basing its plans: what are the concepts behind the programme that will ensure that the various outcomes identified will be reached over the period of time projected? Theory of change evaluation, in common with logic models, asks that projects first establish long-term outcomes and work backwards from these so that intermediate and then early outcomes relate to those long-term objectives.

There are three virtues in the theory of change approach to evaluation. First the evaluator works from the beginning jointly with all stakeholders – local residents, practitioners, managers, councillors – as they shape up the long-term outcomes of any initiative. Second, the very act of doing this helps make explicit what theories are being drawn on to allow stakeholders to have confidence that those outcomes will be reached. Third, the theory of change can blend both process and hard outcomes in framing the first step, that is to say the long-term objectives (Hughes and Traynor 2000). On the other hand critics have said that it can be cumbersome in practice because it strives to factor in all the different stakeholders' points of view as well as the full array of inputs and resources. As an evaluative process then it can take a great deal of time and require skilled facilitation if the theory of change is to work (Coote *et al.* 2004).

Evaluation of the new deal for lone parents

The new deal for lone parents (NDLP), part of the government's general welfare-to-work initiative is a voluntary programme for those lone parents receiving income support and whose youngest child is over five years and three months old. Evaluators of the programme found that, relative to non-participants, the NDLP participants:

*   had more spells in employment
*   had longer spells in employment
*   made less frequent changes in the labour market
*   cycled between benefit and employment states less frequently.

CHILDREN'S FUND NATIONAL EVALUATION

The Children's Fund focused its resources on developing multi-agency partnerships that sought to address the consequences of social exclusion for children between the ages of 5 and 13 right across the country through preventive work in all 149 local authorities in England. It did so by supporting projects that brought schools and parents into closer working relationship. Between 2000 and 2003 it funded after school and breakfast clubs, projects to support pupils in transition to work, improvements in whole-school systems including reduction of school exclusions.

The Fund aimed to reach certain strategic outcomes to:

- expand preventive work and shift the focus in work with children from risk to promoting protective factors and resilience;
- promote partnership in services by pooling budgets and other means in order to prepare the way for children's trusts;
- encourage participation of families in programmes.

A national evaluation of Children's Fund Partnerships was undertaken by the Institute of Education at the University of London, and the University of Birmingham. The first focused on quantitative analysis drawing on the millennium cohort study and national pupil database. The second undertook a qualitative evaluation relying on case studies to provide information as to how Fund partnerships worked at local level. The evaluation found that Fund partnerships accomplished:

- a change in the relationship between families and services;
- reduced both the number of exclusions and the length of time pupils were excluded;
- established the value of intervening before a crisis emerged either within a family or between pupil and school.

Each partnership also conducted its own local evaluation which essentially followed a logic model evaluating the outcomes and impacts the local programmes were intending to deliver. But local evaluations were encouraged not to attempt to evaluate the whole programme but rather to appraise those projects and activities from where the most learning could be gained. Local partnerships were also encouraged to integrate evaluation into the planning of children's services and to construct a timetable over three years that would pinpoint key milestones for decision making.

The evaluators concluded:

> It seems that NDLP participants who did not lose contact with their Personal Adviser had a more straightforward labour market history than those who lost contact with their Personal Adviser. Losing contact with the Personal Adviser was associated with lower employment. (Knight *et al.* 2006)

ACTIVITY 10.2: EVALUATING EVALUATOR'S LANGUAGE

Evaluators of the NDLP explained their results this way: the medium-term impacts on employment and benefit were reasonable in size. After 48 months of participation, the impact of NDLP raised the proportion of parents coming off benefit by about 20 percentage points – 22 percentage points for those with youngest child aged 11 to 16 years and 18 percentage points for those with youngest child aged zero to three years. For those on income support for more than three years and who had been in the programme for 48 months, NDLP raised benefit exit by 26 percentage points while for those on IS for less than three months, this was lower at 16 percentage points.

What does 'benefit exit' mean? Why use the phrase 'after 48 months of participation'? If these are the medium-term impact do you think the short-term impact would be less or more? What do you think would be the long-term impact? Assume there is a steady pool of 100 lone parents in your area and every year 30 came off income support. Assume further that the new deal for lone parents is then introduced into the area and all 100 parents participate. Given the results above how many parents would come off benefits 48 months later?

The practitioner as change agent in the learning organisation

It is tempting to think that you and your colleagues can wait until someone fires the 'time to start tackling social exclusion' gun before taking forward elements of the practice outlined in this book. But that is not a luxury you have. On the contrary your role should be one of catalyst and change agent regardless of your position in the organisation. But to do this you need an understanding of the 'self in the sea of change' to use Gerald Smale's phrase, which is critical to working with the changes in approach, large and small, that tackling social exclusion requires. He frames three important questions that you need to answer, not just about yourself but about your colleagues as well:

1   Are the people you work with active or passive? Will they enthusiastically join, and perhaps lead, innovation or will they resist and have change imposed upon them? Smale reminds us that 'to have the rug pulled out from under you is a very different experience from coming to a decision to reject the old flooring and choose a new carpet' (Smale 1998: 122). In other words imposed or coerced change generates opposition and takes a lot of time to get over.
2   Does the innovation produce a change of identity? The degree of change determines the amount of learning and unlearning that staff will have to do. Tasks will be upgraded and downgraded. Retaining autonomy, respect, dignity in the organisation and breadth of responsibility are all critical factors – often as important as remuneration in a period of change.
3   What do key people win or lose? To understand the impact of change on colleagues and others you work with, for example from other agencies in a prospective partnership, ask who is experiencing what aspect of change as a 'gain' or a 'loss'?

What can you do to help people recognise real gains and build commitment to the new solutions and new situations?

Tackling social exclusion does mean at times going against the grain of current practice – stepping outside of 'silo' thinking, tying practice more closely to social justice outcomes, thinking hard about what constitutes 'preventive work' as opposed to 'defensive work'. Yet it is worth remembering that even in large social service organisations there is no 'single author' writing the script for what the organisation is to do and that the single social worker, the manager, the team, have more authority, power and influence than might be imagined.

Moreover the direction of any organisation is more open to change than one might think with choices continually before it as to whether to follow one direction or another.[10] It is open to practitioners always to create alternative networks, to find out who in the organisation is of like mind that one can speak to, and to decide on what information to give to that person. Watching out for how the whole enterprise of reducing social exclusion in Britain all joins up – even when doing just the small corner of it that comes a practitioner's way as they follow their day-to-day roles and tasks – means they should be ready to supply the message to whoever will listen.

KEY POINTS

❏   Tackling social exclusion requires a change of culture in the agency achieved through continuous learning.

❏   Evaluation is essential to this but the complexity and scale of programmes make any evaluation a contested process, with multiple interests and viewpoints in the frame. Logic models offer one way to judge relative effectiveness of a programme by linking resources and inputs to outputs and outcomes. They can also visualise knowledge and share the lessons learned across the many stakeholders. Both the ABCD approach, and the 'theory of change' are variations of logic models.

❏   Despite the seemingly daunting task of tackling social exclusion practitioners, particularly when networked through shared commitment, are more influential than they might think and can shift the direction of their organisation through persistence and vision.

KEY READING

Anna Coote, Jessica Allen and David Woodhead, *Finding Out what Works: Understanding Complex, Community-based Initiatives* (Kings Fund, 2004).

Joy A. Frechtling, *Logic Modeling Methods in Program Evaluation* (John Wiley and Sons, 2007).

10   I am indebted to Adrian Passmore, chief executive of Regeneration West Midlands, for these thoughts on how practitioners underestimate the influence they have in the organisation in which they work.

BIBLIOGRAPHY

Acheson, D. (1998) *Independent Inquiry into Inequalities in Health*, London: TSO.

Alexander, A. (2000) *Mentoring Schemes for Young People – Handbook*, Brighton and London: Pavilion and National Children's Bureau.

Alinsky, S. (1971) *Rules for Radicals: A Pragmatic Primer for Realistic Radicals*, New York: Vintage Books.

Ames, A., Powell, H., Crouch J. and Tse, D. (2007) *Anti-social Behaviour: People, Place and Perceptions*, London IPSOS Mori.

Anastacio, J., Gidley, B., Hart, L., Keith, M., Mayom, M. and Kowarzik, U. (2000) *Reflecting Realities: Participants' Perspectives on Integrated Communities and Sustainable Development*, Bristol: Policy Press.

Anderson, R., Brown, I., Dowty, T., Inglesant, P., Heath, W. and Sasse, A. (2009) *Database State*, York: Joseph Rowntree Reform Trust.

Apps, J., Reynolds, J., Ashby, V. and Husain, F. (2007) *Family Support in Children's Centres*, London: National Family and Parenting Institute.

Arnstein, S. (1969) 'A ladder of citizen participation', *Journal of the American Institute of Planners* 35, 4: 216–24.

Association of Directors of Social Service (ADSS) (2003) *All Our Tomorrows: Inverting the Triangle of Care*, London: Local Government Association.

Association of Teachers and Lecturers (2008) Poverty and Social Exclusion in Rural Areas, http://www.atl.org.uk/policy-and-campaigns/policies/poverty-and-social-exclusion-in-rural-areas.asp (accessed 15 January 2009).

Audit Commission (2000) *Getting the Best from Children's Services: Findings from Joint Reviews of Social Services*, London: Audit Commission.

—— (2008) *Tired of Hanging Around?*, London: Audit Commission.

Axford, N., Berry, V., Little, M. and Morpeth, L. (2006) 'Developing a Common Language in Children's Services through Research-based Inter-disciplinary Training', *Social Work Education* 25, 2: 161–76.

Bain, E. (2002) *Social Inclusion in Rural Areas: Innovative Projects for Young People*, Edinburgh: Scottish Executive Central Research Unit.

Barnes, J. (2007) *Down Our Way: The Relevance of Neighbourhoods for Parenting and Child Development*, Oxford: Wiley Blackwell.

Barr, A., Drysdale, J. and Henderson, P. (1997) *Towards Caring Communities: Community Development and Community Care*, Brighton: Pavilion.

Barr, A. and Hashagen, S. (2000) *Achieving Better Community Development: Trainer's Resource Pack*, London: Community Development Foundation Publications.

Barr, A., Stenhouse, C. and Henderson, P. (2001) *Caring Communities: A Challenge for Social Inclusion*, York: Joseph Rowntree Foundation.

Barrow Cadbury Trust Commission (2005) *Lost in Transition: A Report of the Barrow Cadbury Commission on Young Adults and the Criminal Justice System*, London: Barrow Cadbury Trust.

Barrow Cadbury Trust (2007) Wolverhampton Asylum and Refugee Services. http://www. bctrust.org.uk/casestudies/deatil.php?csid=2 (accessed 12 December 2008).

—— (2009) Case Studies, http://www.bctrust.org.uk/casestudies/detail.php?csid=2 (accessed 12 January 2009).

Bass, M. and Drewett, R. (1997) *Real Work: Supported Employment for People with Learning Difficulties*, Sheffield: Social Services Monographs.

Bateman, N. (2005) *Practising Welfare Rights*, Abingdon: Routledge.

BBC News (2009) 'NHS age discrimination "common", 27 January, http://news.bbc.co.uk/1/hi/ health/7850881.stm (accessed 28 January 2009).

Bennett, K., Beynon, H. and Hudson, R. (2000) *Coalfields Regeneration: Dealing with the Consequences of Industrial Decline*, Bristol: Joseph Rowntree Foundation and the Policy Press.

Bentley, T. and Gurumurthy, R. (1999) *Destination Unknown: Engaging with the problems of Marginalised Youth*, London: Demos.

Bentley, T. and Oakley, K. (1999) *The Real Deal: What Young People Really Think about Government, Politics and Social Exclusion*, London: Demos.

Berthoud, R. and Hinton, T. (1989) *Credit Unions in the UK*, London: Policy Studies Institute.

Biehal, N., Claydon, J. and Byford, S. (2000) *Home or Away? Supporting Young People and Families*, London: National Children's Bureau.

Biehal, N., Claydon, J., Stein, M. and Wade, J. (1995) *Moving On: Young People and Leaving Care Schemes*, London: HMSO.

Biestek, F. (1961) *The Casework Relationship*, London: Allen and Unwin.

Bobo, L. (1998) 'Mapping racial attitudes at the century's end: has the color line vanished or merely reconfigured?', Paper prepared for the Aspen Roundtable Project on Race and Community Revitalization.

Bonner, A. (2006) *Social Exclusion and the Way Out*, London: John Wiley and Sons.

Boxall, M. (2002) *Nurture Groups in School: Principles and Practice*, London: Paul Chapman.

Bradshaw, J. (2005) *A Review of the Comparative Evidence on Child Poverty*, York: Joseph Rowntree Foundation.

Bradshaw, J. and Richardson, D. (2009) 'An Index of Child Well-being in Europe', *Child Indicators Research* April, 1874-8988 (on line).

Braye, S. (2000) 'Participation and Involvement in Social Care: An Overview', in H. Kemshall and R. Littlechild (eds), *User Involvement and Participation in Social Care*, London: Jessica Kingsley Publishers.

—— (2001) 'Key Workers Can Open Doors', *Community Care* 3–10 May.

Braye, S. and Preston-Shoot, M. (1995) *Empowering Practice in Social Care*, London: Jessica Kingsley Publishers.

Briggs, X. (1997) 'Social Capital and the Cities: Advice to Change Agents', International Workshop on Community Building, Bellagio, Italy

—— (2002) 'The Will and the Way: Local partnerships, Political Strategy and the Well Being of America's Children and Youth', Cambridge, MA: Harvard University Faculty Resource Working Papers.

—— (2004) *Desegregating the City: Issues, Strategies and Blind Spots in Comparative Perspective*, Cape Town: Isandla Institute.

Bronfenbrenner, U. (1979) *The Ecology of Human Development*, Cambridge MA: Harvard University Press.

Brooks-Gunn, I, Duncan, G. and Aber, L. (eds) (1997) *Neighborhood Poverty: Context and Consequences for Children*, New York: Russell Sage Foundation.

Browning, C. and Cagney, K. (2002) 'Neighborhood Structural Disadvantage, Collective Efficacy, and Self Rated Physical Health in an Urban Setting', *Journal of Health and Social Behaviour* 43: 388–99.

Bunting, M. (2006) 'It takes more than tea and biscuits to overcome indifference and fear', *The Guardian*, 16 November.

Burchardt, T., Le Grand, J. and Piachaud, D. (1999) 'Social Exclusion in Britain 1991–1995', *Social Policy and Administration* 33, 3: 227–44.

Burke, B. and Harrison, P. (2001) 'Race and Racism in Social Work', in M. Davies (ed.), *The Blackwell Encyclopaedia of Social Work*, Oxford: Blackwell.

Burleigh, M. (1994) Death and Deliverance: *'Euthanasia' in Germany 1900–45*, Cambridge: Cambridge University Press.

Burns, D., Heywood, F., Taylor, M., Wilde, P. and Wilson, M. (2004) *Making Community Participation Meaningful: A Handbook for Development and Assessment*, Bristol: Policy Press.

Byrne, D. (1998) *Complexity Theory and the Social Sciences: An Introduction*, London: Routledge.

Bytheway, B. (1995) *Ageism*, Buckingham: Open University Press.

Cantel, T. (2001) *Community Cohesion*, London: Home Office.

—— (2008) *Community Cohesion: A New Framework for Race and Diversity*, Basingstoke: Palgrave Macmillan.

Carrier, J. (2005) *Older People, the New Agenda*, London: Presentation to Better Government for Older People Network.

CCETSW (1991) *Rules and Requirements for the Diploma in Social Work*, Paper 30, London: Central Council for Education and Training in Social Work.

Cedersund, E. (1999) 'Using Narratives in Social Work Interaction', in A. Jokinen, K. Juhila and T. Poso (eds), *Constructing Social Work Practices*, Aldershot: Ashgate.

Centre for Social Justice (2007) Breakthrough Britain Vol 2 'Economic Dependency and Worklessness', http://www.centreforsocialjustice.org.uk/client/downloads/economic.pdf.

Chambers, E. (2004) *Roots for Radicals: Organizing for Power, Action and Justice*, New York and London: Continuum International Publishing.

Child Poverty Action Group (CPAG) (latest annual edition) *Handbook on Benefits and Tax Credits*, London: CPAG

Child Poverty Action Group (2007) *Welfare Benefits and Tax Credits Handbook 2007/2008*, London: CPAG.

Child Poverty Action Group, Community Links and the Chartered Institute of Taxation (2007), *Interaction: Benefits, Tax Credits and Moving into Work*, London: CPAG.

Christie, I. (with Mensah-Coker, G.) (1999) *An Inclusive Future? Disability, Social Change and Opportunities for Greater Inclusion by 2010*, London: Demos.

Citizens Organising Foundation (2008) Strangers into Citizens, http://www.londoncitizens.org.uk/strangersintocitizens/index.html (accessed 9 December 2008).

Clark, C. (2000) *Social Work Ethics: Politics, Principles and Practice*, Basingstoke: Macmillan.

Clark, K. and Drinkwater, S. (2002) 'Enclaves, Neighbourhood Effects and Employment Outcomes: Ethnic Minorities in England and Wales', *Journal of Population Economics* 15: 5–29.

Cohen, S. (2001) *Immigration Controls, the Family and the Welfare State*, London: Jessica Kingsley Publishers.

Cole, A., McIntosh, B. and Whittacker, A. (2000) *'We Want Our Voices Heard': Developing New Lifestyles with Disabled People*, Bristol: Policy Press.

Coleman, J. and Hendry, L. (1999) *The Nature of Adolescence* (3rd edn), London: Routledge.

Collier, K. (1993) *Social Work with Rural Peoples*, Vancouver, New Star Books.

Commission for Rural Communities (2008) *Rural Financial Poverty: Good Practice*, Cheltenham: CRC.

Conservative Party (2008) 'Work for Welfare: Real Welfare Reform to Help Make British Poverty History', www.conservatives.com/~/media/Files/Green%20Papers/Welfare_Policy_Paper.ashx.

Coote, A., Allen, J. and Woodhead, D. (2004) *Finding Out What Works: Building Knowledge about Complex, Community-based iInitiatives*, London: King's Fund.

Countryside Agency (2003) *The State of the Countryside 2003*, Countryside Agency Publications.

Craig, G. (2000) 'Introduction', in *Research Matters: Social Exclusion Special Issue*, Sutton: Community Care.

Crime Concern (1999a) *Families in Schools: Best Practice Approaches for Family Literacy and Positive Parenting Programmes*, Swindon: Crime Concern.

—— (1999b) *Reducing Neighbourhood Crime: A Manual for Action*, Swindon: Crime Concern.

Dalrymple, J. and Burke, B. (2006) *Anti-Oppressive Practice: Social Care and the Law* (2nd edn), Buckingham: Open University Press.

Darvill, G. and Smale, G. (eds) (1990) *Partners in Empowerment: Networks of Innovation in Social Work*, London: National Institute of Social Work.

Dawson, C. (2000) *Independent Successes: Implementing Direct Payments*, York: Joseph Rowntree Foundation.

D'Cruz, H. and Stagnitti, K (2008) 'Reconstructing Child Welfare', *Child and Family Social Work* 13, 2, 156–65.

Department for Children, Schools and Families (2006) *The Community Development Challenge*, London: DfCSF.

—— (2007) *Personal Education Allowances for Looked After Children: Statutory Guidance for Local Authorities*, London: DfCSF.

—— (2008) *Outcome Indicators for Looked-after Children*, London: DfCSF.

Department for Communities and Local Government (2006) *The Community Development Challenge*, London: DCLG.

—— (2007) *Tackling Youth Homelessness Policy Briefing* 18, London: Department for Communities and Local Government.

Department for Education and Employment (1999) *Social Inclusion: Pupil Support Circular 10/99*, London: DfEE.

Department for Education and Science (DfES) (2003) *Every Child Matters*, Cm 5860, London: HMSO.

Department for Education and Skills (DfES) (2005) *Higher Standards, Better Schools For All: More Choice for Parents and Pupils*, London: DfES.

Department of Environment, Farming and Rural Affairs (DEFRA) (2003) *Rural Services Standard*, London: DEFRA.

Department of Health (1991) *The Children Act Guidance and Regulations*, London: HMSO.

—— (1995) *Messages from Research*, London: HMSO.

—— (2000a) *Framework for the Assessment of Children in Need and their Families*, London: The Stationery Office.

—— (2000b) *Children (Leaving Care) Act: Regulations and Guidance*, London: The Stationery Office.

—— (2005) *Independence, Well-being and Choice: Our Vision for the Future of Social Care for Adults in England*, Cm 6499, London: DoH

—— (2006) *Our Health, Our Care, Our Say*, London: DoH.

—— (2007) *Putting People First: A Shared Vision and Commitment to the Transformation of Adult Social Care*, London: DoH.

Department of Social Security (1999) *Opportunity for All: Tackling Poverty and Social Exclusion* Cm 4445, London: The Stationery Office.

Department of Work and Pensions (DWP) (2005) *Improving Opportunity, Strengthening Society*, London: DWP.

—— (2007) *Opportunity for all – Indicators*, London: DWP.

—— (2008) *No One Written Off*, London: DWP.

—— (2009) http://www.dwp.gov.uk/lifeevent/benefits/ (accessed 6 January 2009).

—— (2009) *ESA Employment and Support Allowance 2008–9: A Guide to ESA for People with a Disability or Long Term Health Problem*, http://www.dwp.gov.uk/esa/pdfgs/esa-disability-alliance-guide.pdf (accessed 10 May 2009).

Dex, S. (2003) *Families and Work in the Twenty-first Century*, York: Joseph Rowntree Foundation.

Diez-Roux, A. (2001) 'Investigating Neighborhood and Area Effects on Health', *American Journal of Public Health* 91: 1783–9

Dixon, J. and Hoatson, L. (1999) 'Retreat from Within: Social Work Education's Faltering Commitment to Community Work', *Australian Social Work* 52, 2:3–9.

Dobson, B., Middleton, S. and Beardsworth, A. (2001) *The Impact of Childhood Disability on Family Life*, York: Joseph Rowntree Foundation.

Dowling, M. (1998) *Poverty: A Practitioner's Guide*, Birmingham: Venture Press.

—— (1999) *Social Workers and Poverty*, Aldershot: Ashgate.

Ellis, A. (2002) 'Power and Exclusion in Rural Community Development: The Case of LEADER 2 in Wales', PhD thesis, University of Swansea.

Erikson, E. (1969) *Childhood and Society*, London: Pelican.

ESA Employment and Support Allowance 2008–9: A guide to ESA for people with a disability or long term health problem, http://www.dwp.gov.uk/esa/pdfs/esa-disability-alliance-guide.pdf (accessed 10 May 2009).

European Economic Community (1985) 'On specific community action to combat poverty', *Official Journal of the EEC*, 24 February 1985.

Evans, M., Harkness, S. and Arigoni Ortiz, R. (2004) *Lone Parents Cycling Between Benefits and Work*, Research Report No 217, London: Department for Work and Pensions.

Farver, J. and Natera, L. (2000) 'Effects of Neighborhood Violence on Preschoolers' Social Function with Peers', *International Perspectives on Child and Adolescent Mental Health*, Volume 1: Proceedings of the First International Conference 41–57.

Feinstein, L. (2006) *Predicting Adult Life Outcomes from Earlier Signals: Modelling Pathways through Childhood*, London: Centre Research on the Wider Benefits of Learning, Institute of Education, University of London.

Ferguson, R. and Stoutland, S. (1999) 'Reconceiving the Community Development Field', in R. Ferguson and W. Dickens, *Urban Problems and Community Development*, Washington, DC: The Brookings Institution.

Fisher, R and Ury, W. (1982) *Getting to Yes: Negotiating Agreement Without Giving In*, revised 2nd edn, New York: Random House.

Fisher, R., Ury, W. and Patton, B. (1991) *Getting to Yes: Negotiating an Agreement without Giving In* (revised edn), London: Business Books.

Folbre, N. (2001) *The Invisible Heart: Economics and Family Values*, New York: The New Press.

Forrest, R. and Kearns, A. (1999) *Joined-Up Places? Social Cohesion and Neighbourhood Regeneration*, York: Joseph Rowntree Foundation.

Francis, D. and Henderson, P. (1992) *Working with Rural Communities*, Birmingham: BASW.

Frechtling, J. (2007) *Logic Modeling Methods in Program Evaluation*, San Francisco: John Wiley and Sons.

Fulbright-Anderson, K., Kubisch, A. and Connell, J. (1998) *New Approaches to Evaluating Community Initiatives vol. 2*, Washington, DC: The Aspen Institute.

Furlong, A. and Cartmel, F. (2004) *Vulnerable Young Men in Fragile Labour Markets: Employment, Unemployment and the Search for Long-term Security*, York: Joseph Rowntree Foundation.

Garside, R. (2008) *Ten Years of Labour's Youth Justice Reforms: An Independent Audit*, London: Centre for Crime and Justice Studies, King's College, University of London.

Gilchrist, A. (1997) *The Networked Community*, Bristol: Policy Press.

Gilligan, R. (2000) 'Family Support Issues and Prospects', in J. Canavan, P. Dolan and J. Pinkerton, (eds), *Family Support Direction from Diversity*, London: Jessica Kingsley Publishers.

Giloth, R.P. (1998) *Jobs and Economic Development: Strategies and Practice*, Newbury Park, CA and London: Sage.

Glendinning, A., Nuttall, M., Hendry, L., Kloep, M. and Wood, S. (2008) *Sociological Review* 51, 1: 129–56.

Glendinning, C. and Bell, D. (2008) *Rethinking Social Care and Support What Can England Learn from Other Countries*, Viewpoint 2335, York: Joseph Rowntree Foundation.

Goldson, B. (2000) 'Children in Need or Young Offenders? Hardening Ideology, Organizational Change and New Challenges for Social Work with Children in Trouble', *Child and Family Social Work* 5: 255–65.

Gordon, D. *et al.* (2000) *Poverty and Social Exclusion in Britain*, York: Joseph Rowntree Foundation.

Granovetter, M. (1973) 'The Strength of Weak Ties Hypothesis', *American Journal of Sociology* 78, 8: 1360–80.

Green, K. (2008) 'Welfare Reform: A Route to Greater Social Justice', Progress annual conference, London.

Griffiths, R. (1988) *Community Care: Agenda for Action*, London: HMSO.

Griggs, J., Whitworth, A., Walker, R., McLennan, D. and Noble, M. (2008) *Person- or Place-based Policies to Tackle Disadvantage?*, York: Joseph Rowntree Foundation.

Grimshaw, R. and McGuire, C. (1999) *Evaluating Parenting Programmes: A Study of Stakeholders*, London: National Children's Bureau.

Grover, C., Stewart, J. and Broadhurst, K. (2004) 'Transistions to Adulthood: Some Critical Observations of the Children (Leaving Care) Act 2000', *Social Work and Social Sciences Review* 11, 1: 5–18.

Hadley, R., Cooper, M., Dale, P. and Stacy, G. (1987) *A Community Social Worker's Handbook*, London: Tavistock.

Haines, K. and Case, S. (2005) 'Promoting Prevention: Targeting Family-Based Risk and Protective Factors for Drug Use and Youth Offending in Swansea', *British Journal of Social Work* 35: 169–87.

Halliday, S. (2000) 'Institutional Racism in Bureaucratic Decision-making: A Case study in the Administration of Homelessness, Law', *Journal of Law and Society* 27, 3: 449–71.

Hambleton, R., Hoggett, P. and Raazaque, K. (1997) *Freedom within Boundaries: Developing Effective Approaches to Decentralisation*, London: Local Government Management Board.

Handel, R. (1999) *Building Family Literacy in an Urban Community*, New York and London: Teachers College Press.

Hardiker, P. (1999) 'Children Still in Need, Indeed: Prevention Across Five Decades', in O. Stevenson, (ed.), *Child Welfare in the UK*, Oxford: Blackwell Science.

Harris, I. (1995) *Messages Men Hear: Constructing Masculinities*, London: Taylor and Francis.

Harrogate District Council (2006) 'Pensioners profit from pension take up campaign', http://www.harrogate.gov.uk/immediacy-4144 (accessed 14 December 2008).

Havell, C. (1998) 'Homelessness: A Continual Problem for Young People in the UK', *Childright* July/August 148: 12–14.

Hawtin, M., Hughes, G. and Percy-Smith, J. (1994) *Community Profiling: Auditing Social Needs*, Buckingham: Open University Press.

Hayes, D. and Humphries, B. (2004) *Social Work, Immigration and Asylum Debates, Dilemmas and Ethical Issues for Social Work and Social Care Practice*, London: Jessica Kingsley Publishers.

Heenan, D. (2006) 'The Factors Influencing Access to Health and Social Care in the Farming Communities of County Down, Northern Ireland', *Ageing and Society* 26: 373–91.

Henderson, P. and Thomas, D. (2001) *Skills in Neighbourhood Work* (3rd edn), London: Routledge.

Herbert, G. and Napper, R. (2000) *TIPS: Tried and Tested Ideas for Parent Education and Support*, Lyme Regis: Russell House.

Hetherington, P. (2009) 'Uphill strugglers', *Guardian*, 11 February.

Hewitt, R. (1996) *Routes of Racism: The Social Basis of Racist Action*, Stoke on Trent, Trentham Books.

Hickman, M., Crowley, H. and Mai, N. (2008) *Immigration and Social Cohesion in the UK: The Rhythms and Realities of Everyday Life*, York: Joseph Rowntree Foundation.

Hills, J. (1995) *Joseph Rowntree Inquiry into Income and Wealth*, York: Joseph Rowntree Foundation.

Hirsch, D. (2008) *Estimating the Costs of Child Poverty*, York: Joseph Rowntree Foundation.

Hirst, J., Formby, E., Parr, S., Nixon, J., Hunter, C. and Flint, J. (2007) *An Evaluation of Two Intitiatives to Reward Young People*, York: Joseph Rowntree Foundation.

Hollister, R. (forthcoming) *Measuring the Impact of Community Development Financial Institutions' Activities*.

Holman, B. (1998) 'Neighbourhoods and Exclusion', in M. Barry and C. Hallett (eds), *Social Work and Social Exclusion*, Lyme Regis: Russell House.

Home Office and Department for Communities and Local Government (2005) *Citizen Engagement and Public Services: Why Neighbourhoods Matter*, London: DCLG.

Howarth, C., Kenway, P. and Palmer, G. (2001) *Responsibility For All: A National Strategy for Social Inclusion*, London: New Policy Institute and Fabian Society.

Hughes, A. (1997) 'Rurality and "Cultures of Womanhood": Domestic Identities and Moral Order in Village Life', in P Cloke and J Little (eds), *Contested Countryside: Otherness, Marginalisation and Rurality*, London: Routledge.

—— (2004) 'Geographies of Invisibility: The "Hidden" Lives of Rural Lone Parents', in L. Holloway and M. Kneafsey, *Geographies of Rural Cultures and Societies*, Farnham: Ashgate.

—— (n.d.) 'Lone Parents and Paid Work – Case Studies from Rural England', ESRC, end of award report.

Hughes, A. and Nativel, C. (2005) 'Lone Parents and Paid Work: Evidence from Rural England', in J. Little and C. Morris (eds), *Critical Studies in Gender Issues*, Basingstoke: Ashgate.

Hughes, M. and Traynor, T. (2000) 'Reconciling Process and Outcome in Evaluating Community Initiatives', *Evaluation* 6, 1: 37–49.

Hutton, J. (2006) 'Back to work'. BBC Sunday AM, 22 January.

Independent Living Fund (2009) Eligibility – who can apply?, http://www.ilf.org.uk/making_an_application/eligibility/index.html (accessed 14 February 2009).

International Federation of Social Workers (2009) Definition of social work, http:llwww.ifsw.org/f38000138.html1 (accessed 16 February 2009).

Jack, G. (2000a) 'Ecological Perspectives in Assessing Children and Families', in J. Howarth (ed.), *The Child's World: Assessing Children in Need*, London: Jessica Kingsley Publishers.

—— (2000b) 'Social Support Networks', in M. Davies (ed.), *The Blackwell Encyclopaedia of Social Work*, Oxford: Blackwell.

Jack, G. and Jack, D. (2000) 'Ecological Social Work: The Application of a Systems Model of Development in Context', in P. Stepney and D. Ford (eds), *Social Work Models, Methods and Theories: A Framework for Practice*, Lyme Regis: Russell House.

Jack, G. and Gill, O. (2003) *The Missing Side of the Triangle: Assessing the Importance of Family and Environmental Factors in the Lives of Children*, Ilford: Barnardos.

Jackson, S. (1998) 'Educational Success for Looked-after Children: The Social Worker's Responsibility', *Practice* 10, 4: 47–56.

Jackson, S. and Martin, P. (1998) 'Surviving the Care System: Education and Resilience', *Journal of Adolescence*, 21: 569–83.

Jacobs, J. (1961) *Death and Life of American Cities*, New York: Anchor.

Jameson, N. (2001) Director, Citizen's Organising Foundation, personal communication to the author.

Joint Public Affairs Committee for Older Adults (2008) http://www.jpac.org/pdf/may07.jar.pdf (accessed 12 November 2009).

Jones, C. (1998) 'Social Work and Society', in R. Adams, L. Dominelli and M. Payne (eds), *Social Work Themes, Issues and Critical Debates*, Basingstoke: Macmillan.

Jones, C., Ferguson, I., Lavalette, M. and Penketh, L. (2005) *Social Work and Social Justice: A Manifesto for a New Engaged Practice*, http://www.liv.ac.uk/ssp/Social_Work_Manifesto. html (accessed 16 January 2006).

Jordan, B. (1987) *Rethinking Welfare*, Oxford: Blackwell.

Jordan, B. and Jordan, C. (2000) *Social Work and the Third Way: Tough Love as Social Policy*, London: Sage.

Keating, N., Orfinowski, P., Wenger, C., Fast, J. and Derksen, L. (2003) 'Understanding the Caring Capacity of Informal Networks of Frail Seniors: A Case for Care Networks', *Ageing and Society* 23, 115–27.

Kelly, R. and Philpott, S. (2003) *Community Cohesion Moving Bradford Forward Lessons from Northern Ireland*, Bradford: University of Bradford.

Knight, G., Speckesser, S., Smith, J., Dolton, P. and Azevedo, J. (2006) *Lone Parents Work Focused Interviews/New Deal for Lone Parents: Combined Evaluation and Further Net Impacts*, London: Department for Work and Pensions.

Kohli, R. (2007) *Social Work with Unaccompanied Asylum Seeking Children*, Basingstoke: Palgrave Macmillan.

Kubisch, A., Connell, J. and Fulbright-Anderson, K. (2001) 'Evaluating Complex Community Initiatives: Theory, Measurement and Analysis', in J. Pierson and J. Smith (eds), *Rebuilding Community: The Policy and Practice of Urban Regeneration*, Basingstoke: Palgrave Macmillan.

Kubisch, A. and Stone, R. (2001) 'Comprehensive Community Initiatives: The American Experience', in J. Pierson and J. Smith (eds), *Rebuilding Community: The Policy and Practice of Urban Regeneration*, Basingstoke: Palgrave Macmillan.

Langan, M. and Lee, P. (1989) *Radical Social Work*, Today London: Unwin Hyman.

La Valle, I., Arthur, S., Millward, C., Scott, J. and Clayden, M. (2002) *Happy Families? Atypical Work and its Influence on Family Life*, Bristol: Policy Press and Joseph Rowntree Foundation.

Lawrence, K. (2001) 'Structural Racism and Comprehensive Community Initiatives', in J. Pierson and J. Smith (eds), *Rebuilding Community: Policy and Practice of Urban Regeneration*, Basingstoke: Palgrave Macmillan.

Lea, J. (2000) 'The Macpherson Report and the Question of Institutional Racism', *The Howard Journal* 39, 3: 219–33.

Lemos, G. (2005) *The Search for Tolerance: Challenging and Changing Racist Attitudes and Behaviour in Young People*, York: Joseph Rowntree Foundation.

Let's Talk Money, (2007) New Horizons Saving and Loan Scheme, www.nowletstalkmoney. com/m/gb/en/newhorizonsopensitsdoor.html (accessed 17 January 2009).

Levitas, R. (1999) 'Defining and Measuring Social Exclusion: A Critical Overview of Current Proposals', *Radical Statistics* 71: 10–27.

—— (2005) *The Inclusive Society? Social Exclusion and New Labour* (2nd edn) Basingstoke: Macmillan.

Lipset, S. (1996) *American Exceptionalism*, New York: Norton.

Little, M. and Mount, K. (1999) *Prevention and Early Intervention with Children in Need*, Aldershot: Ashgate.

Livingston, M., Bailey, N. and Kearns, A. (2008) *People's Attachment to Place: The Influence of Neighbourhood Deprivation*, Coventry: Chartered Institute of Housing.

Luxmoore, N. (2000) *Listening to Young People in School, Youth Work and Counselling*, London: Jessica Kingsley Publishers.

MacDonald, S. (1991) *All Equal Under the Act*, London: Race Equality Unit.

Maclennan, D. (2000) *Changing Places, Engaging People*, York: Joseph Rowntree Foundation.

MacPhee, J. (2005) *Rural Financial Inclusion and the Challenges Involved*, Ontario: Department for Sustainable Communities.

Macpherson, Sir William (1999) *The Stephen Lawrence Inquiry*, Cm 4262-I, London: The Stationery Office.

Madge, N., Burton, S., Howell, S. and Hearn, B. (2000) *9–13: The Forgotten Years?*, London: National Children's Bureau.

Marsh, P. and Peel, M. (1999) *Leaving Care in Partnership: Family Involvement with Care Leavers*, London: The Stationery Office.

Mayo, M. (1998) 'Community Work', in R. Adams, L. Dominelli and M. Payne (eds), *Social Work Themes, Issues and Critical Debates*, Basingstoke: Macmillan.

McAuley, C., Knapp, M., Beecham, J., McCurry, N. and Sleed, M. (2004) *Young Families Under Stress: Outcomes and Cost of Home-Start Support*, York: York Publishing Services.

McCabe, A., Lowndes, V. and Skelcher, C. (1997) *Partnerships and Networks: An Evaluation and Development Manual*, York: Joseph Rowntree Foundation.

McGhee, D. (2003) 'Moving to "Our" Common Ground – A Critical Examination of Community Cohesion Discourse in Twenty-first Century Britain', *Sociological Review* 51, 3: 376–404.

McLeod, E. and Bywaters, P. (2000) *Social Work, Health and Equality*, London: Routledge.

McLeod, E., Bywaters, P., Tanner, D. and Hirsch, M. (2008) 'For the Sake of their Health: Older Service Users' Requirements for Social Care to Facilitate Access to Social Networks Following Hospital Discharge', *British Journal of Social Work* 38, 1: 73–90.

Miller, J. (1996) *Never Too Young: How Young Children Can Take Responsibility and Make Decisions: A Handbook for Early Years Workers*, London: Save the Children.

Millie, A., Jacobson, J., McDonald, E. and Hough, M. (2005) *Anti-Social Behaviour Strategies: Finding a Balance*, Bristol: Policy Press.

Minsky, S. (1971) *Rules for Radicals: A Pragmatic Primer for Realistic Radicals*, New York: Vintage Books.

Mitchell, W. and Sloper, P. (2000) *User-Friendly Information for Families with Disabled Children: A Guide to Good Practice*, York: Joseph Rowntree Foundation.

Modood, T. (2007) *Multiculturalism*, Cambridge: Polity Press.

—— (2007) 'Multiculturalism and nation building go hand in hand', *Guardian*, 23 May.

Moore, J. (1989) *Hansard*, HC Deb 03 July 1989, vol 156 cc3-6.

Moss, P., Petrie, P. and Poland, G. (1999) *Rethinking School: Some International Perspectives*, Leicester: Youth Work Press and Joseph Rowntree Foundation.

Mullender, A. and Ward, D. (1991) *Self-Directed Groupwork: Users Take Action for Empowerment*, London: Whiting and Burch.

Munro, E. and Calder, M. (2005) 'Where has Child Protection Gone?', *Political Quarterly* 76, 3: 439–45.

Murray, C. (1996) 'Underclass: The Crisis Deepens', in R. Lister, *Charles Murray and the Underclass: The Developing Debate*, London: Institute of Economic Affairs.

Nayak, A. (1999) ' "White English Ethnicities": Racism, Anti-racism and Student Perspectives', *Race Ethnicity and Education* 2, 2: 177–202.

—— (2003) *Racism, Place and Globalization: Youth Cultures in a Changing World*, Oxford: Berg Publishers.

Neighbourhood Initiatives Foundation (2008) *'Planning for Real' User's Guide*, Telford: NIF.

Netten, A., Forder, J. and Shapiro, J. (2006) *Measuring Personal Social Service Outputs for National Accounts: Services for Older People*, Manchester: Personal Social Services Research Unit.

New Policy Institute (2009) 'Help from Social Services' http://www.poverty.org.uk/69/index.shtml (accessed 26 January 2009).

NYHS (2008) http://www.communities.gov.uk/youthhomelessnesslactivities/actionlearning/ (accessed 2 December 2008).

O'Bryan, A., Simons, K., Beyer, S. and Grove, B. (2000) *A Framework for Supported Employment*, York: Joseph Rowntree Foundation.

Office of National Statistics (2009) http://neighbourhood.statistics.gov.uk/dissemination/ LeadTeableview for Chester District (accessed 16 February 2009).

Oliver, M. and Sapey, B. (2006) *Social Work with Disabled People* (3rd revised edn), Basingstoke: Palgrave Macmillan.

Ousley, H. (2001) *Community Pride, Not Prejudice*, Bradford: Bradford City Council.

Palmer, G., MacInnes, T. and Kenway, P. (2007) *Monitoring Poverty and Social Exclusion 2007*, York: Joseph Rowntree Foundation and New Policy Institute.

—— (2008) *Monitoring Poverty and Social Exclusion 2008*, York: Joseph Rowntree Foundation and New Policy Institute.

Parekh, B. (2000) *The Future of Multi-Ethnic Britain: The Parekh Report*, London: Profile Books.

Parkinson, G. (1970) 'I Give Them Money', in Fitzgerald *et al.* (eds) (1977) *Welfare in Action*, London: Routledge and Kegan Paul, cited in Dowling 1999.

Parson, C. (2008) 'Singled out for exclusion?', *Guardian*, Tuesday 22 April.

Participatory Rural Appraisal (PRA) (1999) Relaxed and Participatory Appraisal: Notes on practical approaches and methods, PRA, www.ids.ac.uk/ids/particip.

Parton, N. and O'Byrne, P. (2000) *Constructive Social Work: Towards a New Practice*, Basingstoke: Macmillan.

Patterson, G. (1985) *Anti-Social Boys*, Eugene OR: Castalia Publishing.

Pawson, H., Davidson, E. and Netto, G. (2007) *Evaluation of Homelessness, Prevention Activities in Scotland*, Edinburgh: the Scottish Government, http://www.scotland.gov.uk/ Publications/2007/03/2609514412 (accessed 12 November 2008).

Pearson, C. (2006) 'Direct Payments in Scotland', in J. Leece and J. Bornat (eds), *Developments in Direct Payments: Comparative Perspectives from the UK and Beyond*, Bristol: Policy Press.

Pearson, G. (1989) 'Social Work and Unemployment', in M. Langan and P. Lee (eds), *Radical Social Work Today*, London: Unwin Hyman.

Penketh, L. (2001) *Tackling Institutional Racism: Anti-racist Policies and Social Work Education and Training*, Bristol: Policy Press.

Piachaud, D. and Sutherland, H. (2001) 'Child Poverty in Britain and the New Labour Government', *Journal of Social Policy* 30, 1: 95–118.

Pierson, J. (2008) *Going Local: Working in Communities and Neighbourhoods*, Abingdon: Routledge.

Pierson, J., Worley, C. and Smith, J. (2000) *Local Participation and the New Deal for Communities*, Stoke-on-Trent: Housing and Community Research Unit, Staffordshire University.

Pinkerton, J. and Dolan, P. (2007) 'Family Support, Social Capital, Resilience and Adolescent Coping', *Child and Family Social Work*, 12, 3: 219–28.

Plummer, J. (2000) *Municipalities and Community Participation: A Sourcebook for Capacity Building*, London: Earthscan.

Pollitt, C., Gordon, P. and Plamping, D. (1998) *Decentralising Public Service Management*, Basingstoke: Macmillan.

Power, A. (1997) *Estates on the Edge*, Basingstoke: Palgrave Macmillan.

Power, A. and Mumford K. (1997) 'Negative Pressures on Mass Estates', in A. Power (ed.) *Estates on the Edge*, Basingstoke: Palgrave Macmillan.

—— (1999) *The Slow Death of Great Cities? Urban Abandonment or Urban Renaissance*, York Joseph Rowntree Foundation.

Power, A. and Tunstall, R. (1997) *Dangerous Disorder: Riots and Violent Disturbances in Thirteen Areas of Britain, 1991–92*, York: Joseph Rowntree Foundation.

Pratt, J., Plamping, D. and Gordon, P. (1998) *Partnership: Fit for Purpose?*, London: King's Fund.

Prewett, R. (1999) *Short Term Break, Long Term Benefit. Family Based Care for Disabled Children and Adults*, Sheffield: Social Services Monographs.

Pritchard, J. (2008) *Good Practice in the Law and Safeguarding Adults: Criminal Justice and Adult Protection*, London: Jessica Kingsley Publishers.

Pugh, G. and Statham, J. (2006) 'Interventions in Schools in the UK', in C. McAuley, P. Pecora and W. Rose, *Enhancing the Well-being of Children and Families through Effective Interventions: International Evidence for Practice*, London: Jessica Kingsley Publishers.

Pugh, R. (2000) *Social Work in Rural Areas*, Lyme Regis: Russell House Publishing.

—— (2003) 'Considering the Countryside: Is There a Case for Rural Social Work?', *British Journal of Social Work* 33: 67–85.

—— (2007) 'Dual Relationships: Personal and Professional Boundaries in Rural Social Work', *British Journal of Social Work* 37, 8: 1405–23.

Purdue, D., Razzaque, K., Hambleton, R. and Stewart, M. (2000) *Community Leadership in Area Regeneration*, Bristol: Policy Press.

Putnam, R. (2001) *Bowling Alone: The Collapse and Revival of American Community*, London: Simon and Schuster.

Puttick, K. (2006) *Welfare Benefits and Talc Credits*, Welwyn Garden City: CLT Professional Publishing.

Quilgars, D., Johnsen, S. and Pleace, N. (2008) *Youth Homelessness in the UK*, York: Joseph Rowntree Foundation.

Qureshi, T., Berridge, D. and Wenman, H. (2000) *Where to Turn? Family Support for South Asian Communities – A Case Study*, London: National Children's Bureau.

Randall, B., Paterson, B., Dayson, K. (2005) *Community Access to Money: Housing Associations Leading on Financial Inclusion*, London: Housing Corporation.

Raynes, N., Temple, B., Glenister, C. and Coulthard, L. (2001) *Quality at Home for Older People: Involving Service Users in Defining Home Care Specifications*, Bristol: Policy Press.

Reimer, B. (2006) 'The Rural Context of Community Development in Canada', *Journal of Rural and Community Development* 1: 155–75.

Revans, R. (1982) *The Origins and Growth of Action Learning* Bromley: Chartwell-Bratt, cited in Wilkinson, D. and Applebee, E. *Implementing Holistic Government*, London: Demos.

Riddell, S. (2006) *Disabled People and Direct Payments: A UK Comparative Study – ESRC End of Award Report*.

Roberts, R. (1973) *The Classic Slum*, London: Penguin.

Robinson, C. and Simons, K. (1996) *In Safe Hands? Quality and Regulation in Adult Placements for People with Learning Difficulties*, Sheffield: Social Services Monographs.

Rogers, H. (2000) 'Breaking the Ice: Developing Strategies for Collaborative Working with Carers of Older People with Mental Health Problems in H. Kemshall and R. Littlechild (eds), *User Involvement and Participation in Social Care: Research Informing Practice*, London: Jessica Kingsley Publishers.

Rossi, P., Lipsey, M. and Freeman, H. (2003) *Evaluation: A Systematic Approach*, 7th edn, London: Sage Publications.

Royds Community Association (2008) http://www.royds.org.uk/projects.php (accessed 8 November 2008).

Rural Poverty and Inclusion Working Group (2001) *Poverty and Social Exclusion in Rural Scotland*, Edinburgh: The Scottish Executive.

Rutherford, J. (1997) *Forever England: Reflections on Race, Masculinity and Empire*, London, Lawrence and Wishart.

—— (2003a) *Making the Connections: Final Report on Transport and Social Exclusion*.

Rutter, J. (1994) *Refugee Children in the Classroom*, Stoke-on-Trent: Trentham Books.

Rutter, J. and Hyder, T. (1998) *Refugee Children in the Early Years: Issues for Policy-makers and Providers*, London: Save the Children and the Refugee Council.

Rutter, J. and Jones, C. (1998) *Refugee Education – Mapping the field*, Stoke-on-Trent: Trentham Books.

Rutter, M., Giller, H. and Hagell, A. (1998) *Anti-Social Behavior by Young People*, Cambridge: Cambridge University Press.

Sabel, C. (1993) 'Studied Trust: Building New Forms of Cooperation in a Volatile Economy', *Human Relations* 46: 1133–70.

Saleeby, D. (1992) *The Strengths Perspective in Social Work*, New York: Longman.

Sampson, R. (1999) 'What "Community" Supplies', in R.F. Ferguson and W.T. Dickens (eds), *Urban Problems and Community Development*, Washington DC: The Brookings Institution.

Sampson, R., Morenoff, J. and Gannon-Rowley, T. (2002) 'Assessing "Neighborhood Effects": Social Processes and New Directions in Research', *Annual Review of Sociology* 28: 443–78.

Save the Children (1998) *All Together Now: Community Participation for Children and Young People*, London: Save the Children.

—— (2000a) *Anti-Bias Approaches in the Early Years*, London: Save the Children.

—— (2000b) *We Can Work it Out: Parenting with Confidence. A Training Pack for Parenting Groups*, London: Save the Children.

Sawyerr, A. (1999) 'Identity Project on "Myself" with Pre-schoolers at a Day Nursery', in R. Barns (ed.), *Working with Black Children and Adolescents in Need*, London: British Agencies for Adoption and Fostering.

Scharf, T., Phillipson, C. and Smith E. (2005) *Multiple Exclusion and Quality of Life amongst Excluded Older People in Disadvantaged Neighbourhoods*, London: Office of Deputy Prime Minister.

Scott, J. (1998) *Seeing Like a State: How Certain Schemes to Improve the Human Condition have Failed*, New Haven, CT and London: Yale University Press.

Scottish Executive (2001) *Poverty and Social Exclusion in Rural Scotland: A Report by the Rural Poverty and Inclusion Working Group*, Edinburgh: Scottish Executive.

—— (2001) *Early Education and Childcare Plans 2001–2004: Guidance to Partnerships*, Edinburgh: Scottish Executive.

—— (2006) *Changing Lives: Review of Social Work in the 21st Century*, Edinburgh: Scottish Executive.

Scottish Office (1998) *Policy for Promoting Social Inclusion*, Edinburgh: Scottish Office.

Sellick, P. (2004) *Muslim Housing Experiences: A Research Report for the Housing Corporation*, Oxford: Oxford Centre for Islamic Studies.

Sennett, R. (2007) *The Culture of the New Capitalism*, London: Yale University Press.

Sennett, R. with Cobb, J. (1993) *Hidden Injuries of Class*, New York: Norton and Co.

Shaftesbury Society (2000) *Community Development Work*, London: Shaftesbury Society.

Sheldon, B. and Chilvers, R. (2001) *Evidence-Based Social Care: A Study of Prospects and Problems*, Lyme Regis: Russell House.

Shell, R. (1999) *Bargaining for Advantage: Negotiation Strategies for Reasonable People*, London: Penguin.

Show Racism the Red Card, 'Coaching with a conscience', http://www.theredcard.ie/news/2006/coaching-with-a-conscience/ (accessed 8 January 2009).

Shucksmith, M. (2000) *Exclusive Countryside? Social Inclusion and Regeneration in Rural Britain*, York: Joseph Rowntree Foundation.

—— (2002) *Social Exclusion in Rural Areas: A Review of Recent Research*, Aberdeen: Arkleton Centre for Rural Development Research, University of Aberdeen.

—— (2004) *Social Exclusion in Rural Areas: A Review of Recent Research*, Aberdeen: University of Aberdeen.

Sillett, J. (2008) *Never Too Late for Living*, London: Local Government Information Unit.

Siraj-Blatchford, I. (1994) *The Early Years: Laying the Foundations for Racial Equality*, Stoke-on-Trent: Trentham Books.

Skinner, C. (2003) *How Parents Co-ordinate Childcare, Education and Work*, Bristol: Policy Press for the Joseph Rowntree Foundation.

Skinner, S. (2005) *Assessing Community Strengths*, London: Community Development Foundation.

Sluzki, C. (2000) 'Social Networks and the Elderly: Conceptual and Clinical Issues, and a Family Consultation', *Family Process* 39, 3: 271–84.

Smale, G. (1998) *Managing Change Through Innovation*, London: The Stationery Office.

Smale, G., Tuson, G., Cooper, M., Wardle, M. and Crosbie, D. (1988) *Community Social Work: A Paradigm for Change*, London: National Institute for Social Work.

Smale, G., Tuson, G., Biehal, N. and Marsh, P. (1993) *Empowerment, Assessment, Care Management and the Skilled Worker*, London: HMSO.

Smale, G., Tuson, G., Ahmad, B., Darvill, G., Domoney, L. and Sainsbury, E. (1994) *Negotiating Care in the Community*, London: National Institute of Social Work.

Smale, G., Tuson, G. and Statham, D. (2000) *Social Work and Social Problems: Working Towards Social Inclusion and Social Change*, Basingstoke: Macmillan.

Social Exclusion Data Team (2006) *Child Poverty in London: Income and Labour Market Indicators*, London: Greater London Authority.

Social Exclusion Task Force (2004) *Tackling Social Exclusion: Taking Stock and Looking to the Future*, London: Office of the Deputy Prime Minister.

—— (2006) *Reaching Out: An Action Plan on Social Exclusion*, London: Cabinet Office.

—— (2008) *Think Family: Improving the Life Chances of Families at Risk*, London: Cabinet Office.

Social Exclusion Unit (1998) *Bringing Britain Together: A National Strategy for Neighbourhood Renewal*, London: The Stationery Office.

—— (1999a) *Teenage Pregnancy*, Cm 4342, London: The Stationery Office.

—— (1999b) *Bridging the Gap: New Opportunities for 16–18-year-olds Not in Education, Employment or Training*, London: The Stationery Office.

—— (2000) *National Strategy for Neighbourhood Renewal: A Framework for Consultation*, London: Cabinet Office.

—— (2003) *Better Education for Children in Care*, London: Cabinet Office.

—— (2006) *A Sure Start to Later Life: Ending Inequalities for Older People*, London: Department for Communities and Local Government.

Social Services Inspectorate (1998) *Removing Barriers for Disabled Children*, London: Department of Health.

Stein, M. (1997) *What Works in Leaving Care?*, Ilford: Barnardos.

Stokes, P. and Knight, B. (1997) *Organising a Civil Society*, Birmingham: Foundation for Civil Society.

Stone, R. and Butler, B. (2000) *Core Issues in Comprehensive Community Building Initiatives: Exploring Power and 'Race'*, Chicago, IL: Chapin Hall Centre for Children, University of Chicago.

Street, C. and Kenway, P. (1999) *Food for Thought: Breakfast Clubs and their Challenges*, London: New Policy Institute.

Tamkin, P. (2000) 'Institutional Racism: Daring to Open Pandora's Box', *Equal Opportunities Review* 92: 19–23.

Tanner, D. (1998) *Empowerment and Care Management: Swimming against the Tide*, Health and Social Care in the Community 6, 6: 447–57.

Taylor, M. (1995) *Unleashing the Potential: Bringing Residents to the Centre of Regeneration*, York: Joseph Rowntree Foundation.

—— (2000) *Top Down Meets Bottom Up: Neighbourhood Management*, York: Joseph Rowntree Foundation.

—— (2003) *Public Policy in the Community*, Basingstoke: Palgrave Macmillan.

Thomas, M. (2001) Briefing paper for author, Institute of Social Work, Staffordshire University.

Thomas, M. and Puttick, K. (2009) 'The Local Authority "Corporate Parent": Still Needing Parenting Classes?', *Welfare and Family: Law and Practice* 15, 2, 57–103.

Thompson, E. (1977) *Whigs and Hunters: Origins of the Black Act*, London: Peregrine.

Tönnies, F. (2001; first published 1887) *Community and Civil Society*, Cambridge: Cambridge University Press.

Tosey, P. (2000) 'Making Sense of Interventions: Stranger in a Strange Land', in A. Wheal (ed.), *Working with Parents Learning from Other People's Experience*, Lyme Regis: Russell House.

Townsend, P. (1979) *Poverty in the United Kingdom*, London: Penguin.

Tracy, E. and Whittaker, J. (1990) 'The Social Network Map: Assessing Social Support in Clinical Practice', *Families in Society: The Journal of Contemporary Human Services*, October: 461–70.

Training Organisation for Personal Social Services (TOPSS) (2002) *National Occupational Standards for Social Work and Social Care*, London: Training Organisation for Personal Social Services.

Trevithick, P. (2005) *Social Work Skills*, 2nd edn, Maidenhead: Open University Press.

Troyna, B. and Hatcher, R. (1992) *Racism in Children 's Lives: A Study of Mainly-white Primary Schools*, London: Taylor & Francis.

Turbett, C. (2006) 'Rural Social Work in Scotland and Eastern Canada: A Comparison Between the Experience of Practitioners in Remote Communities', *International Social Work* 49, 5: 583–94.

UN (1995) *The Copenhagen Declaration and Programme of Action for Social Development*, New York: UN Department of Publications.

van Tilburg, W. (1998) 'Losing and Gaining in Old Age: Changes in Personal Network Size and Social Support in a Four Year Longitudinal Study', *Journal of Gerontology Series B: Pyschological Sciences and Social Sciences* 53, 6, S313–23.

Varshney, A. (2002) *Ethnic Conflict and Civic Life,* London, Yale University Press.

Vernon, J. and Sinclair, R. (1999) *Maintaining Children in School: The Contribution of Social Services Departments*, London: National Children's Bureau.

Weatherburn, D. and Lind, B. (2001) *Delinquent-Prone Communities*, Cambridge: Cambridge University Press.

Welsh Assembly (2004) *Settlements, Services and Access: The Development of Policies to Promote Accessibility in Rural Areas in Great Britain*, Cardiff: Welsh Assembly.

Wenger, C. (1997) 'Social Networks and the Prediction of Elderly People at Risk', *Ageing and Mental Health* 1: 311–20.

White, C., Warrener, M., Reeves, A. and La Valle, M. (2008) *Family Intervention Projects: An Evaluation of their Design, Set-up and Early Outcomes*, National Centre of Social Research.

Wilcox, D. (1994) *The Guide to Effective Partnership*, Brighton: Partnership Books.

Wilkinson, D. and Applebee, E. (1999) *Implementing Holistic Government: Joined-up Action on the Ground*, London: Demos.

Williams, J., Toumborurou, J., McDonald, M., Jones, S. and Moore, T. (2005) 'A Sea Change on the Island Continent: Frameworks for Risk Assessment, Prevention and Intervention in Child Health in Australia', *Children and Society* 19, 2: 91–104.

Williamson, H. (ed.) (1995) *Social Action for Young People: Accounts of SCF Youth Work Practice*, Lyme Regis: Russell House.

Wilson, W. (1996) *When Work Disappears: The World of the New Urban Poor*, New York: Alfred Knopf.

Wolfensberger, W. (1975) *The Origin and Nature of Our Institutional Models*, Oakland, CA: Human Policy Press.

Wonnacott, J. and Kennedy, M. (2001) 'A Model Approach', *Community Care* 8–14 March.

Wood, R. L. (1997) 'Social Capital and Political Culture: God Meets Politics in the Inner City', *American Behavioural Scientist* 40, 5: 595–605.

Woodruff, W. (2002) *The Road to Nab End: An Extraordinary Northern Childhood*, London: Abacus.

Worley, C. (2005) '"It's not about race. It's about community": New Labour and "community cohesion"', *Critical Social Policy* 25, 4: 483–96. Yorkshire and Humber Regional Development Agency (n.d.) Active Partners: Benchmarking community participation in regeneration Leeds: Yorkshire and Humber RDA.

Yorkshire and Humber Regional Development Agency (n.d.) *Active Partners: Benchmarking Community Participation in Regeneration*, Leeds: Yorkshire and Humber RDA.

Zetter, R. and Pearl, M. (1999) *Managing to Survive: Asylum Seekers, Refugees and Access to Social Housing*, Bristol: Policy Press

INDEX

ABCD (Achieving Better Community Development) model, social work evaluation 199–201
action learning 61
adolescence 10; *see also* care leavers; young people
adult family placement: people with learning disability 128–9
adulthood: transition into 83, 93, 98, 103, 110, 112, 167
adults, socially excluded 114–31
advocacy, advocate 12, 41, 43–44, 63, 125, 127, 144, 188, 198; citizen advocacy 43; with disability 90, 127; and mentoring 102; parents as 108; and pressure groups 63; self-advocacy 43, 121–2, 131
ageism 118, in the NHS 119
anti-bias 178–9
anti-oppressive practice 31–33; definition 32; and poverty 31; and neighbourhood 30
anti-poverty strategy 31, 48; and credit unions 140; in rural areas 161
anti-racism and social work 31, 178–184; and Central Council for Education and Training in Social Work (CCETSW) 174; and young white people 180–4; Show Racism the Red Card 184; *see also* Macpherson Report; racism
anti-social behaviour 7,10, 36, 73, 96; in young people 104–108; and neighbourhoods 133, and youth offending teams 104
Arnstein's ladder, and participation 64–5
Asian women, training in computer skills 148
assessment of children in need 76, 89–90, 111; common assessment framework 59, 78; holistic 89; work capability 9, 53, 55, 126
asylum seekers, social work 184–189; children as unaccompanied 186–7; promoting inclusion with 188–9; Immigration and Asylum Act 1999 186; National Asylum Support Service (NASS) 185; *see also* refugees

behaviour 2, 9–11, 40, 61; in children 76, 78, 82–4, disruptive 99–100; gender differences in young people and children 96, 179
benefits 48–46; council tax 51–2, 54, 56, 114, 137, 185; eligibility 49, 51, 52, 54, 55; housing 51, 52, 54, 55, 114, 185; income support (IS) 49–52, 54–5; and families 79, 80–1; and adults 126; jobseeker's allowance (JSA) 29, 49, 52, 54; income-based 50–1; and families 79, 81, 82; means-tested 51–53; non-means-tested 54–56; take-up campaigns 55–6; working families' tax credit (WFTC) 50, 54, 75
black majority churches: community work 149
boys: behaviour and crime 21, 96–7 110–111, 136, 137;
breakfast clubs 204
British National Party 172
budgets: individual 117–8; social work agencies 192–3
built environment 21

capacity building 44, 141, 145; with adults 121; definition 137; government promoting of 44; with leaders 148; in neighbourhoods136–139; and Royds Community Association 139;
care leavers: accommodation 108–112 Children (Leaving Care) Act 2000 111–2; criminal behaviour 110; education 108; good practice in working with 111; homelessness 110; social relationships 111; *see also* adolescence; young people
care management 59, 116
Central Council for Education and Training in Social Work (CCETSW), anti-racism 174
child abuse 63, 78; and neighbourhoods 133
child development 76, 85, 100; resilience 106
child poverty 73–75; and lone parents
child protection 26, 31, 36; and partnerships 59, 78; reactive 36

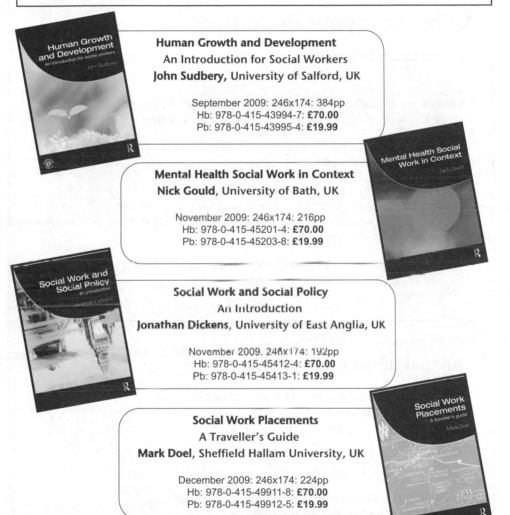